# UNEXPECTED AFFINITIES

While the concept of "type" has been present in architectural discourse since its formal introduction at the end of the eighteenth century, its role in the development of architectural projects has not been comprehensively analyzed. This book proposes a reassessment of architectural type throughout history and its impact on the development of architectural theory and practice. Beginning with Laugier's 1753 *Essay on Architecture*, *Unexpected Affinities: The History of Type in Architectural Project from Laugier to Duchamp* traces type through nineteenth- and twentieth-century architectural movements and theories, culminating in a discussion of the affinities between architectural type and Duchamp's concept of the readymade. Includes over sixty black and white images.

**Pablo Meninato** holds a PhD from the Universidade Federal do Rio Grande do Sul in Porto Alegre, Brazil, and a Master of Architecture from the University of Pennsylvania. He has practiced architecture and urban design in Buenos Aires, Monterrey, and Philadelphia, where he is principal of PMArch. Meninato has lectured at the University of Pennsylvania, Temple University, Philadelphia University, Universidad de Monterrey, and the Universidad de Palermo in Buenos Aires. He has written architectural criticism and essays for *>assemble d3*, *Summa+*, and *Arqtexto*, and the forthcoming "Spatial Seductions—The Everyday Interiorities of Marcel Duchamp, Eduard Kienholz, and Pepon Osorio," in *The Interior Architecture Theory Reader*, Taylor & Francis (March 2018).

# UNEXPECTED AFFINITIES

The History of Type in Architectural Project from Laugier to Duchamp

Pablo Meninato

NEW YORK AND LONDON

First published 2018
by Routledge
711 Third Avenue, New York, NY 10017

and by Routledge
2 Park Square, Milton Park, Abingdon, Oxon, OX14 4RN

*Routledge is an imprint of the Taylor & Francis Group, an informa business*

© 2018 Taylor & Francis

The right of Pablo Meninato to be identified as author of this work
has been asserted by him in accordance with sections 77 and 78 of the
Copyright, Designs and Patents Act 1988.

All rights reserved. No part of this book may be reprinted or reproduced or
utilised in any form or by any electronic, mechanical, or other means, now
known or hereafter invented, including photocopying and recording, or in
any information storage or retrieval system, without permission in writing
from the publishers.

*Trademark notice*: Product or corporate names may be trademarks or
registered trademarks, and are used only for identification and explanation
without intent to infringe.

*Library of Congress Cataloging-in-Publication Data*
A catalog record for this book has been requested

ISBN: 978-0-815-36393-4 (hbk)
ISBN: 978-0-815-36395-8 (pbk)
ISBN: 978-1-351-10498-2 (ebk)

Typeset in Bembo
by Apex CoVantage, LLC

# CONTENTS

| | |
|---|---|
| *List of Figures* | *viii* |
| *Acknowledgments* | *xi* |
| *Preface* | *xiii* |

| | |
|---|---|
| Introduction | 1 |
| *Brief Description of the Book 5* | |

**PART 1**
**Nineteenth Century—Origins, Imitation, Type**     **11**

| | | |
|---|---|---|
| 1 | Towards an Inaugural Definition of Type | 13 |
| | *Antecedents 13* | |
| | *The Little Rustic Hut 16* | |
| | *Quatremère de Quincy 19* | |
| | *Type as Origins, Classification, Imitation 20* | |
| | *Type Versus Model 24* | |
| | *Durand—Architecture as Taxonomy 24* | |
| | *The Précis—Towards a Design Methodology 26* | |
| | *Type as Diagram 28* | |

| | | |
|---|---|---|
| 2 | Semper's Knot | 35 |
| | *Antecedents 35* | |
| | *The Style Paradox 36* | |
| | *Towards a Science of Architecture 38* | |
| | *Origins Reconsidered 39* | |
| | *The Four Elements 41* | |
| | *Knot as Type 43* | |

**vi** Contents

## PART 2
## Twentieth Century—Shifting Considerations      49

3    Modern Architecture's Uncertain Consideration of Type     51
     *Antecedents 51*
     *The "Zero Hour" of History 53*
     *Dreams of Silos 55*
     *Towards a Prototypical Architecture 57*
     *Type, According to Gropius 63*
     *Modernism's Misconstruction of Urbanity 66*

4    Typology Reconsidered     71
     *Antecedents 71*
     *Italians "Rediscovering" the Concept of Type 73*
     *Aymonino and Rossi 75*
     *Type, According to Rossi 77*
     *What Will Be Has Always Been 80*
     *Colquhoun—Expansions of the Concept 83*
     *Vidler's Third Typology 85*
     *The Redeemed Relationship Between Type and City 87*

## PART 3
## Type and Project—Alteration Tactics      93

5    Typological Alterations     95
     *Antecedents 95*
     *Type as a Design Process—Moneo 96*
     *The Elasticity of the Type—Michelangelo and Gaudí 97*
     *The Magnification of Types—Boullée and Oldenburg 102*
     *Abstraction, Juxtaposition, and Assemblage—Ledoux*
       *and Libera 107*
     *Typological Substitutions—Le Corbusier 112*
     *Subtle Transformations—Álvaro Siza 114*

6    Affinities: Typological Displacement and Readymade     124
     *Antecedents 124*
     *The Secret Life of Objects 125*
     *The Fountain, the Maiden, and the Readymade 128*
     *Type, Object, and the Question of Repetition 132*
     *Doors and Windows 134*
     *Unexpected Affinities—Lequeu and Duchamp 136*

Contents **vii**

*The Displaced Column—The Presumed Irony of Loos  141*
*In Praise of the Ordinary—Venturi and Rossi  145*
*Typological Riddles—Herzog & de Meuron  154*

Afterword                                    161

*Bibliography*                               *167*
*Index*                                      *176*

# FIGURES

| | | |
|---|---|---|
| 1.1 | Le Moine, draftsman, Michelinot, engraver. Parallel between ancient and modern temples | 15 |
| 1.2 | Charles-Joseph-Dominique Eisen, draftsman, Jacques Aliamet, engraver. Frontispiece from Marc-Antoine Laugier: *Essai sur l'architecture,* 2nd ed. 1755 | 18 |
| 1.3 | Jean-Nicolas-Louis Durand: *Porches* | 27 |
| 1.4 | Jean-Nicolas-Louis Durand: *Marche à suivre dans la composition d'un projet quelconque* (Procedure to be followed in the composition of any project) | 29 |
| 1.5 | Jean-Nicolas-Louis Durand: *Ensembles d'édifices résultants des divisions du quarré, du parallélogramme et de leurs combinaisons avec le cercle* (Building ensembles, resulting from the divisions of the square, the parallelogram and their combinations with the circle) | 30 |
| 2.1 | Gottfried Semper: "The Caraib Hut" | 41 |
| 2.2 | Gottfried Semper: *Snake ornaments from Greece, Ireland, Egypt and Scandinavia* | 44 |
| 2.3 | Gottfried Semper: *Knots and braids* | 45 |
| 2.4 | Gottfried Semper: *Knots and braids* | 45 |
| 2.5 | Gottfried Semper: *Techniques of weaving* | 46 |
| 3.1 | Gerrit Rietveld: *Schröder House,* 1924 | 54 |
| 3.2 | Erich Mendelsohn: *CHICAGO. Grain Elevator 5. Passage with compartments and distribution bridges.* | 56 |
| 3.3 | Erich Mendelsohn: *CHICAGO. Grain Elevator 5. Distribution of masses at the end of the grain elevator.* | 58 |
| 3.4 | Le Corbusier: *Comparison between Greek temples and automobiles* | 59 |
| 3.5 | Le Corbusier: *Maison Dom-ino,* 1914 | 60 |
| 3.6 | Le Corbusier: *Maison Citrohan,* 1922 | 61 |

Figures **ix**

| | | |
|---|---|---|
| 4.1 | Bramante: *Tempietto di San Pietro in Montorio*, 1502 | 75 |
| 4.2 | Aldo Rossi: *Gallaratese*, 1969–74 | 78 |
| 4.3 | Aldo Rossi: *Città Analoga*, 1976 | 79 |
| 4.4 | Louis Kahn: *Kimbell Art Museum*, 1972 | 81 |
| 4.5 | Louis Kahn: *Suhrawardy Hospital*, 1974 | 81 |
| 4.6 | Louis Kahn: *National Assembly Building of Bangladesh*, 1974 | 82 |
| 4.7 | John Blatteau and Paul Hirshorn: *Comparative study of Philadelphia row houses* | 87 |
| 4.8 | Steven Holl: *Passages between row houses in Reading, PA* | 88 |
| 4.9 | Fernando Diez: *Typological evolution—from the "Roman house" to the "casa chorizo"* | 89 |
| 4.10 | Fernando Diez: *Variations "casa chorizo" according to the lot dimensions* | 90 |
| 5.1 | Michelangelo Buonarroti: *Vestibule of Laurentian Library*, c. 1525 | 98 |
| 5.2 | Michelangelo Buonarroti: *Detail of staircase at Vestibule of Laurentian Library*, c. 1525 | 100 |
| 5.3 | Antoni Gaudí: *Park Güell*, 1900 | 101 |
| 5.4 | Antoni Gaudí: *Park Güell*, 1900 | 101 |
| 5.5 | Michelangelo Buonarroti: *Colossal Order at Palazzo Nuovo*, c. 1545 | 102 |
| 5.6 | Étienne-Louis Boullée: *Bibliothèque Nationale*, 1785 | 103 |
| 5.7 | Étienne-Louis Boullée: *Cénotaphe à Newton*, 1784 | 104 |
| 5.8 | Frank Gehry and Claes Oldenburg: *Chiat/Day building*, 1985 | 105 |
| 5.9 | Claes Oldenburg: *Clothespin*, 1976 | 106 |
| 5.10 | Claude-Nicolas Ledoux: *Axonometric study of the Barrières*, 1785 | 109 |
| 5.11 | Claude-Nicolas Ledoux: *Vue perspective de la ville idéale de Chaux*, 1804 | 109 |
| 5.12 | Ledoux: *House and office of Inspector of Loue River* | 110 |
| 5.13 | Adalberto Libera: *Casa Malaparte*, 1942 | 111 |
| 5.14 | Le Corbusier: *Ville Savoye—detail of pilotis* | 113 |
| 5.15 | Le Corbusier: *Ville Savoye—detail of roof garden* | 113 |
| 5.16 | Le Corbusier: *Ville Savoye—detail of horizontal window* | 114 |
| 5.17 | Le Corbusier: *Casa Curutchet—detail of ramp* | 115 |
| 5.18 | Álvaro Siza: *Variations of U-shaped courtyards*. Left: Casa *Beires-Póvoa de Varzim*, 1976. Center: *Faculdade de Arquitectura da Universidade do Porto*, 1974. Right: *Rectorado para la Universidad de Alicante*, 1998. | 117 |
| 5.19 | Álvaro Siza: *Church of Santa Maria en Marco de Canaveses* | 119 |
| 5.20 | Álvaro Siza: *Church of Santa Maria en Marco de Canaveses, interior* | 120 |
| 6.1 | Marcel Duchamp: *Nu descendant un escalier*, 1912 | 126 |
| 6.2 | Marcel Duchamp: *Broyeuse de chocolate*, 1913 | 127 |
| 6.3 | Marcel Duchamp: *Roue de bicyclette*, 1913 | 129 |
| 6.4 | Marcel Duchamp: *Fountain*, 1917 | 130 |
| 6.5 | Jean-Jacques Lequeu: *Et nous aussi, nous serons mères . . .* | 137 |
| 6.6 | Jean-Jacques Lequeu: *La porte de la chasse du Prince et l'étable* | 139 |
| 6.7 | Jean-Jacques Lequeu: *Temple à la divination* | 140 |
| 6.8 | Jean-Jacques Lequeu: *Tombeau de Porsenna, roi d'Étrurie* | 140 |

**x** Figures

| | | |
|---|---|---|
| 6.9 | Jean-Jacques Lequeu: "*The Cow Byre faces south on the cool meadow*" | 141 |
| 6.10 | Adolf Loos: *Chicago Tribune competition*, 1922 | 143 |
| 6.11 | Venturi, Scott Brown and Associates (Principal: Robert Venturi with Denise Scott Brown), *Ironic Column*, Allen Memorial Art Museum, Oberlin College, 1973–1977 | 147 |
| 6.12 | Venturi, Scott Brown and Associates (Frederic Schwartz, draftsman), *The Big Apple at Times Square Center*, 1984 | 148 |
| 6.13 | Aldo Rossi: *Teatro Faro, Toronto*, 1988–1989 | 151 |
| 6.14 | Filarete: *Ca' del duca Palace*, c. 1469 | 152 |
| 6.15 | Aldo Rossi: *Friedrichstasse*, 1981 | 153 |
| 6.16 | Herzog & de Meuron: *Porta Volta* in Milan, 2014 | 155 |
| 6.17 | Herzog & de Meuron: *House Rudin in Leymen*, 1998 | 156 |

# ACKNOWLEDGMENTS

Over the years of writing this book I have had the privilege of receiving many people's ideas, support, and advice. I am very grateful to the colleagues and friends who reviewed the various versions of the manuscript, offering observations and suggestions, including my former doctoral advisors, Carlos Eduardo Comas, Claudia Cabral, and Fernando Diez. I also greatly benefited from the criticism and advice of Jean-Michel Rabaté and David Leatherbarrow, who read drafts of the manuscript at various stages. While writing this book I was associated with various institutions to which I am very grateful, including Temple University, University of Pennsylvania, Philadelphia University, and the Universidade Federal do Rio Grande do Sul. I am particularly grateful to my research assistants Abby Freed and Joanna Kozole, who were very instrumental in the completion of this project, as well as Emily Bamforth, for her help reviewing the final version of the manuscript. I want to especially acknowledge my gratitude to my editor at Routledge, Katharine Maller, who persistently expressed confidence in the project.

I want to acknowledge the generosity of Nicola Goretti, who was instrumental in helping me obtain many of the photographs, including some of his own. I am especially grateful to those who lent their photographs and images: Leonardo Finotti, Marc Llimargas i Casas, Naquib Hossain, Maite Iriarte, Irma de Arrascaeta, Roberto Pasini, Fernando Diez, Ariel Vazquez, John Blatteau, and Paul Hirshorn. Personnel at libraries, archives, and institutions have been a great help in finding source material and images for the book, including Charlette Caldwell, Harry Bolick, and Denise Scott Brown, from Venturi Scott Brown Associates, Greg O'Malley, from Steven Holl Architects, Anthony Vidler, Isabelle Godineau, from the Fondation Le Corbusier, Maria Elena Murguia, from the Artists Rights Society, Chiara Spangaro, from the Fondazione Aldo Rossi, Carlos Basualdo and Allison McLaughlin,

**xii** Acknowledgments

from the Philadelphia Museum of Art, Sarah Sherman, from the Getty Research Institute, and Heather Isbell Schumacher, from The Architectural Archives of the University of Pennsylvania. I would like to thank friends and colleagues for their help and encouragement during this long journey, including Pablo Güiraldes, Allan Irving, Ignacio Ros de Olano, Josh McIlvain, Alessandra Fassio, Ivano D'Angella, Brian Johnston, Peter Rudd, Patricio Ortiz, and my sister, Irene Meninato.

Finally and foremost, I am grateful for my wife, Silvana, my daughter, Paula, and my son, Lorenzo, for their infinite patience and support.

# PREFACE

*. . . and almost always my walk ended in the gallery district, perhaps because arcades and galleries have always been my secret country.*

—Julio Cortázar[1]

Buenos Aires, 1940s. While strolling around the center of the city, the young man deliberates about the fundamental aspects of his life: his youthful anxieties, a dull job at the bourse, his engagement with Irma, who provokes in him the most ambivalent feelings: "she is the kindest and most generous of women. I would never dream of talking to her about the things that count most for me."[2] We soon find out that he is approaching the *Güemes Arcade*, a glass-covered street that cuts through a city block. For the narrator, the arcade represents his most intimate and secret desires, something impossible to share with anyone else. If Irma "knew," he seems to confess, "how I liked the Güemes Arcade she would not fail to be shocked." As he gets closer to his destination, the protagonist feels the promise of adventure, the escape from routine, the excitement of the unexpected. The large vaulted space appears as a secret shelter, the "the treasure cave in which a glimpse of sin and mint drops deliciously mixed, where they cried out the evening editions with crimes on every page, and the lights burned in the basement theater where they showed restricted blue movies."[3]

When the narrator finally enters the expansive semi-covered space, the story takes an unexpected turn. We are now in Paris in 1868; the Buenos Aires passage of "dirty windows and stuccoes with allegorical figures" has transfigured into the *Galerie Vivienne* in the heart of France. The protagonist ponders his imminent appointment with Josiane, who initiated him sexually and receives her "customers" in an attic in "the upper levels" of the *Galerie Vivienne*. The naive expectation of the

**xiv** Preface

Buenos Aires *flâneur* has transformed into an imminent rendezvous with Parisian eroticism. The urban passage sublimates an intimate experience, the transition from adolescence into adulthood, the breaching of innocence by carnal initiation. It is also a metaphysical tunnel, capable of reversing in time while connecting two cities that are *a world apart*:

> It's still hard for me to cross the Güemes Arcade without feeling ironically tender toward that memory of adolescence at the brink of the fall; the old fascination still persists, and that's why I liked to walk without a fixed destination, knowing that at any moment I would enter the region of the galleries, where any sordid, dusty shop would attract me more than the show windows facing the insolence of the open streets . . . its short cuts which end in a secondhand book shop or a puzzling travel agency, where perhaps nobody ever even bought a railroad ticket, that world which has chosen a nearer sky.[4]

The story "El Otro Cielo" (The Other Sky, 1966) by Julio Cortázar is structured as an improbable oscillation between two different geographical and temporal conditions—one tedious and predictable Buenos Aires of mid-twentieth century, the other the bohemian and menacing nineteenth-century Paris.[5] The character slides between worlds that cannot (or should not) meet. The intersection of these two realities occurs in a space remarkable for its ambivalence: it is covered though open at both ends; it can be seen as both an interior and exterior space, as a public or private setting. While it is part of the city—on rainy days people use the arcades as protection from the elements and to shorten walks—it is also an autonomous urban moment. The arcades, according to this logic, are various places and a singular one; with all their differences they seem uncannily similar. To visit an arcade (any arcade) is to immerse oneself into an experience replicated in many other times and spaces; it is the nostalgic feeling of *déjà vu*—the remembrance of a moment not yet lived.

Probably the most comprehensive essay on arcades is Walter Benjamin's *Das Passagen-Werk* (*The Arcades Project*, 1927–1940),[6] a literary *collage* dedicated to analyzing the history and cultural significance of this urban initiative. The structure of *The Arcades Project* resembles a mosaic of fragments resulting in the intersection of art and technology, economics and consumption, architecture and history. Benjamin starts by citing a precise definition of this urban space extracted from an *Illustrated Guide of Paris*:

> These arcades, a recent invention of industrial luxury, are glass-roofed, marble-paneled corridors extending through whole blocks of buildings, whose owners have joined together for such enterprises. Lining both sides of these corridors, which get their light from above, are the most elegant shops, so that the passage is a city, a world in miniature.[7]

If for Cortázar the arcade constitutes a nostalgic and marginal urban landscape, for Benjamin those continuous glass vaults represent *the architectural emblem of modernity*. Modern architecture, according to this premise, was originated after the development of new construction technologies sparked by the discovery of new materials, as "for the first time in the history of architecture, an artificial building material appears: iron. It undergoes an evolution whose tempo will accelerate in the course of the century."[8] The innovative concept of the arcade, adds Benjamin, supports the modern narrative of *breaking with the past*: "At the same time, what emerges in these images is the resolute effort to distance oneself from all that is antiquated—which includes, however, the recent past."[9] However, afterwards Benjamin seems to contradict himself, commenting that those forms do not constitute *genuine* architectural inventions, but instead derive from an extensive genealogic chain. Their etymological roots can be found in Fourier's nineteenth-century *phalanstery*, or in ancient types, such as the *Persian bazaar* and the *Roman vaulted basilica*. The arcade, according to Benjamin, can be understood as a paradoxical oscillation between innovation and replication, or between tradition and modernity.

The pendular oscillation between convention and innovation that Benjamin observes in the development of the urban passage reflects clear affinities with the understanding of the concept of *repetition* within the architectural discourse. Gilles Deleuze has observed that "repetition changes nothing in the object repeated, but does change something in the mind which contemplates it."[10] In other words, it is the *meaning* (and not the form) of the repeated object that is bound to be altered. As the character of Cortázar's story can attest, the insertion of an individual into a different context—whether real or metaphysical—produces an alteration of the perception of that person. While the young man *seems to be the same* while walking through the arcades of Buenos Aires or Paris, it becomes evident that the translocations affect both his perception of reality and of himself. Human nature after all—just like objects or architectural types—is defined, and signified, by its interaction with the environment.

## Notes

1 Cortázar, Julio, "The Other Sky." In Suzanne Jill Levine (ed.), *All Fires the Fire*. New York: Random House/Pantheon Books, 1973, 129–130. Julio Cortázar (1914–1984) was a Belgium-born Argentine writer. While he is most well-known for his short stories, most critics consider his masterpiece *Rayuela* (*Hopscotch*; 1963), a fragmented novel, where the reader is invited to rearrange the sequence of the different chapters according to alternative options prescribed by the author. Similarly to the main character in "The Other Sky," Cortázar's life oscillated between Buenos Aires and Paris.

2 Cortázar, "The Other Sky," 129.

3 Cortázar, "The Other Sky," 129.

4 Cortázar, "The Other Sky," 130.

5 For a literary analysis of Cortázar's story see Schwartz, Marcy, *Invenciones Urbanas*. Ediciones Corregidor, 2010, 92–102.

6 The *Passagenwerk* or *The Arcades Project* was written by Walter Benjamin between 1927 and 1940, the year he died under uncertain circumstances on the French-Spanish border.

**xvi** Preface

Benjamin entrusted the manuscript to his friend Georges Bataille before fleeing Paris under Nazi occupation. The full text was published only in 1999. For more information see "Translator's Foreword" (transl. Howard Eiland and Kevin McLaughlin), ix–xvi, in Benjamin, Walter, *The Arcades Project*. Cambridge: Harvard University Press, 2002.

7  Benjamin, *The Arcades Project*, 8.
8  Benjamin, *The Arcades Project*, 4.
9  Benjamin, *The Arcades Project*, 5.
10 Deleuze, Gilles, *Difference and Repetition*. New York: Columbia University Press, 1994, 70.

# INTRODUCTION

*Now, if the very notion of the avant-garde can be seen as a function of the discourse of originality, the actual practice of vanguard art tends to reveal that "originality" is a working assumption that itself emerges from a ground of repetition and recurrence.*

—Rosalind Krauss[1]

The architect faces two seemingly incompatible conditions upon starting a new project: the aspiration of creating new and original forms, and the assumption that the conception of those forms will be affected or influenced by previously assimilated images, forms, or ideas. Since the origins of humankind, these ostensibly conflicting interests have defined the evolution of architecture and the other arts, perhaps best summed up as an inevitable tension produced by the coexistence of the tradition of past forms and the search for original resolutions. The aim of this work is to examine the presence of type in the architectural project. While the concept of type has been a persistent presence in the architectural discourse, its role in the development of the architectural project has not been subjected to a comprehensive and exclusive analysis. My main contention is that "type," like all kinds of preexisting images and forms, should be taken as foundational in most architectural projects, and understood in diverse and inventive ways.

The study of the idea of type in architecture, as discussed in this work, argues for a preliminary definition of the term. Last decades registered numerous and diverse interpretations of the meaning of type; while some appeared simple and practical, others introduced sophisticated philosophical disquisitions. In simple terms, the concept of architectural type can be understood as the formal features shared by a group of buildings. The type "roman courtyard house," for instance, is characterized by the presence of a central space open to the sky, enclosed by columns or arcades, which in turn define a perimeter loggia. Buildings registering that formal

**2** Introduction

distribution belong to that type. In a strict sense, a type can be described but not shown. Therefore, a single example of a courtyard house does not represent the type; it is after identifying various instances that share those formal features that a type is determined. Type, consequently, is a mental construct; it is the capacity of identifying and extrapolating formal analogies constant in various buildings.

You cannot "invent" a type. The architect can create a first formal solution that—after it is imitated in posterior projects—will evolve into a type. For example, Rafael Moneo comments on how Brunelleschi "created" the type "lantern" as a crowning of the dome of *Santa Maria del Fiore* in Florence.[2] While effectively Brunelleschi was the first to devise such particular solution, the consolidation of the "lantern" type happened only *after* other architects and builders adopted it into their projects. In this respect, type behaves like language.[3] While anyone can propose a new word, a term will be incorporated into language only after a group of people starts using it. Words, like types, acquire meaning through repetition.

The question of meaning leads towards the most paradoxical aspect of architectural type, which is the *indifference* to the notion of function. In principle, the architectural project is a response to a given program, in turn dictated by conventional use. A project for a "house," or a "hospital," will result in a certain disposition, an arrangement of forms reflecting the designer's reaction towards that program. This idea, which at first instance appears as an obvious argument and common sense, will be questioned initially by Giulio Carlo Argan[4] and, more emphatically, by Aldo Rossi.[5] According to Rossi, the architectural type should be understood solely as an arrangement of building forms capable of hosting a multiplicity of uses. His argument was that the actual performance of architecture resides in its forms, which are "permanent,"[6] while the activities occurring under those forms may vary and fluctuate. When, in the early 1960s, Argan, Rossi, and many other Italian architects and thinkers formulated these theories, they were seen as a battle cry against one of the pillars of modernism—that there is a prevailing relation between functions and forms in architecture. This subject was later discussed by Alan Colquhoun,[7] who, based on structural linguistic studies by Ferdinand de Saussure, Claude Lévi-Strauss, and Roland Barthes,[8] questioned the correspondences between sign and meaning, which, translated into architecture, resolved the discrepancy between form (or type) and function.[9]

The notion of type blurs the distinction between "high" and "low" architecture. Its spectrum contemplates vernacular or utilitarian constructions, such as huts, barracks, bazaars, factories, arcades, row houses, or igloos realized by anonymous builders, as well as palazzos, museums, and skyscrapers designed by the most celebrated architects. If, as Aldo Rossi says, "type is the very idea of architecture,"[10] then the history of architecture is the history of the evolution of types. It is compelling, then, that since ancient times, generations of architects constructed the history of architecture by repeating, varying, and altering the typological heritage.

So far, the notion of type has been discussed mainly as a classification tool, a strategy for identifying, grouping, and dividing the building inventory. In common parlance this is the most typical consideration of the term. In addition, the notion of type may be considered as an instrument for the development of the architectural project, which is the main subject of this study. The concept of type as a design mechanism was initially introduced into the architectural discourse by archaeologist and architect Quatremère de Quincy. In his entry titled "Type," from the 1825 edition of the *Encyclopédie Méthodique*,[11] Quatremère defines the term as response to the *origins* of architecture, an instrument for *classifying* the building inventory, and an artistic process derived from the Aristotelian doctrine of *imitation*. The history of architecture, according to this idea, is a continuous sequence of mimetic operations, where each building is both a derivation of anterior precedents and an original model. The complex and abstract qualities of Quatremère's definitions help explain, on one hand, the challenges that face framing a discussion around the notion of type. On the other hand, however, they demonstrate how such a framework has inspired, and continues to inspire, multiple and diverse interpretations.

The suggestive ambiguity regarding the operational meaning of Quatremère's definitions became evident in the works of two nineteenth-century thinkers. In the first place, Jean-Nicolas-Louis Durand, a contemporary of Quatremère, established a design methodology based on taxonomy of types (although opting for the terms "parts," "elements," and "genres"), understood as formal synthesis of building components. Unlike Quatremère, for whom the architectural project was advanced under the spectrum of imitation, Durand assumes the building precedent as a "given," a formal presence ready to be disposed as a combinatorial and compositional strategy. The second nineteenth-century figure proposing an alternative consideration of type was Gottfried Semper. Semper coincides with Quatremère in explaining the origins of architecture as a mimetic activity, but unlike Quatremère's identification of building type as the foundation of architecture, he considers that the first space defined by humans was the gathering around the *hearth*, in turn manifested in communal weaving. Transpiring ethnological theories, Semper describes the *knot* as the method for producing the first dressings as well as the inaugural building enclosures. The knot, according to this view, can be interpreted as the notion of type in its most minimal expression.

During the first decades of the twentieth century, the art world began experiencing radical changes. As the "daughter" of the avant-garde,[12] modern art was signaled by the illusion of abstraction and originality[13] (a position later advocated by thinkers such as Sigfried Giedion, Theodor Adorno, and Clement Greenberg).[14] For those for whom the ultimate goal of the architectural project was abstraction and sheer originality, type was implicitly associated with figuration, predictability, and repetition,[15] its inevitable connection to nineteenth century canceling the promise of novelty. Type, together with "style," was seen as a "ghost" of the neoclassical past, from which modernism intensively desired to differentiate itself. It is for these same reasons that modern architectural doctrines—and their latest iteration in contemporary expressionist manifestations—have expressed suspicion or rejection of the concept of type. We hear this sense of condemnation in the words of contemporary critic Alberto Pérez-Gómez, affirming that the difficulty of type in

**4** Introduction

the architectural project is its tendency towards repetition, ultimately denying "our real capacity for invention and imagination."[16]

In the 1960s, the world of art evidenced a reappreciation of the "other" modernism,[17] which, rather than focusing on "retinal" and abstraction aspects, dwelled on conceptual and figurative explorations. Art, according to this view, is no longer dependent on abstraction and formal alteration; the emphasis is now on assembling and recontextualizing images and objects. Of course the lineage of this approach can be traced to the works and ideas of Marcel Duchamp, who during the first decades of the century started exploring the subtle and hidden qualities of everyday objects and artifacts, eventually speculating around the notion of "designating" some of those objects as "works of art." This seemingly simple task, later known as *readymade*, redefined the most fundamental conception of the artistic act, since the artist is no longer the one who produces the work of art, but instead he "chooses" it. Guided by the iconoclastic legacy of Duchamp, the second half of the twentieth century witnessed the emergence of a new generation of artists, such as Richard Hamilton, Robert Rauschenberg, Jean Tinguely, Yves Klein, Jasper Johns, Edward Kienholz, and Joseph Beuys, who reintroduced figuration by disposing into their artworks mundane and "ordinary" objects.

During this same period, initially in Italy and later in most of the Western world, can be detected a denunciation of modern architectural principles. In what can be interpreted as either an "antimodern" reaction or an attempt to correct modernism's path, theoreticians and architects such as Argan, Aymonino, Tafuri, and Rossi proposed a "return to the notion of type"[18]—which by default implied revisiting Quatremère's conception of type. Type, in this new context, entails, on the one hand, a tool for a better understanding of the inexorable correspondence between architecture and the city, and, on the other, a return of repetition as a mechanism for the realization of the architectural project. According to this view, historical forms, such as loggias, cortiles, domes, vaults, galleries, and courtyards, were again acceptable mimetic precedents.

One could say that each generation of architects, in its revelatory character, is bound to discover its own interpretation of type. This notion is reflected in Rafael Moneo's 1978 essay "On Typology," suggesting that the (contemporary) typological project could continue operating under the spectrum of *mimesis*, thus listing mechanisms such as transformation, distortion, alteration of scale, and juxtaposition.[19] And just as type is a framework that is constantly being rediscovered, it becomes, paradoxically, a context where the architect feels at liberty. What is striking about type is that it can be viewed as an actual exercise of freedom within cultural and historical boundaries.

While for those who think that the origins of the architectural project are not to be found in the *tabula rasa* so much as in the reconsideration and reappropriation of reality, the power of type lies in its capacity to bridge between collective memory and the individual object, between the idea of the object and its materiality, between singular and communal manifestations, where architecture can be seen as a prolonged cultural chain. Perhaps it is because of this sense of connection with the origins of building, of embracing history while developing the yet to come, that architects (knowingly or unknowingly) have taken up the type as the medium within which to work. It is as though they tended to reduce architecture to a schematized synthesis where repetition becomes an act of originality.

It is within this context that this study examines the affinities between the notions of *typological displacement* and *readymade*. Both tactics avoid the temptation of formal alteration, whereby variation of meaning is achieved through dislocation. The prerequisite for this examination is identifying the analogies between type and object, or between imitation and replication. These antecedents help explain why type and readymade have been associated with the act of copying, imitating, replicating, and repeating—initiatives that appear contrarian to the ideals of modernism. This opposition was examined by Rosalind Krauss, who in her essay "The Originality of the Avant-Garde"[20] (1981) discusses how precepts of originality and repetition become relevant for considering the notions of convention and innovation in contemporary art. According to Krauss, there is no originality without repetition, and there is no repetition without originality; this is the basis of the present-day quest of reassessing the relationship between innovation and copy. As will be discussed later on, some projects by Lequeu, Loos, Rossi, Venturi, and Herzog & de Meuron are exemplary in this respect.

In his book *The Shape of Time: Remarks on the History of Things*[21] (1962), anthropologist George Kubler anticipates some of the issues discussed by Rosalind Krauss, describing the pendulum between originality and repetition as a constant of humankind: "Human desires in every present instant are torn between the replica and the invention, between the desire to return to the known pattern, and the desire to escape it by a new variation."[22] In architecture, the notions of originality and repetition must be considered as false opposites; type can become a reconciling instrument.

## Brief Description of the Book

This book is divided in three parts. The first part examines the origins and interpretations of the concept of type through the eighteenth and nineteenth centuries, and the second part analyzes the oscillating consideration of type during the twentieth century. The third part, which conveys the main argument of the study, examines how type can become an agent in the development of the design process. While Chapter 5 discusses various morphological alteration tactics, the final chapter examines parallels between typological displacement and the "readymade" as conceived by Marcel Duchamp. This latter topic has never been discussed in connection with Duchamp.

Chapter 1 starts with the Enlightenment's interest in the notion of *origins*, as attested by Abbé Marc Antoine Laugier's *Essai sur l'architecture*, in which he identifies the "primitive hut" as humankind's first dwelling. Echoing the thinking of Rousseau, Laugier's "rustic hut" evokes man's blissful primeval natural state, the principle and measure of all architecture, the original seed that would reproduce

**6** Introduction

and evolve into all buildings realized by humankind. Following, the storyline moves to Quatremère de Quincy, who posited that the origins of architecture can be traced to "three original types"—the *hut*, the *tent*, and the *cave*—in his 1785 essay *Mémoire sur l'architecture Égyptienne*. While Quatremère's thesis concentrated on the origins of architecture, his theory also has contemporary resonances: each present-day building was seen as the culmination of an extensive chain of variations and transformations whose origins can be traced to one of those inaugural types.

Chapter 1 closes by examining the figure of Jean-Nicolas-Louis Durand, who developed a distinctive interpretation of type, understood as a classification strategy and a design methodology. Durand's ambition, one that would pose a lasting influence well into the twentieth century, was to conceive a theory of architecture substantiated on scientific premises, thus employing similar methodologies as those implemented by the biological sciences, such as anatomy, botany, and zoology. Durand manifests his theoretical agenda in two texts: the *Recueil*, in which he developed a formal taxonomy of historical buildings, and the *Précis*, in which he advances a design methodology. Durand's attitude towards type can be interpreted as counterpoint to the principles argued by Quatremère; while Quatremère assumed that the creation of forms was substantiated in the doctrine of *imitation*, Durand conceived the architectural project as a combination and disposition of predetermined building components.

Chapter 2 focuses on the German architect and thinker Gottfried Semper, who, during the second half of the nineteenth century, developed a reinterpretation of various subjects earlier discussed by Quatremère. These include the question of the origins of architecture, the concept of imitation, and the criteria for classifying buildings and objects. Substantiated by his interests in ethnology, Semper developed a novel theory on the origins of architecture. Rather than conceiving the first architectural dwelling as a "construction" (i.e., a fixed building type), he argued that the original space shared by humankind was the gathering around the campfire, a ritual that encouraged the first social interactions. Fire (or *hearth*) was the first of the "Four Architectural Elements." The other three were the *roof*, the *enclosure*, and the *mound*. Semper then introduces the notion of the *knot*, an elastic and flexible device that allowed for the first weavings and dressings, the same technique that developed the building enclosures. Semper referred to the knot as the "oldest technological symbol," the necessary antecedent of all architectural endeavors. Semper's conceptualization of the knot can be interpreted as the type in its minimal expression—thus, the generation of architecture is produced through a series of transformations and iterations in which original motifs are gradually adapted to new needs and conditions.

*The second part*, combining Chapters 3 and 4, examines the oscillating consideration of type during the twentieth century. Chapter 3 centers on the advent of modernity, where three divergent positions coexist: first, the avant-garde groups, such as *de Stijl* and *suprematism*, who vehemently rejected any consideration of type; second, the evolving interest by Gropius, Mendelsohn, Le Corbusier, and Mies in *alternative typological precedents*, such as silos, factories, and grain elevators; and third, Le Corbusier's fascination with forms and imageries derived from new industrial machineries, such as ships, airplanes and automobiles. From the third position derives the notion of the *prototype*, a strategy that can be interpreted either as a substitution of the type or as the assimilation of *mass production* as an alternative mimetic tactic.

Chapter 4 analyzes the *renewed consideration of the concept of type* attested during the second half of the twentieth century. This interest was initially sparked by the theories of Saverio Muratori and Giulio Carlo Argan—the first with his typological analysis of Veneto's housing, the second with his influential article "On the Typology of Architecture." Following, I turn my attention to the group known as *La Tendenza*, architect-authors like Aldo Rossi and Carlo Aymonino who studied the relationship between the concept of type and topics such as city, history, and memory. I continue by examining the emergence of Louis Kahn, a contemporary of Aymonino and Rossi, whose ambition was to develop a modern architectural vocabulary impregnated with the presence of ancient types. This chapter concludes with an examination of Anthony Vidler's seminal essay "The Third Typology," an analysis of the enduring correspondences between the concept of type and the configuration of the city.

*The third part* (Chapters 5 and 6) presents the main argument of this study, which is the consideration of type as an instrument for generating the architectural project. After reviewing Rafael Moneo's description of a typological design process, Chapter 5 lists and investigates the implementation of various morphological alteration tactics, as exemplified by the works of Michelangelo and Gaudí (*distortion*), Boullée and Oldenburg (*magnification*), and Ledoux and Libera (*assemblage* and *juxtaposition*). Following, based on a reassessment of Le Corbusier's "five points," I examine the notion of *typological substitution*, a strategy wherein conventional architectural elements (e.g., column, roof, window, and staircase) are redefined by their "modern" versions. This chapter concludes with the notion of *subtle typological alterations*, a strategy that proposes a range of transformations characterized by its restraint rather than by its spectacularity, as demonstrated by the works of Álvaro Siza.

Chapter 6 investigates the correspondences between typological displacement and the tactic of readymade as conceived by Marcel Duchamp. It introduces Duchamp's persistent consideration of architectural "openings" (i.e., doors and windows), and his recurrent interest in the notions of *displacement* and *repetition*. Then the chapter analyzes the correspondences between *type* and *object*: while type has been traditionally developed under the umbrella of imitation (i.e., the alteration of forms), the object is produced through duplication. The chapter's final segment considers the parallels between *typological displacement* and *readymade* under the spectrum of the architectural project. For this, I explore four "case studies": Lequeu's *fantastic* explorations, in which type fuses with figurative sculpture; Adolf Loos's ostensibly *ironic* proposal for the *Chicago Tribune*, a gigantic column proposing the inauguration of the "skyscraper type"; Rossi and Venturi's renewed interest in the notion of the "ordinary," the capacity of mundane buildings and objects to convey unforeseen meanings; and Herzog & de Meuron's *typological riddles*, in which the

**8** Introduction

tactics of typological repetition and displacement revolve around the iconic image of the archetypal house.

## Notes

1 Krauss, Rosalind E., "The Originality of the Avant-Garde: A Postmodernist Repetition." *October, Vol. 18* (Autumn, 1981) MIT Press, 54. The essay was also published in Krauss, Rosalind E., *The Originality of the Avant-Garde and Other Modernist Myths*. Cambridge, MA: MIT Press, 1986.
2 Moneo, Rafael, "On Typology," *Oppositions #13*. Cambridge, MA: MIT Press, 1978, 24.
3 The affinities between the concepts of type and language have been discussed by Alan Colquhoun, who noted that "just as language always preexists a group or individual speaker, the system of architecture preexists a particular period or architect. It is precisely through the persistence of earlier forms that the system can convey meaning." See Colquhoun, Alan, "Postmodernism and Structuralism: A Retrospective Glance." In Nesbitt, Kate (ed.), *Modernity and the Classical Tradition: Architectural Essays, 1980–1987*. Cambridge, MA: MIT Press, 1989, 247–248.
4 Argan, Giulio Carlo, "On the Typology of Architecture." In Nesbitt, Kate (ed.), *Theorizing a New Agenda for Architecture: An Anthology of Architectural Theory, 1965–1995*. New York: Princeton Architectural, 1996, 242–246. Argan first published this article as "Sul concetto di tipologia architettonica," *Progetto e destino*, Milan, 1963. In his essay, Argan introduces the notion that architectural type is indifferent to function: "typological series do not arise only in relation to the physical functions of buildings but are tied to their configuration: The fundamental 'type' of the circular shrine for instance, is independent of the functions, sometimes complex, which such buildings must fulfill," 244.
5 As discussed in Chapter 4, a central subject of *The Architecture of the City*, first published in 1966 with the title *L'Architettura della Città*, is the questioning of the notion of function in architecture and urbanism. This is particularly discussed in the section titled "Critique of Naïve Functionalism." See Rossi, Aldo, *The Architecture of the City*. Cambridge, MA: MIT Press, 1982.
6 The description of the notion of type as a "permanent" presence in architecture and the city is a recurrent subject in Rossi's theory. Subscribing to this idea, his initial definition of architectural type is "something that is permanent and complex, a logical principle that is prior to form and that constitutes it." See Rossi, *The Architecture of the City*, 40.
7 In Colquhoun, "Postmodernism and Structuralism: A Retrospective Glance," 243–254.
8 Colquhoun defines a "structuralist" approach to language and meaning as "the ability of signs to convey meaning, within any sign system whatever, depends on an arbitrary and conventional structure of relationships within a particular system, and not on the relation of signs to preexistent or fixed referents in outside reality." In Colquhoun, "Postmodernism and Structuralism: A Retrospective Glance," 246.
9 "We can see," posits Colquhoun, "that structuralism was able to provide the rationale for an attack on two dogmas—functionalism and historical determinism—that were fundamental to the theory and practice of modernism." Colquhoun, "Postmodernism and Structuralism: A Retrospective Glance," 247.
10 Rossi, *The Architecture of the City*, 41.
11 See definition of "Type," in Quatremère, De Quincy, and Samir Younés, *The Historical Dictionary of Architecture of Quatremère De Quincy*. London: Andreas Papadakis, 1999, 254–257.
12 As summed by Jürgen Habermas, "Modernity then unfolded in various avant-garde movements and finally reached its climax in the Café Voltaire of the Dadaists and in surrealism." Habermas, Jürgen, "Modernity—An Incomplete Project." In Foster, Hal (ed.), *The Anti-Aesthetic: Essays on Postmodern Culture*. Port Townsend, WA: Bay Press, 1987, 5.
13 Krauss, "The Originality of the Avant-Garde," 56.

Introduction **9**

14 While coming from different disciplines, Siegfried Giedion, Theodor Adorno, and Clement Greenberg were the main theoretical "apostles" of modernism. Giedion was the author of modern architecture's most influential book, *Space, Time and Architecture: The Growth of a New Tradition*, first published in 1941; Theodor Adorno discussed modern art from the perspective of philosophical aesthetics, as in his essay *Aesthetic Theory* of 1970; and Clement Greenberg became modernism's most well-known art critic after the Second World War, arguing for the continuation of formalism and abstraction in modern art. One of Greenberg's most influential essays was "Modernist Painting," originally given as a radio broadcast, and published in 1961.

15 Again, Colquhoun discusses the impact of repetition in the development of the architectural project: "One of the many reasons why a typology of forms might have more impact on practice in architecture than in the other arts is the inherent reproducibility of architecture and its dependence on prototype. In the past, all the arts depended, to a greater or a lesser extent, on the faithful reproduction of prototypical elements. In classical artistic theory this use of prototypes was, so to speak, sublimated into the theory of mimesis, insofar as this applied to the imitation of models of classical art." See Colquhoun, "Postmodernism and Structuralism: A Retrospective Glance," 247.

16 Here is the full quote of Pérez-Gómez's criticism of the consideration of type in the development of the architectural project: "Even in its most sophisticated formulations, the positing of typology ultimately denies our real capacity for invention and imagination. It hampers the primary mission of architecture, which must be to constitute the vision of a new order from an authentic mimesis of history, the *storia* of the poet." See Pérez-Gómez, Alberto, "Architecture Is Not a Convention." In Rockcastle, Garth (ed.), *Type and the (Im)Possibilities of Convention*. Midgard Monograph, 1991, 18.

17 I am referring principally to Dada and the surrealist movement.

18 Colquhoun uses the expression "we must return to the notion of type" to convey the theoretical landscape of the 1960s and 1970s, when type was seen as an alternative to modern architecture's conventional practices. See Colquhoun, "Postmodernism and Structuralism: A Retrospective Glance," 254.

19 Moneo, "On Typology," 23.

20 Krauss, "The Originality of the Avant-Garde," 56.

21 Kubler, George, *The Shape of Time: Remarks on the History of Things*. New Haven, CT: Yale University Press, 1962.

22 Kubler, *The Shape of Time*, 72.

**PART 1**

# Nineteenth Century—Origins, Imitation, Type

# 1

# TOWARDS AN INAUGURAL DEFINITION OF TYPE

*The actual causes of a thing's origin and its eventual uses, the manner of its incorporation into a system of purposes, are worlds apart; that everything that exists, no matter what its origin, is periodically reinterpreted.*

—Friedrich Nietzsche[1]

## Chapter 1—List of Contents

| | |
|---|---|
| *Antecedents* | *13* |
| *The Little Rustic Hut* | *16* |
| *Quatremère de Quincy* | *19* |
| *Type as Origins, Classification, Imitation* | *20* |
| *Type Versus Model* | *24* |
| *Durand—Architecture as Taxonomy* | *24* |
| *The Précis—Towards a Design Methodology* | *26* |
| *Type as Diagram* | *28* |

## Antecedents

The eighteenth century in Europe became known as the *Enlightenment*, a period characterized by dramatic changes in science, philosophy, society, and politics. The term "Enlightenment" was introduced by Immanuel Kant in his brief 1748 essay ("What Is Enlightenment?"),[2] where he defined the concept as humankind's new phase, defined by its capability of emerging from its "self-imposed immaturity. Immaturity is the inability to use one's own understanding without another's guidance."[3] Man, according to Kant, should be capable of thinking by himself, thus becoming liberated from traditions and institutions, such as the church or political and governmental structures. "This enlightenment," he posits, "requires nothing

**14** Nineteenth Century—Origins, Imitation, Type

but *freedom*—and the most innocent of all that may be called 'freedom': freedom to make public use of one's reason in all matters."[4] The principal guiding principles of the new era, according to Kant, are science and philosophy.

Two fundamental issues marked the transformative developments in the sciences throughout the Enlightenment: the notions of *classification* and *origins*. With the publication of *Systema Naturae* (1735),[5] Carolus Linnaeus became one of Europe's leading scientists advancing the notion of classification in the biological sciences, developing a strategy that would be extremely influential in all areas of knowledge. Linnaeus proposed a division of living things into *Classes*, *Orders*, *Genera*, and *Species*,[6] establishing a correlation between the species' physical characteristics and their progeny, where each present form was the result of a prolonged evolutionary chain. The strategy was supplemented with a novel *nomenclature* criterion combining the names of the organism's specie and its genus. Linnaeus's ideas were very influential in all areas of knowledge; architecture was no exception. It became apparent that the built environment could be examined and analyzed according to similar taxonomic criterion. As posited by Anthony Vidler, "If Linnaeus was able to establish a classification of the zoological universe in Classes, Orders, and Genera (with their attendant species and varieties), why should not the architect similarly regard the range of his own production?"[7]

The consideration of classification in the sciences influenced the thinking of French architect and professor of the *Académie Royale d'Architecture* Jacques-François Blondel. In his *Cours d'Architecture* of 1771,[8] Blondel compiled an extensive list of varieties of buildings, such as theaters, libraries, prisons, and lighthouses, designating each of those groups of buildings as "genres" (the term suggesting a biological connotation). The *Cours* proposed an original strategy for understanding the history of architecture: rather than focusing on particular architects or monuments, the emphasis was placed on categorizing the building inventory as a collective endeavor developed over time, where authorship was relegated or eliminated.

An alternative approach for classifying the architecture of the past was advanced by French historian Julien-David Le Roy (1724–1803). In his *Les Ruines des plus beaux monuments de la Grèce* (1758),[9] Le Roy developed an innovative study of Greek temples. Instead of following chronological or stylistic criterion, he listed groups of buildings according to formal similitudes. The matrix of buildings deployed by Le Roy displays a notable resemblance to Linnaeus's biological rubrics, thus advancing an innovative (and scientific) methodology for analyzing and classifying the built environment. This idea is illustrated in the figure titled "Parallel Between Ancient and Modern Temples" (Figure 1.1), where temples of different historical periods and styles drawn at the same scale were grouped according to planimetric similitudes, their positioning and alignment suggesting an evolutionary process. A notable feature of Le Roy's approach was the coexistence of some of the most celebrated monuments together with lesser-known edifications—subscribing to the argument that science shouldn't have qualitative predilections.[10]

The other issue impacting the eighteenth century's intellectual debate was the notion of *origins*. Following a questioning of the biblical depictions of the beginnings

Towards an Inaugural Definition of Type **15**

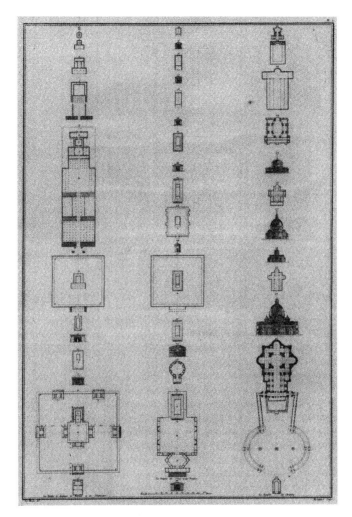

FIGURE 1.1   Le Moine, draftsman, Michelinot, engraver. Parallel between ancient and modern temples. From Julien-David Le Roy, *Les ruines des plus beaux monuments de la Grèce*, 2d ed. (Paris: Louis-François Delatour, 1770), plate 1. Getty Research Institute, Los Angeles.

of humankind, thinkers and scientists developed various theories regarding the origins of ideas, religions, languages, architecture, and artifacts created by early humans.[11] Intellectuals and philosophers such as Voltaire, Montesquieu, Rousseau, and Condillac expressed a strong interest in the first civilizations, leading to the publication of numerous texts and essays explaining the beginnings of humankind. This interest was fueled by several factors, including recent archaeological discoveries in Egypt and Greece and publications about the colonial experiences in the American continents.

**16**  Nineteenth Century—Origins, Imitation, Type

The Enlightenment's academic and scientific interest in the question of origins had a profound influence on eighteenth-century architectural theory. As noted by Anthony Vidler,[12] a consequence of this concern about the beginnings of architecture was the renewed consideration of the writings of Vitruvius. In Book 2, Chapter 1 of his treatise, Vitruvius describes how the first men gathered together around "the warm fire," and "began in that first assembly to construct shelters."[13] Humankind's first dwelling, according to this narration, was not a physical structure but a space delimited by the warmth emanated from the hearth. Architecture, therefore, was primarily a social setting.[14]

Vitruvius then discusses the evolution of architecture, establishing a linkage between the first constructions and their posterior developments:

> By observing the shelters of others and adding new details to their own inceptions, they constructed better and better kinds of huts as time went on. And *since they were of an imitative and teachable nature*, they would daily point out to each other the results of their building, boasting of the novelties in it; and thus, with their natural gifts sharpened by emulation, their standards improved daily.[15]
>
> *(Italics added)*

With this statement Vitruvius evinces the influence of the Aristotelian doctrine of imitation or *mimesis*, the process of adopting and later transforming a certain formal precedent. The history of architecture, according to this idea, is a prolonged chain of transformative iterations, where each building is both a derivation of anterior precedents and a new and original instance.

## The Little Rustic Hut

The figure that best represents the impact of the question of origins in the architectural discourse during the Enlightenment is the Jesuit abbé Marc-Antoine Laugier[16] (1713–69). With his *Essai sur l'architecture* (*An Essay on Architecture*, 1753), Laugier exemplifies the ideological shift developed during the eighteenth century: a priest depicting an account of the origins of architecture that differs from the Catholic doctrine. In his preface, Laugier lays out the fundamental principles of architecture, concluding with what could be described as an intellectual epiphany:

> Suddenly a bright light appeared before my eyes. I saw objects distinctly where before I had only caught a glimpse of haze and clouds. I took hold of these objects eagerly and saw by their lights my uncertainties gradually disappear and my difficulties vanished.[17]

What Laugier "sees" is the inevitable connection between the origins of architecture and its posterior development. His vision is epitomized by the image of the "rustic hut," a form predestined to be endlessly imitated, the initiation of a sequence that would continue on through contemporary times.

Laugier's account presents both similarities and differences to Vitruvius's narrative. The most notable discrepancy is that while Vitruvius describes the first constructions as distant and historical events, Laugier presents the "rustic hut" as a metaphor of contemporary significance, an original form that would become a central concept for the architectural debate of his time. Laugier's intention was to create the foundation of a theory that "firmly establishes the principles of architecture, explains its true spirit, and proposes rules for guiding talent and defining taste."[18] The primitive hut, therefore, may also be understood as an *allegory*,[19] a guide to be considered and reflected upon by his contemporaries. Reaffirming this notion, Laugier writes, "All splendors of architecture ever conceived have been modeled on the little rustic hut I have just described."[20]

Laugier's "technological" accounts were much more detailed than those of Vitruvius. He describes the process of building the hut, how it starts with the selection of a site next to the banks of a river, follows with the assortment of materials (branches and logs), continues with the conversion of those natural elements into architectural parts, and concludes with the final assembly of the dwelling:

> Some fallen branches in the forest are the right material for his purpose; he chooses four of the strongest, raises them upright and arranges them in a square; across their top he lays four other branches; on these he hoists from two sides yet another row of branches which, inclining towards each other, meet at their highest point. He then covers this kind of roof with leaves so closely packed that neither sun nor rain can penetrate. Thus, man is housed.[21]

While in the iconic image (Figure 1.2) the hut appears to be an indivisible unit, Laugier describes its construction as an arrangement of different "components." Initially, "man" collected trunks and branches of various sizes and shapes, and—after minimal alterations and repositioning—those parts were converted into building elements. In this way, the hut can be understood as an *assemblage*, where each element is independently defined:

> Let us never lose sight of our little rustic hut. I can only see columns, a ceiling or entablature and a pointed roof forming at both ends what is called a pediment . . . If each of these parts is suitably placed and suitably formed, nothing else need be added to make the work perfect.[22]

A *semantic operation* is evidenced in Laugier's text: what he previously referred to as "branches and logs" he later designates as "column," "entablature," and "pediment." While he describes the gradual transformation and relocation of the natural components, he starts referring to them as *architectural elements*. Not surprisingly, he dedicates the following chapter to "The Column,"[23] and lists a series of recommendations for its proper form and disposition. "The column," states Laugier,

**18**  Nineteenth Century—Origins, Imitation, Type

**FIGURE 1.2**  Charles-Joseph-Dominique Eisen, draftsman, Jacques Aliamet, engraver. Frontispiece from Marc-Antoine Laugier: *Essai sur l'architecture*, 2nd ed. 1755. Getty Research Institute, Los Angeles.

must be: (1) strictly perpendicular; (2) freestanding, so that its origin and purpose are expressed in a natural way; (3) round because nature makes nothing square; (4) tapered from bottom to top in imitation of nature where this diminution is found in all plants; (5) resting directly on the floor as the posts of the rustic hut rest directly on the ground.[24] Just as the "rustic hut" would become the ideal precedent for the

Towards an Inaugural Definition of Type **19**

future conception of buildings, the erected trunk will constitute the model for future "columns," the precursor of an architectural element destined to be forever imitated.

Laugier's depiction of the origins of the primitive hut presents suggestive similarities with Rousseau's description of the origins of language. In his *Essai sur l'origine des langues* (*Essay on the Origin of Languages*, 1781),[25] Rousseau states that in its inception, language possessed an absolutely transparent structure—words had an unequivocal meaning, which meant that communication among men was exempted of misunderstandings. Over time, this perfect language was affected by the use of metaphors and mannerisms, obfuscating the communication among men. Laugier develops a similar argument, applying it to the origins and development of architecture. His "column" becomes equivalent to Rousseau's *words*, entities that in their original state displayed diaphanous and evident meanings, though over time, men decorated and adorned them, muddling their comprehension. As suggested by Wolfgang Herrmann and others, Laugier's essay subscribed to an agenda designed for his contemporaries, which conveyed the principles of a rational architecture— epitomized by the freestanding structural columns—against the decorative excesses of the Rococo style so prevalent in France at the beginning of the eighteenth century.[26]

In the face of this problem, it became clear that rather than developing a better understanding of the actual beginnings of humankind, Rousseau and Laugier's primary goal was to advance a theoretical agenda. This idea was precisely articulated by Alan Colquhoun, who in his essay "Vernacular Classicism" commented,

> The postulation of a common, primitive culture, which Laugier shares to some extent with Rousseau, does not involve the empirical discovery of an actual vernacular, it is an hypotheses based on what logically should have been the case, conflating the logical with the chronological. We don't know a great deal about the pre-monumental architecture of ancient Greece, but what we do know leads us to believe that it had no relation to Laugier's primitive hut. Nor it is certain what the sources of Greek monumental architecture were. Laugier was no more concerned with the "real" Mediterranean vernacular than was Rousseau with a historical primitive society. He was with a distillation of a classical culture. He was not seeking to return to the earliest hours of man, but to the pure sources of classical architecture.[27]

## Quatremère de Quincy

The questions of origins and classification of architecture would come together in the theoretical corpus of Antoine-Chrysostome Quatremère de Quincy (1755–1849). Born and raised in Paris, Quatremère initially studied law before taking art courses at the *Collège de Louis-le-Grand*. During this period, he also attended the sculpture ateliers of professors Guillaume Coustou and Pierre Julien.[28] After graduating, Quatremère was awarded a residence in Italy, where he had the opportunity

**20**  Nineteenth Century—Origins, Imitation, Type

to survey the archaeological sites of Paestum and Pompeii,[29] an experience that awakened his interest in archaeology and the origins of architecture.

Like so many artists and intellectuals of his time, Quatremère suffered the effects of the 1789 revolution.[30] While he initially supported the uprising—in 1791 he briefly served as a deputy to the Legislative Assembly—during the *Reign of Terror* he was incarcerated for two years (1793–1795), during which time he was almost executed twice. In 1797 Quatremère went into exile in Germany, where he became familiar with the ideas of Immanuel Kant and Gotthold Lessing.[31] The following year, he was allowed to return to Paris, where he soon gained enormous prestige in academic circles. During the first decades of the nineteenth century, Quatremère became one of France's most renowned and influential scholars, as demonstrated by his appointment as *Secrétaire Perpétuel de l'Académie des Beaux-Arts*, a position he held from the institution's foundation in 1815 to his retirement in 1839.

Throughout his extensive academic career, Quatremère demonstrated a broad understanding of multiple and varied topics, such as archaeology, philosophy, linguistics, history, art, and architecture. The continuing variation and evolution of his theories—with notable thematic shifts—were reflected in his writings. Broadly speaking, the main three themes that defined his career were the question of *origins*, the notion of *imitation*, and the concept of *type*. While the focus of his interests varied, he simultaneously developed *intellectual continuities*, since many of the themes he discussed at one stage he would later reexamine under the framework of a new topic.

## Type as Origins, Classification, Imitation

In the third volume of the *Dictionnaire d'architecture*, published in 1825, Quatremère included the entry "Type," a term he had used before, but without offering a precise definition. In what became a pattern for most of the *Dictionnaire*'s entries, Quatremère starts the article by identifying the etymology of the term, and then listing its various uses throughout history into modern times. "Type," he informs, comes from the ancient Greek word *typos*, which represented the act of engraving, marking, tracing, or leaving a figure over a surface. The word was also associated with the creation of a *mold*, a *model*, or a *pattern*, to be used as a reference for future iterations, an action closely related to notions of repetition, reproduction, transcription, and replication. For Quatremère words, just like buildings, objects, and artworks, carry a progeny ready to be exhumed, and the scholar's task is to identify that genealogy.

Quatremère's definition of "Type" is an amalgamation of the principal topics he engaged throughout his academic career (and, as Sylvia Lavin pointed out, the question of "character" also became one of his central preoccupations).[32] Successively and alternatively, Quatremère defined type as: (1) a response to the question of *origins*; (2) a tool for *classifying* architecture; and (3) an agent of *imitation* for the development of the artistic process. Thus type, according to Quatremère, is a *polysemic concept*—it can alternatively or simultaneously adopt various meanings.

This factor helps explain the inherent complexity in launching a discussion on the concept, and why it has been subject to such diverse (sometimes contradictory) interpretations.

## Origins

Quatremère's first mention of the term "type" was in his essay *De l'Architecture Égyptienne*, completed in 1785, but published only in 1803.[33] In this study, Quatremère examined the early Egyptian constructions, which he compared to the temples of ancient Greece. His initial hypothesis was that the primitive hut originated in Egypt, and was only later adopted by the Greeks.[34] However, he later rectified this theory, arguing that the genesis of Egyptian architecture was the "cave," the "hut" being a form conceived and developed exclusively by the Greeks. This reassessment derived from his observation of Egyptian architecture's main features: the emphasis placed on volume, interiority, and "heaviness," contrastingly different traits than Greek architecture, characterized by its structural lightness.

After arguing for the existence of two *original forms*—the hut and the cave—Quatremère noticed that the tents assembled by the nomadic peoples of North Africa and the Middle East, traditionally made with canvas and light structures, were remarkably different from their Egyptian and Greek counterparts. This led him to introduce a third primary form, "the tent," whose conception and development showed quite distinct features from the other original constructions. Thus, Quatremère arrived at the conclusion that the beginnings of architecture can be traced to *three original types*: the *hut*, the *tent*, and the *cave*, respectively developed by communities of hunters, shepherds, and farmers. According to this theory, each one of those forms was developed independently due to particular geographical, climatic, and cultural conditions, where every building realized throughout the history of architecture denotes a certain lineage, an affiliation with one of the original types:

> We observe also how all inventions, in spite of subsequent changes, have conserved their elementary principle in a manner that is always visible, and always evident to feeling and reason. This elementary principle is like a sort of nucleus around which are assembled, and with which are consequently coordinated, all the developments and the variations of form to which the object was susceptible . . . This is what ought to be called *type* in architecture as in every other area of human invention and institution.[35]
>
> *(Italics in original)*

In Quatremère's description and analysis of the three original dwellings, "type" is considered both a taxonomic and genetic concept, the "elementary principle" from which all branches of architecture initiated. By establishing a relationship between the origins of architecture and the notion of type, this last one acquires a *genealogical* rooting, a necessary link between the original forms and contemporary buildings.

## Classification

The second meaning of type, according to Quatremère, is as a *classification tool*. Although the ability of cataloguing the built forms is the most conventional consideration of the concept of type, Quatremère discusses the subject only succinctly. Quatremère's notion of classifying architecture according to morphological criterion derived from his earlier theory of the three originating types, where he divided humankind's inaugural constructions into three *typological chains*—the hut, the cave, and the tent. Years later he expanded this idea by elaborating on the evolution of the hut into the Doric temple,[36] stating that while the transformation evidenced an abrupt change of materials (from wood to stone), the morphological progress displayed a clear continuity. In the 1825 edition of the *Dictionnaire*, Quatremère reinforces this notion, arguing that the division of the building inventory must be realized according to a morphological criterion: "type," he states, may be considered "to designate certain general forms which are characteristic of the building that receives them,"[37] a position that appears aligned with Le Roy's tables of buildings organized according to formal similitudes.

Quatremère's morphological understanding of type cancels an alternate approach for classifying buildings—according to their function. As previously commented, in his *Cours d'Architecture*, Blondel proposed an organization of the building inventory according to programs—theaters, schools, prisons, and so forth. In a strict sense, this criterion is incompatible with a morphological taxonomy of types. Buildings associated with two different programs, such as a school and a prison, belong to the same formal type if they have similar floor plan layouts. While Quatremère didn't elaborate on the relationship between type and function, it transpires from his theory of the three original types that buildings derived from those forms can host a variety of functions.[38]

## Imitation

The third meaning of type according to Quatremère derives from the concept of *imitation* or *mimesis*. As commented earlier, imitation was a central topic in the articulation of his theory of the three original types, affirming that the evolutionary nature of architectural forms developed through mimetic processes.[39] Years later he expanded his ideas on the subject in his 1823 essay *De l'imitation*,[40] introducing two notions that would become critical for his understanding of type. In the first place he established the differentiation between repetition and resemblance—that is, between the exact copy and (Aristotelian) imitation—"the one identical, being in fact only the repetition of a thing by the thing itself; the other imitative, being the repetition of a thing by some other which becomes the image of it."[41] The other simmering issues that Quatremère discusses are the different approximations towards imitation in architecture and the other arts.[42] In painting and sculpture, he argues, the mimetic model is the natural world; the artist therefore emulates the elements, species, and all visible forms that populate the earth. "To imitate in the fine arts is to produce the resemblance of a thing, but in some other thing which becomes the image of it."[43] Without a natural model, architecture was founded on abstract and intellectual concepts, such as the instrumentalization of norms and mathematical relationships, "but that she imitates no reality; that her form is for the mind, only a combination of relations, proportions, and reasons, which please inasmuch as they are simply expressed."[44] These abstract qualities, he concludes,[45] posit architecture as the most sophisticated of the arts, "apparently more enslaved by matter than the other two arts, [and] [. . .] in fact more ideal, more intellectual, and more metaphysical than they are."[46]

A remarkable aspect of Quatremère's theory of imitation—which would transpire in his conception of type—is the *integration* of the doctrines of mimesis advanced by Plato and Aristotle. As commented on by Panofsky in his essay *Idea*[47] (1929), procuring the reconciliation of Plato's and Aristotle's theories of imitation had been a central question since the Renaissance. The consideration of Plato is a complex one, since in principle he rejected the conception of art as a mimetic process.[48] Artistic imitation, according to this view, is a falsification of reality, and therefore a distancing from the truth. As posited by Panofsky, starting in the sixteenth century Plato's theories were reinterpreted under a new light; "it was possible that precisely the concept of 'idea,' from which Plato himself had so often deduced the inferiority of artistic activity, is now used almost as a specifically art-theoretical concept."[49] Following this view, the work of art is conceived under the spell of an *idea* or *concept*,[50] an originating form that anticipates and dictates the development of the artistic process.

The other doctrine of imitation considered by Quatremère was that advanced by Aristotle. Contrary to his master, Plato, Aristotle embraced a positive opinion of the imitative act, up to the point of considering imitation one of the main features that distinguishes humans from other species. In his *Poetics*,[51] Aristotle discriminates between two kinds of mimetic processes: the one that represents things *as they are*, and the one that represents things *as they ought to be*.[52] This last option is associated with the artistic process, the faculty of creating something *differentiated* and (if possible) *superior* to what already exists. Aristotle's conception of artistic process implies the selection of preexisting forms, images, or ideas, and appealing to diverse mimetic procedures (e.g., transformation) results in the generation of original iterations.

Quatremère's characterizations of imitation as an idea and as an artistic process lead him to a consideration of the architectural project developed under the domain of the type. The typological project, according to this notion, is realized in two instances. The initial stage is the identification of type as an ideal form "within an artist's imagination," comprising "the idea of an element which must itself serve as a rule for the model."[53] The following instance is the process of formal definition involving "all the developments and the variations of form to which the object was susceptible."[54] While the initial stage conveys the manifest influence of Platonic doctrine, the subsequent process of formal definition derives from the Aristotelian conception of mimesis, understood as the adoption and transformation of preexisting forms or images.

**24** Nineteenth Century—Origins, Imitation, Type

## Type Versus Model

To clarify the significance of the concept of "type" in the artistic process, Quatremère establishes a dialectic contrast with what he refers to as the "model" (as observed by Sylvia Lavin, Quatremère's utilization of the term "model" implies a remarkable semantic adjustment from previous texts, since on various occasions, particularly in his essay on Egyptian architecture, he used the words "type" and "model" interchangeably).[55] In his entry of 1825, Quatremère presented the concepts of "type" and "model" as opposite and antithetical: while type is understood as a *formal idea* to be imitated, the model is defined as a concrete and precise *replica*:

> The model, understood in the sense of practical execution, is an object that should be repeated as it is; contrariwise, the type is an object after which each artist can conceive works that bear no resemblance to each other. All is precise and given when it comes to the model, while all is more or less vague when it comes to the *type*.[56]

> *(Italics in original)*

The opposition between type and model advanced by Quatremère echoes his earlier identification of two "kinds of resemblance" for developing an artistic process: "identical" and "imitative."[57] In his definition of "type," Quatremère presents a similar contrast for describing the architectural project: while the "model" implies an "identical" replication, an operation that demands precise similitude[58] between the precedent and its copy, the "type" is considered "imitative," an exploratory process where the development of the new iteration is defined through Aristotelian imitation.

Towards the end of the entry, Quatremère makes a quite unexpected comment, establishing a correlation between type and object: "No one is unaware that a multitude of pieces of furniture, tools, seats, and clothes have their necessary type."[59] The statement posits that "objects," or mechanically produced things, can be designated as "types," seemingly contradicting his previous comments that precisely replicated elements constitute "models." The statement also reverses his recurring argument contrasting the notions of imitation and replication. It could be argued, however, that Quatremère is establishing a *disciplinary distinction* for considering the concept of type: when assumed within the field of architecture, he advocates a mimetic (Aristotelian) artistic process (therefore rejecting the model), though when he discusses industrially designed and manufactured objects ("furniture, tools") he accepts them as "types." This situation (which is further discussed in the following section dedicated to Durand) suggests the possibility of expanding the conventional definition of architectural type, where the distinctions between type and object become increasingly ambiguous.

## Durand—Architecture as Taxonomy

There are two interrelated issues that define Quatremère de Quincy's theoretical legacy. On the one hand, there is the abstract character of his thought, which in various passages resembles more the enquiries of a philosopher than of an art scholar. His texts denote a timeless "aura," with a remarkable capacity to navigate the most diverse disciplines, such as archaeology, linguistics, art, or architectural theory. Although in certain passages Quatremère appears to be favoring a "classical" conception of art (e.g., when he considers the Greek temple an unsurpassable model),[60] he does not promote a stylistic agenda. Quite on the contrary, his arguments consistently refer to conceptual and metaphysical[61] concepts beyond circumstantial deliberations. These qualities help explain the permanence and validity of his theories, which—particularly since the 1960s—have been the subject of continuous examinations and interpretations.

Another characteristic of Quatremère's texts is the absence of examples and graphic references. In this regard, his bibliographic position appears paradoxical. During a period when the theoretical production of architecture begins to rely on graphic evidence—it suffices to recall Leroy's treatise— Quatremère, following Alberti's legacy, continues discussing ideas and concepts independent of circumstantial examples or projects. This posture is reflected in his conception of type, understood both as an idea and as a synthesis resulting from comparing multiple buildings that share similar features, and therefore it cannot be represented by images.

Against this background, it is necessary to contrast Quatremère with his contemporary, Professor Jean-Nicolas-Louis Durand (1760–1835). While both agreed on the need to reformulate a theory of architecture substantiated in building classification, their strategies were clearly different. While Quatremère advanced his theory of type as a set of reflections, and left to the reader's imagination the visualization of those ideas, Durand's theoretical corpus was structured around plates and tables with plans, sections, elevations, and diagrams. If Quatremère insisted on the impossibility of representing a type, Durand's self-imposed task was to visually expose all known types by cataloguing groups of buildings sharing similar characteristics.

Born in Paris and raised by a family of humble resources, Durand[62] won a scholarship at the *Collège Montaigu*, one of the city's most respected educational institutions. Early on, he displayed a notable interest in art and design, excelling in drawing, sculpture, and history courses. After obtaining the second prize of Rome's Grand Prix in two consecutive years (1778 and 1780), he was hired by Étienne-Louis Boullée, where he collaborated on various projects, such as the *Hôtel Royal des Invalides*, and the expansions of the *Opéra* and the *Métropole*. In 1795, he was offered a professorship at the recently inaugurated *École Polytechnique*, where he was in charge of teaching architectural principles and design to engineering students. Shortly after, he reformulated the architectural courses' syllabus, diagraming a program of weekly lessons distributed throughout the academic year.

During his first years at the *Polytechnique*, Durand wrote two seminal books that, from different angles, examine the notion of type. Continuing the ambitions of various eighteen-century thinkers, his aim was to establish the basis of a novel "science of architecture," structured around a comparative method of classification. For the development of this task, he absorbed the legacy of two figures who also influenced Quatremère.[63] On the one hand, he followed the strategies advanced by his former teacher Julien-David Leroy, who developed an extensive analysis of ancient Greek temples according to morphological similitudes. On the other hand, he considered Linnaeus's method of classification of biological species. Leroy's thinking and Linnaeus's thinking are particularly palpable in Durand's first book, the *Recueil et parallèle des édifices de tout genre, anciens et modernes* (*Collection and Parallel of Buildings of Every Genre, Ancient and Modern*, 1799), which includes brief commentaries by his colleague, the historian Jacques-Guillaume Legrand. Echoing the Enlightenment's fixation on taxonomy, the Recueil consisted of a series of plans illustrating all known building types organized "according to their kinds, arranged in order of degree of likeness and drawn to the same scale."[64]

The *Recueil* acknowledged one of the central questions posed by the concept of type: it cannot be represented with a single image. Therefore Durand presents a series of floor plans sharing similar features, allowing the reader to "construct" the type through the comparison and synthesis derived from those plans. This strategy is evidenced in the table titled "*Temples ronds*," composed of a series of circular plants from various historical periods, where their placing criteria is based on formal similitudes rather than chronological of stylistic considerations.[65] The table can be understood as a visual corroboration of the type (in this case the "circular temple"), defined by the persistence of certain common features. Type, in this context, is assumed as both a classification tool and abstraction process, an instrument that helps one to understand the immense building inventory.

## The Précis—Towards a Design Methodology

The second treatise Durand wrote is the *Précis des leçons d'architecture données à l'École royale Polytechnique* (*Précis of the Lectures on Architecture at the École Royale Polytechnique*), published between 1802 and 1805, where he discusses various mechanisms for developing the architectural project. The design strategy starts with the selection of predetermined *elements*,[66] such as columns, vaults, and walls. The elements, according to Durand, are the most simple and essential components; indivisible in architectural terms, they are to architecture as "notes are to music; without a perfect knowledge of which it is impossible to proceed further."[67] The following step is the assemblage of those elements into parties (or parts), such as stairs, porches, or courtyards, allowing an increased level of complexity (Figure 1.3). At this point, Durand discusses the different ways those parts may be disposed: "The elements of buildings may be placed side by side, or one above the other . . . We shall therefore distinguish between two kinds of disposition: horizontal, as represented by plans; and vertical, as represented in sections and elevations."[68] The architectural project, according to this idea, is the art of combining and connecting distinctive building elements and parts.

For Durand, both the elements and the parties are products of a distillation process, where the architect doesn't need to shape those forms—they are *available collective constructs*, just like words are a precondition for the learning and utilization of language. This question brings back Quatremère's problematic distinction between the notions of *type* and *model*. In a strict sense, Quatremère's understanding

Towards an Inaugural Definition of Type 27

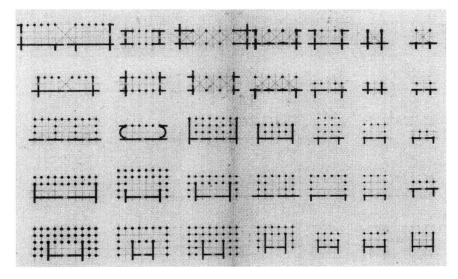

FIGURE 1.3   Jean-Nicolas-Louis Durand: *Porches*. From *Précis des leçons d'architecture données à l'École polytechnique*. Part II, Composition in General. Plate 9. Getty Research Institute, Los Angeles.

of type differs from Durand's definitions of architectural *element* or *part*. According to Quatremère, type stems from an idea whose form and appearance will be shaped through a mimetic process. In turn the model implies the exact repetition of a certain precedent. Durand considered that—following a process of cataloguing and classification—formal precedents could be condensed into single and "standard" forms, ready to be assembled and distributed in a larger scheme. Thus his approach appears like a replication tactic and consequently beyond Quatremère's typological realm. However, it has been noted that towards the end of his entry on *type* Quatremère contradicts his previous statements, commenting that repetitive pieces "have their necessary type."[69] This situation (which is further discussed in Chapter 6) suggests the possibility of expanding the conventional definition of architectural type, where the distinctions between type and object (or model) become increasingly ambiguous.

In the third section of the second volume of the *Précis*, Durand examines the relationship between the city and its main constituents: building typologies. While he insists on identifying the correspondences between the parts and the whole, he delineates a distinction between public and private buildings: "Just as walls, columns, and so on, are the elements of which buildings are composed, buildings are the elements of which cities are composed."[70] The ruling recalls the categorization by Giambattista Nolli for his plan of Rome (1748), where public buildings' (mostly churches and convents) interiors were assumed as part of the urban inventory, while private buildings (presumably housing) are represented as containers of the urban

**28** Nineteenth Century—Origins, Imitation, Type

fabric. The idea of the city advanced by Durand follows this *typological hierarchy*, commanded by urban landmarks and monuments, such as temples, courthouses, and libraries, and supplemented by "generic" residential typologies that shape the urban fabric.

## Type as Diagram

Once identified the building parts, the *Précis* introduces a methodology for integrating those parts under a single plan: the architectural composition. Again, for conveying the design mechanism, Durand appeals to an artistic analogy: "the elements are to architecture what words are to speech, what notes are to music."[71] The architectural project, according to this view, is advanced as a gradual progress from simple to complex, from general to specific, deducing the appropriate disposition of the diverse elements and parts. "Architecture," Durand wrote,

> is the composition of the whole of buildings which is nothing other than the result of the assemblage of their parts. It is necessary to know the former before occupying oneself with the latter; as these parts are solely a compound of the basic elements of buildings, and as all particular principles must be derived after the study of general principles, it will be these basic elements that constitute the prime object of the architect's study.[72]

A notable aspect of the *Précis* is that it proposes different design methodologies depending on the scale of the intervention. For developing an entire building, rather than selecting and combining the elements and parts, Durand advances a process ruled by the *elements of composition*, such as grids and axes, geometrical and immaterial entities that assist the designer in "composing" a building. Anthony Vidler has commented on how Durand was influenced by his colleague at the *École Polytechnique*, Professor Gaspard Monge, credited as the inventor of descriptive geometry. As posited by Vidler, Monge developed "a method for representation—a code of points, lines, and planes to be organized on the newly introduced graph paper."[73] Just like those geometric entities defined by Monge, the elements of composition introduced by Durand provide a framework for the development of the architectural project.

Durand's consideration of the elements of composition in the development of the architectural project is illustrated in the plate titled *Marche à suivre dans la composition d'un projet quelconque* (Procedure to be followed in the composition of any project), a sequence of five drawings, each representing a step towards the realization of an architectural project (Figure 1.4). The first drawing is a *diagram* with a few intersecting axes inscribed in a grid, a very abstract image with minimal architectural information. The next drawing includes various "sub-grids," laying the basis for the inclusion of four equidistant rectangles. Following he adds the walls' thicknesses, suggesting a distinction between interior and exterior spaces. The concluding drawing is a quite detailed floor plan of a circular

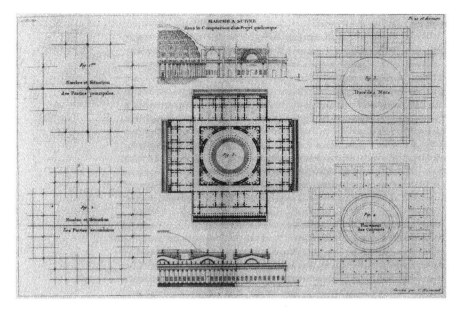

**FIGURE 1.4** Jean-Nicolas-Louis Durand: *Marche à suivre dans la composition d'un projet quelconque* (Procedure to be followed in the composition of any project). From *Précis des leçons d'architecture données à l'École Polytechnique*. 4th ed. (Paris, the author, 1825), vol. 2, plate 21. Getty Research Institute, Los Angeles.

space surrounded by four porticoes, a composition reminiscent of Palladio's *Villa Rotonda*. As posited by Leandro Madrazo, "What Durand actually described is a step-by-step transformation of a rough scheme into a detailed representation of a building, that is to say, a transformation of geometry into architecture."[74] Thus, the initiating diagram can be interpreted as the preliminary representation of the type; its level of abstraction and indefinition allows the project to be developed in multiple and varied ways.

The power of the diagram is more intensively explored in the plate *Ensembles d'édifices résultants des divisions du quarré, du parallélogramme et de leurs combinaisons avec le cercle* (Building ensembles, resulting from the divisions of the square, the parallelogram and their combinations with the circle; as Madrazo observed, in spite of the title there are no buildings represented in this illustration).[75] *Ensembles d'édifices* displays an array of diagrams constructed by geometrical entities such as lines, circles, arches, and squares (Figure 1.5). Each drawing can be interpreted as a synthesis derived from similar floor plans as well as the originating signature for the development of the architectural project, where the essential properties of the architectural project are already present in the figure. The diagram, according to this idea, reaffirms the relationship between type and geometry; it is both an abstraction of preceding buildings and the originator of the architectural form.[76]

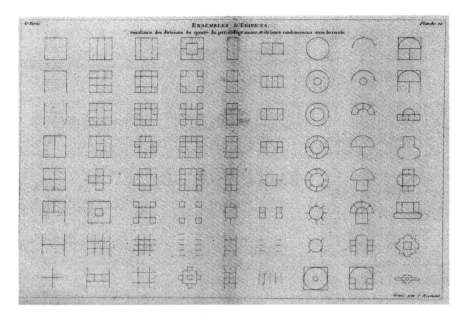

**FIGURE 1.5** Jean-Nicolas-Louis Durand: *Ensembles d'édifices résultants des divisions du quarré, du parallélogramme et de leurs combinaisons avec le cercle* (Building ensembles, resulting from the divisions of the square, the parallelogram and their combinations with the circle). From *Précis des leçons d'architecture données à l'École polytechnique*. Part II. Composition in General. Plate 20. Getty Research Institute, Los Angeles.

The notion of diagram as originator of the architectural project echoes the previously discussed equivalences between type and model. The subjacent question is if Durand's diagrams, elements, and parts can be considered under the domain of the type,[77] a subject that has sparked intense debate between contemporary architects and critics.[78] Rafael Moneo has categorically rejected the possibility of equating the notions of type and diagram, affirming that "types, in my view, resist representation. I don't believe that types can be drawn . . . and as a result of that, using Durand to speak about typology is misleading."[79] In turn, Leandro Madrazo accepts the correspondences between Durand's diagrams and Quatremère's concept of type, commenting that "the method described by Durand . . . suggests that the initial geometric scheme can be considered the type."[80]

What lies behind Moneo's and Madrazo's contrasting positions is the *precise* definition of type, and more specifically, its standing in the contemporary architectural scene. While with his statement Moneo subscribes to Quatremère's definition of type as a mental construct, which cannot (or shouldn't) be represented in graphic terms, Madrazo argues for an expanded understanding *and* scope of the concept of type, particularly considering the role of diagram as originator of the architectural project. In the following chapters the consideration of type will oscillate between these two positions. On the one hand, this study accepts Quatremère's definition of type as origins, classification, and imitation as a vital and indispensable reference. On the other hand, this work also assumes the need of a continual reassessment of the concept of type, particularly when considering its protagonism within the realm of the architectural project.

## Notes

1  Nietzsche, Friedrich, *On the Genealogy of Morals*. New York: Knopf Doubleday, 2010, 77.
2  Kant, Immanuel, and Hans Reiss. "An Answer to the Question: 'What Is Enlightenment?'" *Kant: Political Writings*. Cambridge: Cambridge University Press, 1970, 54–60.
3  Kant, "What Is Enlightenment?" 54.
4  Kant, "What Is Enlightenment?" 55.
5  Linnaeus, Carolus, *Systema naturae, 1735*. (Facsimile of the 1st edition). Nieuwkoop, B. de Graff, 1964. For a thorough discussion of Linnaeus's theories and influence on his contemporaries, see Andrew Polaszek (ed.), *Systema Naturae 250 — The Linnaean Ark*. Boca Raton, FL: CRC Press, 2010.
6  See David Quammen, "Linnaeus, A Passion for Order," 5–10. In Polaszek (ed.), *Systema Naturae*, 250.
7  Vidler, Anthony, "The Idea of Type: The Transformation of the Academic Ideal, 1750–1830," *Oppositions 8*. Cambridge, MA: MIT Press, 1977, 445.
8  For a thorough review of François Blondel's treatise, see Robin Middleton, "Jacques François Blondel and the 'Cours d'Architecture.'" *Journal of the Society of Architectural Historians*, Vol. 18, No. 4, 1959, 140–148. DOI: 10.2307/987903.
9  Le Roy, David, *The Ruins of the Most Beautiful Monuments of Greece*. Los Angeles: Getty Research Institute, 2004. For a comprehensive examination of the work of Le Roy and his influence on his contemporaries, see Christopher Drew Armstrong: *Julien-David Le Roy and the Making of Architectural History*. London: Routledge, 2012.
10  Mari Hvattum developed an extensive commentary on Le Roy's text. See Hvattum, Mari, *Gottfried Semper and the Problem of Historicism*. Cambridge: Cambridge University Press, 2004, 117.
11  For a detailed account of the eighteenth-century interest in the question of the origins in France, see Vidler, Anthony, *The Writing of the Walls—Architectural Theory in the Late Enlightenment*. Princeton: Princeton Architectural Press, 1987, 7–21.
12  Anthony Vidler examined Vitruvius's influence on various eighteenth-century thinkers, particularly the work of Lafitau, Rousseau, and Dafoe. See Vidler, *The Writing of the Walls*; particularly the chapter "Rebuilding the Primitive Hut," 7–21.
13  Vitruvius, *The Ten Books of Architecture*. Translated by M. H. Morgan. Cambridge, MA: Harvard University Press, 1914, The Project Gutenberg EBook no. 20239. www.gutenberg.org. Release date 31 December 2006.
14  As discussed in Chapter 2, the consideration of the hearth as the first human dwelling became a central topic in Gottfried Semper's "Four Elements of Architecture."
15  Vitruvius: *The Ten Books of Architecture*. See Book 2, "The Origin of the Dwelling House," 38–42.
16  Laugier's life illustrates the peculiarities of the period: a Jesuit priest with a solid intellectual education developing one of the most influential theories about the origins of architecture, thus contradicting the Old Testament's catechism. Laugier was raised in a well-off family; his father owned and managed properties, while his mother was from a noble lineage. As the youngest brother and following the tradition, the young Marc-Antoine consented to pursue the career of priest. A few years after entering the novitiate, he stood out for his intellectual and oratorical skills, having the honor of preaching before the king and his court at the chapel of Versailles. In 1753 he published the *Essai*, initially

## 32 Nineteenth Century—Origins, Imitation, Type

anonymously, trying to avoid any controversy with the Church's hierarchy. However, a few months after publication it became evident who had been the real author of the text, creating a conflict with the Jesuit order. In 1754 he was transferred to the Benedictine order, allowing him to focus almost exclusively on academic and intellectual activities. For a detailed biography, see Herrmann, Wolfgang, *Laugier and Eighteenth-Century French Theory*. London: Zwemmer, 1985.

17 Laugier, Marc-Antoine, *An Essay on Architecture*. Los Angeles: Hennessey & Ingalls, 1977, 4.
18 Laugier, *Essay*, 1.
19 Richard Etlin has argued that Laugier's primitive hut should be interpreted as an allegory. See Etlin, Richard A., *Frank Lloyd Wright and Le Corbusier: The Romantic Legacy*. Manchester: Manchester University Press, 1994, 205.
20 Laugier, *Essay*, 12.
21 Laugier, *Essay*, 12.
22 Laugier, *Essay*, 12–13.
23 Laugier, *Essay*. See "Article I" titled "The Column," 14–22.
24 Laugier, *Essay*, 14.
25 Rousseau, Jean-Jacques, and Johann Gottfried Herder, *On the Origin of Language*. London: University of Chicago Press, 1986.
26 Herrmann, *Laugier and Eighteenth Century French Theory*, 66–67.
27 Colquhoun, Alan, "Vernacular Classicism." In *Modernity and the Classical Tradition: Architectural Essays, 1980–1987*. Cambridge, MA: MIT Press, 1989, 30.
28 The main biographical data was obtained from the website *Dictionary of Art Historians:* "Antoine Quatremère de Quincy." www.dictionaryofarthistorians.org/quatremeredequincya.htm. Accessed November 20, 2014.
29 Lavin, Sylvia, *Quatremère de Quincy and the Invention of a Modern Language of Architecture*. Cambridge, MA: MIT Press, 1992, 18.
30 *Dictionary of Art Historians*, "Quatremère."
31 *Dictionary of Art Historians*, "Quatremère."
32 In the chapter "The Characters of Classicism" (*Quatremère de Quincy and the Invention of a Modern Language of Architecture*, MIT Press, 1992, 126–147) Sylvia Lavin comments that the notion of "character" preoccupied Quatremère at various moments of his academic career. In a simple manner, "character" (and the similar term "decorum") can be defined as the capacity of a building to express its purpose. The notion of character was a central eighteenth-century architectural topic, as attested by the works of Germain Boffrand (*Livre d'architecture,* 1745) and Jacques-François Blondel (*Cours d'architecture,* 1771), two of the main architects who discussed the concept. A central aspect of Quatremère's definition of "character" is that it can convey different meanings depending on the context in which it is employed. He defined three kinds of "character": *essential, relative,* and *accidental,* according to the approach regarding imitating nature. For additional information, see Francis Mallgrave's abbreviated version of Quatremère's 1788 rubric dedicated to "Character." Mallgrave, Harry Francis (ed.), *Architectural Theory: An Anthology From Vitruvius to 1870*. Malden, MA: Blackwell, 2006, 206–209. Also, for a brief review of the notion of character in Quatremère's theoretical evolution, see Di Palma, Vittoria, "Architecture, Environment and Emotion: Quatremère de Quincy and the Concept of Character." *AA Files 47*, September 2002, 50.
33 Lavin, *Quatremère de Quincy*, 88–90.
34 Sylvia Lavin developed a detailed analysis of Quatremère's essay on the origins of Egyptian architecture. See Lavin, *Quatremère*, 18–30.
35 Quatremère De Quincy, and Samir Younés, *The Historical Dictionary of Architecture of Quatremère De Quincy*. London: Andreas Papadakis, 1999, 255.
36 Quatremère discusses this subject in the entry "On the Origin of the Doric Order," *The Historical Dictionary of Architecture*, 146–149.
37 Quatremère, *The Historical Dictionary of Architecture*, 256.

Towards an Inaugural Definition of Type **33**

38 The relationship between type and function, which would become a central topic at various moments of the twentieth century, is extensively discussed in Chapters 3 and 4.

39 In his *De l'architecture egyptienne*, Quatremère stated that "we have indeed seen that primitive dwellings, suggested by need, became everywhere a kind of model offered to the imitation of art" (SL 107).

40 Quatremère de Quincy, *An Essay on the Nature, the End, and the Means of Imitation in the Fine Arts*. London: Smith, Elder, Cornhill, 1837. Text also referred to as *De l'imitation*, original print 1823.

41 "Having distinguished two kinds of resemblance, the one identical, being in fact only the repetition of a thing by the thing itself; the other imitative, being the repetition of a thing by some other which becomes the image of it." Quatremère de Quincy, *De l'imitation*, 31.

42 The question of Quatremère's distinction between imitation in the fine arts and architecture is thoroughly discussed in Lavin: *Quatremère*, particularly the chapter "The Language of Imitation," 102–113.

43 Quatremère, *De l'imitation*, 11.

44 Quatremère, *The Historical Dictionary*, 87.

45 "Consequently, only time and customs must have imperceptibly developed a general system of proportions." Quatremère, *The Historical Dictionary*, 147.

46 Quoted in Lavin, *Quatremère*, 107.

47 Panofsky, Erwin, *Idea: A Concept in Art History*. Columbia: University of South Carolina Press, 1968 (Orig. Ed. 1929).

48 Plato, *The Republic*, translated by Allan Bloom. New York: Basic Books, 1991.

49 Panofsky, *Idea*, 7.

50 For a thorough examination of the Renaissance's notion of *concetto* (concept), see David Summers, *Michelangelo and the Language of Art*. Princeton: Princeton University Press, 1981, 279–282.

51 Aristotle, *Rhetoric and Poetics*. New York: The Modern Library, New York, 1954.

52 "the distinction between historian and poet is not in the one writing prose and the other verse . . . it consists really in this, that the one describes the thing that has been, and the other a kind of thing that might be." Aristotle, *Poetics*, 1451b.

53 Quatremère, *The Historical Dictionary*, 254.

54 Quatremère, *The Historical Dictionary*, 255.

55 Observed by Lavin in *Quatremère*, particularly in the chapter "The Transformation of Type," 89–91.

56 Quatremère, *The Historical Dictionary*, 254–255.

57 Quatremère, *De l'imitation*, 31.

58 "The model compels a formal resemblance." Quatremère, *The Historical Dictionary*, 255.

59 Quatremère, *The Historical Dictionary*, 256.

60 In the entry *Doric* Quatremère comments about the preeminence of the Doric temple, "the originating type . . . the result of the experience and taste of many centuries . . . it is rather the very perfection of art." See Quatremère, *The Historical Dictionary*, 146.

61 In his introductory commentary on the *Historical Dictionary*, Samir Younés argues about the "metaphysical" qualities of Quatremère's theories. See Quatremère, De Quincy, and Samir Younés, *The Historical Dictionary*, 10.

62 For additional details of Durand's life, see Villari, Sergio, *J.N.L. Durand (1760–1834): Art and Science of Architecture*, New York: Rizzoli, 1990.

63 The influence of Le Roy and Cuvier in Durand's taxonomic criterion was examined by Anthony Vidler, "The Idea of Type," 450.

64 Quoted in Vidler, "The Idea of Type," 451.

65 The design tactic described by Durand presents clear similarities with Quatremère's definition of type: "This elementary principle is like a sort of nucleus around which are assembled, and with which are consequently coordinated, all the developments and the variations of form to which the object was susceptible." Quatremère, *The Historical Dictionary*, 255.

**34** Nineteenth Century—Origins, Imitation, Type

66  Durand, Jean-Nicolas-Louis, *Précis of the Lectures on Architecture; With, Graphic Portion of the Lectures on Architecture.* Los Angeles, CA: Getty Research Institute, 2000, 74.
67  Introduction by Antoine Picon in Durand, *Précis*, 29.
68  Durand, *Précis*, 119.
69  Quatremère, *The Historical Dictionary*, 256.
70  Durand, *Précis*, 143.
71  Quoted in Westfall, Carroll William, *Architecture, Liberty and Civic Order: Architectural Theories From Vitruvius to Jefferson and Beyond.* New York: Routledge, 2016.
72  Quoted in Villari, *J.N.L. Durand (1760–1834)*, 59.
73  Vidler, "Diagrams of Diagrams," 9.
74  Madrazo, Leandro, "Durand and the Science of Architecture," *Journal of Architectural Education Vol. 48, No. 1*, (Sept. 1994), 17. DOI: 10.2307/1425306, 18.
75  Madrazo, "Durand and the Science of Architecture," 18.
76  See Sam Jacoby, "Typal and Typological Reasoning: A Diagrammatic Practice of Architecture," *The Journal of Architecture* (2015): accessed February 28, 2016. DOI: 10.1080/13602365.2015.1116104.
77  In his introduction to the English translation of the *Précis*, Antoine Picon comments on Durand and Quatremère's divergent conceptions of type: "Here, again, the gulf that separates Durand's compositions from those of Quatremère de Quincy is striking." Durand, *Précis*, 48.
78  These last decades the diagram has become a critical theoretical and practical subject, occasionally discussed in relation to the notion of type. Anthony Vidler examined the subject in various texts, such as "Diagrams of Diagrams: Architectural Abstraction and Modern Representation," *Representations, No. 72*, 2000, 1–20. Most recently, the apparent equivalence between the notions of type and diagram was discussed by Sam Jacoby and Hyungmin Pai. Pai examines the subject within the framework of his research on the North American Beaux-Arts system of composition and its posterior collapse as a consequence of the rise of modernism (see Pai, Hyungmin, "The Diagrammatic Construction of Type." *The Journal of Architecture* (2015), 1088–1104; also the book evolving from his doctoral dissertation: Hyungmin Pai, *The Portfolio and the Diagram: Architecture, Discourse and Modernity in America.* Cambridge, MA, The MIT Press, 2002). Sam Jacoby's focus on the subject starts at the historical moment Hyungmin Pai concludes his thesis: his concern is how modernism's infatuation with the diagram affected the conventional (what could be summed as the *Quatremère-Argan-Rossi lineage*) conception of type. Jacoby argues that the diagram should be understood as a strategy to be developed under the ample spectrum of type, thus generating what he refers to as a "typological diagram." In Jacoby's words, "The eventual demise of type in the twentieth-century architectural discourse encouraged a turn to diagrams. However, as Le Roy recognized, architectural diagrams rely on typological production. He also understood that a diagrammatic function depends on abstraction, an abstraction of architectural form that considers history, context and culture as discursive arguments and limits. The typological diagram therefore simultaneously envisions architecture as a specific object and a generic possibility of objects. The diagram limits the possibilities of architectural speculation without determining a finite formal representation." See Jacoby, "Typal and Typological Reasoning," 957.
79  Moneo made this comment during a roundtable session at the conference "Type Versus Typology." See Sam Jacoby and María José Orihuela, "Conversations on Formal and Social Diagrams," *The Journal of Architecture* (2015): accessed February 28, 2016. DOI: 10.1080/13602365.2015.1117186.
80  Madrazo is referring to Giulio Carlo Argan's essay on typology, which recounts Quatremère's inaugural definition of the concept of type. See Madrazo, Leandro, "Durand and the Science of Architecture," 18.

# 2

# SEMPER'S KNOT

*The nocturnal sky shows glimmering nebulae among the splendid miracle of stars—either old extinct systems scattered throughout the universe, cosmic dust taking shape around a nucleus, or a condition in between destruction and regeneration. They are a suitable analogy for similar events on the horizon of art history. They signify a world of art passing into the formless, while suggesting at the same time a new formation in the making.*

—Gottfried Semper[1]

## Chapter 2—List of Contents

| | |
|---|---|
| *Antecedents* | *35* |
| *The Style Paradox* | *36* |
| *Towards a Science of Architecture* | *38* |
| *Origins Reconsidered* | *39* |
| *The Four Elements* | *41* |
| *Knot as Type* | *43* |

## Antecedents

During the nineteenth century, Germany went through rapid and profound changes. Prompted by intense industrial development, the country went from a heavily rural culture to extraordinary growth and modernization. As a result of a remarkable process of industrialization, by the beginning of the twentieth century the country had become the second largest economy in Europe. In philosophy and the arts Germany also experienced outstanding developments; intellectuals such as Immanuel Kant, Lessing, Goethe, and Schiller were considered among the Enlightenment's principal thinkers. It is within this historical context that the surge of Gottfried Semper (1803–1879) can be best understood. While he developed a very successful

**36** Nineteenth Century—Origins, Imitation, Type

professional practice, Semper's principal legacy resides in his writings on architectural theory, which exerted a notable influence among his contemporaries and followers.[2]

Gottfried Semper was born into a modest family in Hamburg and raised in Dresden, where in 1823 he registered to study mathematics at the University of Göttingen. After a short period he enrolled in the Academy of Fine Arts in Munich, where he took some architectural courses. In 1826, he moved to Paris to complete his studies under the direction of the German architect Franz Christian Gau (a former student of Durand), where he familiarized himself with the theoretical discussions at the city's two most influential schools: the *École de Beaux-Arts* and the *École Polytechnique*. Thanks to Gau's recommendation, in 1834 Semper returned to Dresden, where he was appointed director of the *Bauakademie* (Academy of Fine Arts). During his tenure at the Academy, he restructured the pedagogical program of the school of architecture, recommending the studio format and the integration of practical and theoretical courses. Due to his participation in the 1849 failed revolt against the monarchy, he was forced into exile. Initially he moved to Paris, though after a few months he settled in London, where he was eventually offered a position in the Department of Practical Art, an institution formed by his friend Henry Cole in 1852.[3] After five years in London, Semper moved to Zurich to assume the direction of the newly formed *Politechnikum* (currently the *Eidgenössische Technische Hochschule*, commonly referred to as ETH Zurich).

During the following decades Semper developed a very successful career as a practicing architect, teacher, and theoretician, having most of his architectural projects built in Dresden, Zurich, and Vienna. In Dresden the two versions of the *Hoftheater*[4] (the earlier one destroyed by fire in 1869 and rebuilt in 1878) stand out, as well as the synagogue and the city's art gallery. In Zurich he carried out projects for the astronomical observatory, the train station, and the *Politechnikum*. His last grand projects were in Vienna, where he was responsible for the urban planning of the "Imperial Forum," which included designs for the museums of historical art and natural history.

## The Style Paradox

Semper's contrasting positioning towards the notion of style in his buildings and in his writing can be defined as *paradoxical*. Throughout his professional career, he consistently designed his buildings in "Neo-Renaissance style," arguing that it "offered a great freedom in the use of symbols"[5] derived from classical antiquity. The question of historical styles should be considered from a historical perspective. It was the nineteenth century's most dominant subject, as epitomized by Heinrich Hübsch's polemic book *In What Style Should We Build?*[6] of 1828, conceding that the selection of the appropriate historical style had become among the most relevant architects' tasks. It is within this particular context that can be better understood Semper's consideration of ornamental vocabularies in his architectural projects.

In his writings, however, Semper demonstrates a very sophisticated interpretation of the concept of style, a question that appears disassociated from how he faces the subject in his architectural projects. His most extensive and important writing was *Der Stil in den technischen und tektonischen Künsten oder praktische Ästhetik* (*Style in the Technical and Tectonic Arts or Practical Aesthetics*, 1860–3),[7] where he developed an integral theory of the evolution of the arts, craftsmanship, and architectural forms structured around the notion of style. Rather than defining style as a fixed ornamental vocabulary, Semper understands it as a dynamic process evolving over time. Just like language, style cannot be the invention of an individual, but rather a collective endeavor that includes the creation and manufacturing of all kinds of elements and objects produced by the community—from artworks, crafts, and garments to tools and buildings. Style, according to this view, explains how culture evolves and manifests, and what makes each culture particular and unique.

If examining solely Semper's theoretical output, it becomes evident that he was far ahead of his times at many levels. He was among the first to anticipate the impact of industrialization and standardization in the architectural project,[8] foreseeing that the discovery of new building materials would derive in the realization of novel forms, and realizing that new programs derived from the industrialization of society would embolden the development of new formal typologies. As summarized by Harry Mallgrave, Semper "was one of the first architects of the nineteenth century to articulate the problem of modernity."[9]

However, when acting on the question of style in the architectural project Semper faced a riddle impossible to solve. At various moments, he declared the ambition of developing a vocabulary in accordance to his times, observing that "A vast field of inventiveness will be revealed to us once we try to make use of *our* social needs as factor in the style of *our* architecture."[10] Yet in other instances, he acknowledged the difficulty of achieving this task, until finally lamenting the fact that neither he, nor anyone of his generation, would be able to conceive a "style for their time." In the last paragraph of his lecture, titled *Ueber Baustyle* ("On Architectural Styles," 1869), Semper arrived at a pessimistic conclusion about his generation solving the dilemma of style:

> People reproach us architects for a lack of inventiveness too harshly, since nowhere has a new idea of universal importance, pursued with force and consciousness, become evident. We are convinced that wherever such an idea should really take the lead, one or the other of our young colleagues will prove himself capable of endowing it with a suitable architectural dress. Until that time comes, however, we must reconcile ourselves to make as best as we can with the old.[11]

Semper's words convey a sense of despair, surrender, and loss; acknowledging that under the existing social and cultural conditions the conception of a "style for our time" had become a virtually impossible task. As will be discussed in the following chapter, this mission would fall on the next generation of architects and designers, who at the beginning of the twentieth century would develop an architectural

**38** Nineteenth Century—Origins, Imitation, Type

vocabulary capable of reflecting the outstanding social, political, artistic, and technological changes.

## Towards a Science of Architecture

As a student in Paris, Semper had the opportunity to attend lectures by Jean-Nicolas-Louis Durand and Quatremère de Quincy, figures who exerted notable influence in his future development.[12] In various instances Semper expressed opinions that conflicted with Durand's. On the one hand he condemned the systematic utilization of the grid insofar it encourages simplistic and mechanistic design solutions,[13] while on the other he appreciated Durand's aim of developing a theory of architecture based on scientific methodologies. Semper's respect for Durand is best appreciated in a letter to his editor, where he acknowledged the French professor's work towards developing a science of architecture:

> To regain our course we have divided the immense material into different subjects, and a particular doctrine has been assigned to each subject. Only few writers have tried to show the connection between these arbitrarily separated doctrines, and these few have kept to the grooves of the trend especially familiar to them, so that without noticing it they have been led away from the goal they set for themselves, as if on a forced path. The Frenchman Durand has come closest to this goal.[14]

Semper's familiarity with the works and ideas of Durand aroused his interest in Baron Georges Cuvier's systems of anatomical and biological classification. It should be noted, however, that the French anatomist had an understanding of taxonomy that was more complex and sophisticated than Durand's. One of Cuvier's main arguments was that all natural species are constantly evolving; therefore, he conceived a dynamic system of classification contemplating continual transmutations and transformations. On various occasions, Semper expressed his admiration for Cuvier's ideas, as attested in his lecture at the Department of Practical Art in London in 1853:

> When I was a student at Paris I went often to the *Jardin des Plantes*, and I was always attracted, as it were by a magic force, from the sunny garden into those Rooms ... In this magnificent collection, the work of Baron Cuvier, we perceive the types for all the most complicated forms of the animal empire, we see progressing nature, with all its variety and immense richness, most sparing and economical in its fundamental forms and Motives; we see the same skeleton repeating itself continually, but with innumerable varieties, modified by gradual developments of the Individuals and by the conditions of existence which they had to fulfill.[15]

Influenced by Cuvier, Semper establishes a distinction between morphological and functional classification principle. As Hvattum points out, "In a certain sense,

Semper's reinterpretation of Durand resembled Cuvier's reinterpretation of Linnaeus: the transition from a comparison based on the appearance of parts to a comparison based on a set of internal relations."[16] While from different perspectives, Semper and Durand shared the understanding of architecture as an evolutionary process. While for Durand, the architect accepts a sort of typological standard distilled from the past and therefore ready to be disposed, Semper, on the other hand, echoing Cuvier, assumes architecture as a complex organism, a system where each part fulfills particular and specific functions, and all parts are interdependent and interrelated.

## Origins Reconsidered

The other personality who influenced Semper during his stay in Paris was Quatremère de Quincy.[17] Many themes he would later consider, such as a renewed theory of the origins of architecture, a reinterpretation of the concept of type, and the notion of architectural evolution through imitation, were subjects extensively discussed by Quatremère. For Semper, just like for Quatremère half a century earlier, a necessary step towards formulating a theory of architecture was an understanding of its origins.[18] As he would later state in his first volume of *Der Stil*, rather than demonstrating "how to create a particular art-form" his interests revolved around "how it comes into being."[19]

Semper shared Quatremère's interest in the correspondence between the origins of architecture and language. Both thinkers found a correlation between linguistic etymology and the first constructions, assuming that language and architecture developed as collective undertakings. Discussing the subject, Kenneth Frampton commented on Semper's understanding of language and architecture as a communal experience, seeing "artistic culture as an evolving language in which certain root forms and operations are transposed over time."[20] As discussed in the previous chapter, a similar notion was advanced by Quatremère, contending that "the invention of architecture should be considered as aligned with that of language, in the sense that both inventions cannot be attributed to one individual, but rather attributes of humanity."[21]

Quatremère's influence on Semper is evidenced in his early theory of originating types, arguing that all European constructions derived from two principal typologies: the gable-roof structures of northern Europe and the wall-dominated interior patios developed in Mediterranean regions. As noted by Harry Mallgrave,[22] Semper affirmed that these architectural forms were determined by climate and geography; while in the northern European regions the roof is the most important component, in the benevolent climate of southern Europe the wall assumes greater prominence. Those two typologies help explain the fundamental characteristics of each culture, the northern more reserved and isolated, while the Mediterranean more prone to social exchange.[23]

In his book *The Four Elements of Architecture*[24] (1851) Semper developed a theory of the origins of architecture that was clearly different from his previous "two typologies," and by extension, from Laugier and Quatremère. Rather than

**40** Nineteenth Century—Origins, Imitation, Type

identifying the seminal architectural instance as a building type, he affirmed that the first space defined by humans was the gathering around the *Herd* (hearth). This idea was greatly influenced by the work of the ethnographer Gustav Klemm[25]—his contemporary in Dresden and author of the *General Cultural History of Mankind* (1843–52)—who identified the origins of culture in humankind's initial interactions and rituals, such as communal music and dance.[26] Echoing Klemm, Semper asserted that architecture originated when the first humans started developing group activities, such as singing, dancing, and making handicrafts around the space delimited by the warmth emanated by the *fire*:

> The first sign of human settlement and rest after the hunt, the battle, and wandering in the desert is today, as when the first men lost paradise, the setting up of the fireplace and the lighting of the reviving, warming, and food-preparing flame. Around the hearth the first groups assembled; around it the first alliances formed; around it the first rude religious concepts were put into the customs of a cult. Throughout all phases of society the hearth formed that sacred focus around which the whole took order and shape. It is the first and most important, the moral element of architecture.[27]

According to Semper's account, the confirmation of his theory of "the four elements" derived from a relatively fortuitous event. While exiled in London he visited the 1851 Great Exhibition, which took place at the celebrated *Crystal Palace* by Joseph Paxton, a vast wrought iron structure volume entirely clad by glass. At the "Colonial" section of the exhibit Semper noticed "The Carib Hut" (Figure 2.1), a replica of the dwellings made by the aborigines of the Caribbean island of Trinidad, built mainly with bamboo canes.[28] In the hut, Semper identified each of the subjects listed in his "four elements": it had a central "hearth" (or fire pit), the perimeter's walls were the "enclosure," the "roof" was built with timber, and the whole assembly was raised on a "mound" or platform.

The paradigm of a hut as the original architectural model evidences resonances of the writings of Laugier and Quatremère. Semper, however, discards these assumptions, arguing that the evolution of the hut into the Greek temple is impossible to corroborate, and is therefore constructed upon "strange and fruitless speculations."[29] In turn, he states that the consideration of the Caribbean hut as the original dwelling was "no phantom of the imagination, but a highly realistic exemplar of wooden construction, borrowed from ethnology."[30] Rather than a formal prototype, Semper considers the Caribbean hut a "context" resulting from humankind's first activities. The "Carib Hut," he argues, demonstrates that the four elements of architecture are the product of the interrelationship between ritual activities and artisanal works initiated by the first men. As Frampton pointed out, Semper "will no longer classify architecture with painting and sculpture as a plastic art but rather with dance and music as a cosmic art, as an ontological, world-making art evocative of nature in action."[31]

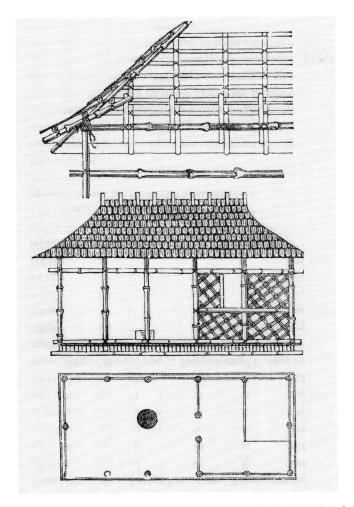

**FIGURE 2.1**  Gottfried Semper: "The Caraib Hut." *Der Stil* (2nd ed. 1878), vol. 2, p. 263. Heidelberg University.

## The Four Elements

Semper considers "fire" the first and most important of the four elements, the moment that initiates a practical and symbolic ritual. Following, he lists the other elements: the "enclosure," the "roof," and the "mound." Introducing an anthropological dimension, Semper considers that each of the four elements corresponds to an activity or craft, each craft associated with a certain material. From the "fire," for example, rises the baking of *clay*, which leads to the creation of ceramic techniques; the "mound" elevates the whole ensemble, safeguarding it from the dampness of

**42** Nineteenth Century—Origins, Imitation, Type

the earth and the stalking of animals, and is associated with the work with *stone*; the "wall" allows the enclosure of the structure, a weaving process aligned with *textile fabric*; finally the fourth element is the "roof," which, in using wood as the main material, is associated with the *carpentry* trade. The origin of architecture is therefore inevitably linked to humankind's first activities and socialization, developed by the community as a whole.

Of the four elements, the "wall," or enclosure, is the one Semper that discusses more exhaustively, noting that it is the constituent that has a greater impact in defining the architectural experience. Echoing Quatremère's fascination with etymology, Semper notices that the Germanic word *Wand* (wall) has the same root and basic meaning as *Gewand* (garment), both terms alluding to the notion of spatial enclosure and protection from the elements.[32] Rather than assuming the wall is a monolithic barrier made of brick or stone (its most conventional understanding), the primal enclosure is an enclosing membrane. "The beginning of building," he declared, "coincides with the beginning of textiles."[33] Therefore the wall, just like dressing and drapery, is conceived of as a textile fabric, manufactured as an artisanal and communal activity. Consequently, *architecture shares its origins with dressing*—or one should say, architecture *is* dressing. Both activities were born as a response to the need for sheltering and protection from the inclemency of the weather, promptly attaining symbolic value. Following, Semper details the technique for building the wall as an assembly of structural posts and filler partitions woven by branches and *Wandbereiter* (wickerwork). As Semper wrote,

> The use of wickerwork for setting apart one's property, the use of mats and carpets for floor coverings and protection against heat and cold and for subdividing the spaces within a dwelling in most cases preceded by far the masonry wall, and particularly in areas favored by climate. The masonry wall was an intrusion into the domain of the wall fitter by the mason's art, which had evolved from building terraces according to very different conditions of style. Wickerwork, the original space divider, retained the full importance of its earlier meaning, actually or ideally, when later the light mat walls were transformed into clay tile, brick, or stone walls. Wickerwork was the *essence of the wall*.[34]

As proof of the correspondence between the concepts of "wall" and "dress," Semper recalls the principle of *Bekleidung* (cladding).[35] An example of this technique he refers to is the presence of carpets in Assyrian architecture, which were used as spatial divisors as well as cladding, ornamentation, and pigmentation of surfaces. "Hanging carpets," posits Semper, "remained the true walls, the visible boundaries of space . . . Even where building solid walls became necessary, the latter were only the inner, invisible structure hidden behind the true and legitimate representatives of the wall, the colorful woven carpets." "The wall," he adds,

> retained this meaning when materials other than the original were used, either for reason of greater durability, better preservation of the inner wall, economy, the display of greater magnificence, or for any other reason. The

inventive mind of man produced many such substitutes, and all branches of the technical arts were successively enlisted.[36]

## Knot as Type

The correspondence between the theories of Quatremère and Semper is a complex subject.[37] Throughout his life, the German architect expressed ambivalent and contradictory opinions about the *Secrétaire Perpétuel de l'Académie des Beaux-Arts*. As stated earlier, after meeting Quatremère during his early stay in Paris, Semper's work displayed clear influences of his ideas. During the next decades he would revisit many subjects discussed by Quatremère, such as the concepts of origins, type, and imitation and developing a theory of architecture informed by the novel sciences of ethnography, archaeology, and linguistics. At various moments, however, Semper departs from and even challenges aspects of Quatremère's thinking, such as when he rejects the theory of the three original types on the grounds it lacked empirical evidence.[38]

The two concepts that more succinctly epitomize the theoretical corpus of Quatremère and Semper are respectively *type* and *knot*, a subject that deserves a particular discussion. In principle, the differences between both concepts are evident: while Quatremère defines the type as a morphological principle, Semper identifies *knot* as a pre-formal notion: "It looks for the constituent parts of form that are not form itself but rather the idea, the force, the material, and the means—in other words, the basic preconditions of form."[39] However, if Semper's knot is examined under the umbrella of Quatremère's "theoretical universe," both concepts present clear affinities: (1) they share an intrinsic relation with the *origins* of the architecture; (2) they can be evaluated according to *taxonomic* criteria; and (3) they constitute the matrix of an *imitation* process capable of allowing innumerable variations.

Quatremère and Semper concurred in advancing a theory of architecture derived from a reconsideration of the question of origins, particularly identifying what they considered the *original instance*. After years researching on Egyptian and Greek architecture, Quatremère developed his theory of the three original dwellings based on the concept of *type*. For Semper, instead, architecture originated with the communal activity of weaving developed through the technique of the *knot*, which in this view was the method for producing the first dressings as well as the original building enclosures.[40] As Semper wrote, the knot is "perhaps the oldest technical symbol and, as I have shown, the expression for the earliest cosmogonic ideas that arose among nations."[41]

After recognizing the type and the knot as the *originating* instance, Quatremère and Semper proceeded to analyze their development according to taxonomic criterion. Quatremère postulated the original division of building inventory in three originating types: the cave, the hut, and the tent. As observed by Mari Hvattum,[42] Semper's understanding of the categorization of the knot is quite more intricate and elaborate, echoing Baron Cuvier's contemporary scientific developments, which asserted that rather than in its visible members, the essential features of zoological and botanical species reside in the *cells* that conform the organs. According

**44** Nineteenth Century—Origins, Imitation, Type

to this idea, instead of focusing on visual appearances (forms and proportions), anatomy is understood as a combination of microorganisms in a permanent process of transmutation. The analogy between "knot" and "cell," hence between architectural tectonics and biology, suggests a novel relationship between architecture and the human body. Unlike the doctrine inaugurated by Vitruvius[43] establishing a correspondence between human's proportions and architecture, the analogy proposed by Semper assumes the knot as an evolving microorganism, "simultaneously a functional technique and a symbolic means of representation."[44]

A third correspondence between Quatremère's type and Semper's knot is around the notion of *imitation*.[45] While Quatremère identified the mimetic condition of type as the origin of a continuous mimetic process, Semper developed a similar argument around the knot, understood "as a complex series of transformations in which original motifs are gradually modified in response to new needs and conditions."[46] Semper envisioned the tectonic and symbolic evolution of the knot as an imitative process: initially simple and rustic, with the passage of time they begin exhibiting a varied range of straps, braids, and fabrics, later evolving into the first *motifs* (motives), which in turn become "patterns" that varied according to ways of connecting and assembling, available materials, climate conditions, and geographical settings (Figures 2.2, 2.3, 2.4, and 2.5). The conception of knot as a mimetic

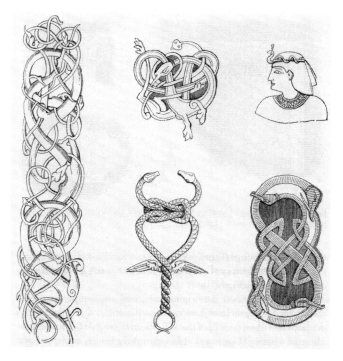

**FIGURE 2.2** Gottfried Semper: *Snake ornaments from Greece, Ireland, Egypt and Scandinavia.* From *De Stil* (2nd ed. 1878), vol. 1, pp. 77–78. Heidelberg University.

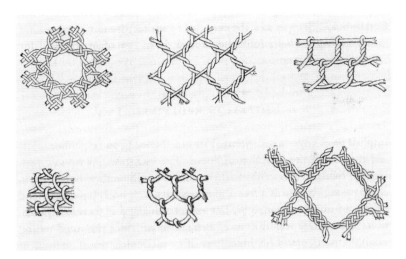

**FIGURE 2.3** Gottfried Semper: *Knots and braids*. From *De Stil* (2nd ed. 1878), vol. 1, pp. 169–72. Heidelberg University.

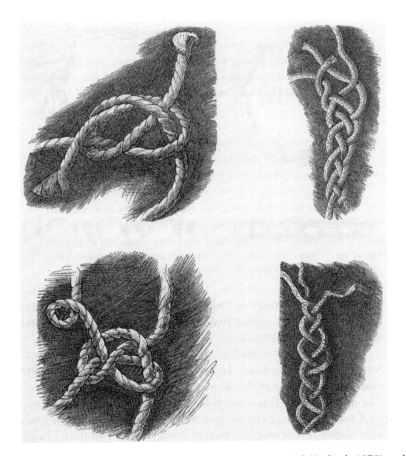

**FIGURE 2.4** Gottfried Semper: *Knots and braids*. From *De Stil* (2nd ed. 1878), vol. 1, pp. 169–72. Heidelberg University.

## 46 Nineteenth Century—Origins, Imitation, Type

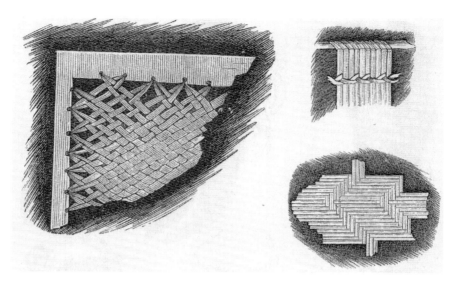

**FIGURE 2.5** Gottfried Semper: *Techniques of weaving*. From *Der Stil* (2nd ed. 1878), vol. 1, p. 177. Heidelberg University.

mechanism summarizes Semper's conception of "style," where the developments of different and variable kinds of knots mark the particular characteristics of clothing, decoration, ornamentation, and construction associated with each culture.

Semper and Quatremère considered imitation the force behind artistic production, where the history of architecture and the arts can be interpreted as an extensive mimetic chain going back to the beginnings of humankind. It could be argued that Semper's knot can be analogically assumed as the concept of type in its most minimal expression: they both embody originating architectural instances for becoming catalysts of imitative processes. This question suggests an expansive understanding of the concept of type, in terms of its role both as mimetic precedent and as imitative process, a subject to be further discussed in the following chapters.

## Notes

1 Semper, Gottfried, "Prolegomena" to *Style in the Technical and Tectonic Arts, Or, Practical Aesthetics*. Translated into English by Harry F. Mallgrave and Michael Robinson. Los Angeles, CA: Getty Research Institute, 2004, 71.
2 Harry Mallgrave commented on how Semper's studies in math influenced his later theoretical evolution. See Mallgrave, Harry Francis, *Gottfried Semper: Architect of the Nineteenth Century*. New Haven: Yale University Press, 1996, 12.
3 London's Department of Practical Art had been formed in 1852, mainly as Henry Cole's initiative, as the central administration of the Schools of Design. See Herrmann, Wolfgang, *Gottfried Semper: In Search of Architecture*. Cambridge, MA: MIT Press, 1984, 65.
4 According to Mallgrave, Semper received the Hoftheater commission thanks to the recommendations of Richard Wagner and Frederick Schinkel. See Mallgrave, *Gottfried Semper*, 117.

Semper's Knot **47**

5  On various occasions Semper discussed the range of design possibilities offered by the Renaissance style. Mallgrave, *Gottfried Semper*, 120.
6  Hübsch, Heinrich, *In What Style Should We Build?: The German Debate on Architectural Style*. Santa Monica, CA: Getty Center for the History of Art and the Humanities, 1992.
7  Semper, *Style*.
8  In "Science, Industry, and Art," Semper discusses the relationships between artistic creation, craftsmanship, standardization, and mass production. See Semper and Mallgrave: *The Four Elements*, 130–167.
9  Mallgrave, *Gottfried Semper*, 4.
10  Cited in Hvattum, Mari, *Gottfried Semper and the Problem of Historicism*. Cambridge: Cambridge University Press, 2004, 156.
11  Transcription of the conference "On Architectural Styles" offered at the Rathaus in Zurich in 1869. Semper, *The Four Elements*, 284.
12  Mallgrave narrates Semper's experiences during his stay in Paris. See Mallgrave, *Gottfried Semper*, 35–40.
13  Mallgrave, Harry Francis, *Modern Architectural Theory: A Historical Survey, 1673–1968*. Cambridge: Cambridge University Press, 2009, 132.
14  Semper, Gottfried, *The Four Elements of Architecture and Other Writings*. Translated into English by Harry F. Mallgrave and Wolfgang Herrmann, Cambridge: Cambridge University Press, 1989. Section titled "Prospectus Comparative Theory of Building" (1852), 169.
15  Quoted in Mallgrave, Rykwert, and Semper, "London Lecture," 8.
16  Hvattum, *Semper*, 130.
17  For an extended commentary of Quatremère's influence on Semper, see Hvattum, *Gottfried Semper*, 42.
18  In *The Four Elements* Semper argues that in order to formulate a contemporary theory of architecture he needs to articulate and understand its origins, "At the risk of falling into the same error that I criticize, I see myself forced to go back to the primitive conditions (*Urzustiinde*) of human society in order to come to that which I actually propose to set forth." Semper, *The Four Elements*, 102.
19  Semper, *Style*, 71.
20  Frampton, Kenneth, and John Cava. *Studies in Tectonic Culture: The Poetics of Construction in Nineteenth and Twentieth Century Architecture*. Chicago, IL: Graham Foundation for Advanced Studies in the Fine Arts, 2001, 88.
21  Cited by Samir Younés in "Architecture and Language," in Quatremère, De Quincy, and Samir Younés, *The Historical Dictionary of Architecture of Quatremère De Quincy*. London: Andreas Papadakis, 1999, 37. The quote is from Younés's translation of Quatremère's *De l'architecture égyptienne*, 12.
22  Semper's theory of the "two original types" was discussed by Mallgrave. See Mallgrave, *Gottfried Semper*, 180. Herrmann also commented on this theory in Herrmann, *Gottfried Semper: In Search of Architecture*, 168.
23  In his 1853 "London Lecture" Semper revisited the correspondences between type and origin, though he describes a more abstract and generic process not uniquely related to architecture. Semper wrote, "Types as we have seen are primitive forms, prescribed by necessity, but modified after the first materials, which were used for their embodiment." See Semper, Gottfried, "London Lecture of November 11, 1853," edited with a commentary by Harry Francis Mallgrave and preface by Joseph Rykwert, in *RES: Anthropology and Aesthetics*, 6 (1983), 16.
24  Semper, *The Four Elements*.
25  Mari Hvattum developed an exhaustive analysis on how Klemm's ideas influenced Semper, particularly regarding the origins of architecture. See Hvattum, *Semper*, 42–46.
26  Hvattum, *Semper*, 43.
27  Semper, *The Four Elements*, 102.
28  Herrmann, *Gottfried Semper: In Search of Architecture*, xii.
29  Wolfgang Herrmann discusses this issue in the chapter "Semper's Position on the Primitive Hut," in Herrmann, *Gottfried Semper: In Search of Architecture*, 165–173.

**48** Nineteenth Century—Origins, Imitation, Type

30 Cited in Hvattum, *Gottfried Semper*, 36.
31 Frampton, *Studies in Tectonic Culture*, 88.
32 Semper, *Style*, 248.
33 Hvattum, *Gottfried Semper*, 70. From *Der Stil*, vol. 1, 213.
34 Semper, *The Four Elements*, 103–104 (italics in original).
35 Hvattum, *Gottfried Semper*, 70–71.
36 Semper, *The Four Elements*, 104.
37 It should be noticed that the discussion of the concept of type under Semper's theoretical discourse, together with the correspondences between Quatremère and Semper's theories, was extensively examined in the unpublished doctoral dissertations of Sam Jacoby and Leandro Madrazo. See Jacoby, Sam, *The Reasoning of Architecture—Type and the Problem of Historicity* (unpublished doctoral dissertation, Technischen Universität Berlin, 2013), 145–207. Jacoby later revisited the subject in his lecture at the Architectural Association symposium "Type Versus Typology" of 2015, later published as Sam Jacoby, "Typal and Typological Reasoning: A Diagrammatic Practice of Architecture," *The Journal of Architecture*, 2016, 20:6, 938–961. DOI: 10.1080/13602365.2015.1116104. See also Madrazo, Leandro, *The Concept of Type in Architecture: An Inquiry Into the Nature of Architectural Form* (unpublished doctoral dissertation, Swiss Federal Institute of Technology, 1995), 239–253.
38 Hvattum comments on Semper's "sarcastic" rejection of Quatremère's threefold origin type: "scholars who tired themselves out in making ingenious deductions to prove that Chinese architecture had derived from the tent." Cited in Hvattum, *Gottfried Semper*, 42.
39 Quoted in Mallgrave, *Modern Architectural Theory*, 153.
40 In Hvattum, *Gottfried Semper*, 70. From *Style*, vol. 1, 213.
41 Semper, *The Four Elements*, 217.
42 See Hvattum, *Gottfried Semper*, 42–46.
43 According to Frampton, "Semper's four elements represent a fundamental break with the Vitruvian triad of *utilitas, firmitas, venustas*." See Frampton, *Studies in Tectonic Culture*, 85.
44 Hvattum, *Gottfried Semper*, 67.
45 For an analysis of Semper's consideration of Imitation, see Hvattum, *Semper*, 72–83.
46 Hvattum, *Gottfried Semper*, 73.

**PART 2**

# Twentieth Century— Shifting Considerations

# 3

# MODERN ARCHITECTURE'S UNCERTAIN CONSIDERATION OF TYPE

*Since the first decades of the 20th century, from Loos and Behrens to Gropius and Le Corbusier, among others, a constant trip was made back and forth from architecture to industrial building—until then at the margins of what was properly considered architecture—a trip that still is a characteristic of contemporary architecture.*

—Reyner Banham[1]

## Chapter 3—List of Contents

| | |
|---|---|
| *Antecedents* | *51* |
| *The "Zero Hour" of History* | *53* |
| *Dreams of Silos* | *55* |
| *Towards a Prototypical Architecture* | *57* |
| *Type, According to Gropius* | *63* |
| *Modernism's Misconstruction of Urbanity* | *66* |

## Antecedents

In architecture, the nineteenth century ended with a sense of heaviness and pessimism. As discussed in the previous chapter, one of the issues that defined this period was the question of *style*, or as some referred to, the "battle of the styles."[2] Towards the end of the century, most European and American cities evidenced the emergence of buildings with the most varied ornamental styles, such as neoclassic, neo-Gothic, Romanesque, or Byzantine. The ambitious objective expressed by Semper and others of producing a "style of our time" will become a pending matter for the next generation of architects. Many considered the *École des Beaux-Arts*, Europe's oldest and most influential school of architecture, mainly responsible for this situation. The teachings of Professor Julien Guadet compiled in his treatise *Eléments*

## 52 Twentieth Century—Shifting Considerations

*et théorie de l'Architecture*[3] (1900–1904) represent the *École*'s final and unsuccessful attempt at continuing nineteen-century academicism's theoretical and pedagogic norms into the twentieth century.

Two factors evolving during the nineteenth century help explain the origins of *modernism*.[4] The first was the industrial revolution. While this process started in England, it was in Germany where the impact on architecture of industrial developments was more intensely discussed by designers, industrialists, and scholars. The realignment of interests from England to Germany is epitomized in the figure of Gottfried Semper, who during his exile in London wrote the essay "Science, Industry and Art,"[5] examining the conflicting relationship between industrial progress and building design. Semper anticipates many issues that will greatly impact the evolution of the arts the following century, such as the relationship between artistic creation and standardization (i.e., between *individuality* and *type*), and between design and mass production, as well as the influence of scientific and technological innovations in the development of architecture.

The technological innovations that dramatically impacted the development of twentieth-century architecture were laid down in the second half of the nineteenth century by engineers using cast and wrought iron in the construction of train stations, arcades, factories, and markets. As discussed in the preface, Walter Benjamin[6] analyzed the phenomenon of the emergence of the covered arcade, a structure that can be understood as anticipations of new building type, or as radical reformulations of a traditional type. A notable example of this second option is Joseph Paxton's *Crystal Palace* in London of 1851. The building resembled a Roman barrel and was realized with cast iron and glass; its construction process took advantage of "new design guidelines" such as standardization and division of labor.

The other factor affecting the beginnings of modernism was the tendency towards *abstraction* in the arts. The rise of abstraction suggested the possibility of an artwork liberated from the past, the promise of a new beginning with norms and rules yet to be determined. From a certain perspective, the tendency towards abstraction was both the end and a beginning of an era; it represented a challenge to realism and figuration as well as the opportunity to develop new and original creations. In architecture, the rejection of figuration implied the dismissal of historical ornamental vocabularies, including classicism which had been the prevailing language for the last five centuries.

The impact on the initial developments of modern architecture of the industrial revolution and abstraction in the arts resulted in a renewed consideration of architectural type. While modernism conveyed numerous and disparate attitudes towards the notion of type in the architectural project,[7] this chapter focuses on four distinctive approaches: (1) the advances by various *avant-garde* groups rejecting any notion of type or formal precedent; (2) the early moderns' consideration of industrial and rural constructions as alternative typological precedents; (3) the substitution of the notion of type for prototype; and (4) Gropius's assumption of type as a standardized and fixed building form. A fifth strategy, "typological substitutions" as advanced by Le Corbusier, is discussed in Chapter 5.

## The "Zero Hour" of History

A defining ambition of early twentieth-century avant-garde groups, such as *de Stijl*, *suprematism*, and *constructivism*, was developing an art free from figurative and iconographic precedents. This position was advanced by *suprematist* artist Kazimir Malevich, advocating an art independent of any influences, even of his own contemporaries: "Suprematism originated neither from Cubism nor from Futurism," wrote Malevich, "neither from the West nor from the East. For non-objectivity could not originate from something else; the single significant question is whether something is cognized or not."[8] Malevich proposed a "return to *zero*" of art, identifying that number (or *non-number*) with a reset of history.[9] With *Black Square* (1915) and *White on White* (1918), Malevich pushed this radical reductionism to an extreme. Both canvases should be considered as the "genuine point zero" of art, an irresistible process of abstraction leading towards a *"point of no return."* (What can be more abstract than an entirely white canvas?) Shortly after *White on White* Malevich quit painting, returning with figurative works only more than a decade later.

The notion of *restarting history* through a relentless process of abstraction is also present in the work and ideas of Dutch architect Theo van Doesburg, one of the principal figures of the group *de Stijl*. In his manifesto "Towards a Plastic Architecture" (1924), van Doesburg proposes the elimination of all architectural precedents, arguing that "Instead of using earlier styles as models and imitating them, the problem of architecture must be posed entirely afresh."[10] The agenda includes canceling the consideration of type in the architectural project. "The new architecture is formless and yet exactly defined; that is to say, it is not subject to any fixed aesthetic formal type . . . In contradistinction to all earlier styles the new architectural methods know no closed type, no basic type."[11] Unlike other avant-garde architects and thinkers whose criticisms were focused on the nineteenth century's stylistic adventures, van Doesburg argued for an explicit rejection of the concept of type in the design process.

In his 1923 *Contra-Construction* project, van Doesburg explored many of the ideas presented in his manifesto. The proposal can be understood as an ensemble of geometrical elements (planes and lines) seemingly disassociated from any typological reference. The composition blurs the distinctions between inside and outside spaces, top and bottom, and front, side, and rear elevations:

> The new architecture possesses no single passive factor. It has overcome the *opening* (in the wall). With its *openness* the window plays an active role in opposition to the *closedness* of the wall surface. Nowhere does an opening or a gap occupy the foreground; everything is strictly determined by contrast.[12]

As transpires from the quote, with *Contra-Construction* van Doesburg not only proposes substituting typological precedent with formal invention but also recommends a radical redefinition of the most conventional architectural elements, such as doors and windows. The door, for example, rather than being an element in its own right (consisting of a frame and a panel) is perceived as the absence of the wall. Likewise, the windows are not punctures in the wall but rather openings that are left between the planes. The project seems to have been conceived as a formal laboratory whose ultimate goal was to substantiate the manifesto's points. By canceling the past, and by extension the concept of type, the "new architecture" was ready to initiate its path towards the future.

Van Doesburg's thesis inspired Gerrit Rietveld to design his Schröder House in Utrecht in 1924 (Figure 3.1). Located in a neighborhood of traditional brick townhouses, the house appears provocatively disjointed from the existing urban context. Color is among the project's most distinctive features, the horizontal and vertical planes were painted in white and in four shades of gray, while railings and frames displayed the three primary colors: blue, red, and yellow.[13] The house materializes most of the ideas advanced in *Contra-Construction*: walls, roofs, and balconies are disposed as a three-dimensional arrangement of interlocking of planes, while windows and doors are interruptions of the planar composition. With the Schröder House, de Stijl's ambition of developing an architecture "not subject to any fixed aesthetic formal type" seems to have been finally materialized.

**FIGURE 3.1**   Gerrit Rietveld: Schröder House, 1924.

Photograph courtesy of Ariel Vazquez.

## Dreams of Silos

While the positions advanced by avant-garde groups had a great impact on the initial development of modern architecture, their influence gradually diminished. It could be argued that the irrepressible tendency towards abstraction and the continual demand for original creations became objectives impossible to attain.[14] In his book *A Concrete Atlantis* (1986),[15] Reyner Banham identified a "causal, cultural, and conscious connection" between several of the principal pioneers of modern architecture and North American utilitarian and anonymous constructions. Images of factories, silos, and grain elevators became the inspiration for the posterior developments in modern architecture. The first architect to express interest in the "healthy" qualities of American utilitarian constructions, posits Banham, was Walter Gropius, who in an article for the 1913 *Deutsche Werkbund* journal wrote the following:

> The grain elevators of Canada and South America, the coal bunkers of the big railroads, and the most recent work halls of the North American industrial corporations impress one as having a monumental strength that can almost stand comparison with the buildings of ancient Egypt. They have an architectural image of such convincing impact that the spectator cannot help but grasp the meaning of the building. What these buildings are is self-evident, and their monumental effect cannot be explained as inherent in their size. It seems that their designers have retained an independent, healthy, and pure feeling for massive, compact, and integrated forms. Therein lies for us a valuable hint: that we should abandon our historical nostalgia and any other intellectual considerations which dim our modern European artistic creativity and obstruct our artistic immediacy.[16]

It should be noted that when drafting the article Gropius had not seen those constructions; his observations came from photographs given to him by the industrialist Karl Benscheidt, who had recently commissioned him for the Fagus Factory.[17] Therefore his commentaries of American constructions were assumptions based on a handful of pictures of constructions he was partly imagining. For Gropius, as for many other European architects, America, "the motherland of industry,"[18] was becoming an aspiration, a romantic tale about immeasurable landscapes and unlimited resources. The new continent could become the ideal setting for laying the grounds of an abstract and functional architecture, with utilitarian structures devoid of any "historical nostalgia."

Contemporary to Gropius, his compatriot and colleague Erich Mendelsohn also expressed strong interest in North American agro-industrial constructions. Likely influenced by the *Deutsche Werkbund* article, in 1923 Mendelsohn embarked on a journey to the United States and Canada, an experience he later recounted in his book *Amerika*.[19] The text is a sort of traveler's chronicle, alternating between personal notes, photographs of cities such as New York and Chicago, and snapshots of ports, factories and grain elevators (Figures 3.2 and 3.3). At various moments, Mendelsohn's comments adopt a candidly poetic tone, such as when referring to the grain elevator, where "A bare practical form becomes abstract beauty."[20] In a moving letter to his wife, Mendelsohn shares his feelings after facing the monumental silos of the port of Buffalo: "I took photographs like mad. Everything else so far now seemed to have been shaped interim to my silo dreams. Everything else was merely a beginning."[21]

**FIGURE 3.2** Erich Mendelsohn: *CHICAGO. Grain Elevator 5. Passage with compartments and distribution bridges*. From *Amerika*. Dover Publications, 1993, page 49.
Public domain.

Modern Architecture's Uncertain Consideration of Type **57**

Another architect influenced by Gropius's publication was Le Corbusier. In 1919 he borrowed from Gropius the photos of the American grain elevators for use in various articles for his magazine *L'Esprit Nouveau*, most of which were later included in *Vers une Architecture* (1923).[22] Le Corbusier was the one modern pioneer who argued with great impact that the morphological and iconographic qualities of American agricultural and industrial constructions were the "models" for developing a new architecture. He articulates this idea in a provocative juxtaposition of a sixteenth-century Renaissance courtyard with images of warehouses and factories, "the reassuring first fruits of our age."[23]

Le Corbusier referred to silos and grain elevators as abstract volumes of primary geometries ("cubes, cones, spheres, cylinders, or pyramids"),[24] utilitarian constructions that compose the reference for developing a new architectural vocabulary. "Mass and surface," he pondered, "are the elements by which architecture manifests itself."[25] In the chapter "Three Reminders for Architects" Le Corbusier describes in distinctly lyrical terms the qualities of those anonymous buildings: "Thus we have the American grain elevators and factories, the magnificent FIRST-FRUITS of the new age ... It is for that reason that these are *beautiful forms, the most beautiful forms*."[26]

Together with Gropius, Mendelsohn, and other emerging modern architects, Le Corbusier was indicating an alternative path to the one initiated by the avant-garde groups. While it is clear that these groups of "pioneers" agreed with the avant-garde's rejection of academic tradition, rather than proposing a *tabula rasa*, they searched for a typological lexicon with genealogical roots sufficiently differentiated from nineteenth-century stylistic experiences. What those modern pioneers "saw" in these utilitarian constructions—absence of ornamentation and simple geometrical volumes derived from functional needs—was the possibility of a morphological language that has not already been "contaminated" by the doctrines of the *École*. "Architecture," claims Le Corbusier, "has graver ends; capable of the sublime, it impresses the most brutal instincts by its objectivity; it calls into play the highest faculties by its very abstraction."[27]

## Towards a Prototypical Architecture

The interest awakened by young modern architects in manufacturing and industrial structures not only involved the search for a range of typologies differentiated from those associated with the *École des Beaux-Arts* but also sparked a reassessment of the "margins of architecture," now "expanded" to include the most prosaic buildings. As stated earlier, the other issue that greatly impacted the beginnings of modern architecture was the emergence of new technologies. The industrial revolution stimulated the irruption of new transportation mechanisms, such as the automobile, the airplane, and the ocean liner, imposing a novel relationship between man and territory. Simultaneously, the construction industry incorporated new materials, such as steel and reinforced concrete, allowing a generation of new building typologies, such as the covered gallery, the train station, and the skyscraper.

**58** Twentieth Century—Shifting Considerations

The impact of new materials and machineries on the development of modern architecture is evident in the emergence of two groups: the German Werkbund and the Italian futurists. Propelled by different ideologies, both groups coincided in their fascination for new technologies. The Werkbund was founded in 1907, with the purpose of establishing a partnership of design professionals and product manufacturers with the goal of improving the competitiveness of German products in global markets. Many of its members—some of whom later founded the Bauhaus—considered the association an alternative to the eclecticism's aesthetic agenda, arguing that the century's new values were *rationalization, standardization, economy*, and *mass production*.[28] In turn, the Italian futurists assumed the *macchina* as a device with high symbolic and political voltage, its presence fostering the transformation of society upon the reinvention of art, architecture, and the city. "We must

**FIGURE 3.3** Erich Mendelsohn: *CHICAGO. Grain Elevator 5. Distribution of masses at the end of the grain elevator.* From *Amerika.* Dover Publications, 1993, page 51.
Public domain.

invent and rebuild our Futurist city," pondered Antonio Sant'Elia, "like an immense and tumultuous shipyard, active, mobile, and everywhere dynamic, and the Futurist house like a gigantic machine."[29]

One of the issues raised by both the Werkbund and the Futurists was dissolving the differentiation between "high" and "low" architecture. Le Corbusier presented the question as a choice between "Architecture" (capitalized), implicitly associated with the classicist programs of the *École des Beaux-Arts*, and the "Engineer's Aesthetic," represented by utilitarian constructions.[30] "The engineers of to-day," he wrote, "find themselves in accord with the principles that Bramante and Raphael had applied a long time ago."[31] In the chapter conspicuously titled "Eyes Which Do Not See,"[32] Le Corbusier argues for an even greater expansion of the margins of the discipline by proposing ocean liners, automobiles, and airplanes as references for an emerging modern architecture (Figure 3.4). With his characteristic aphoristic prose, he asks the reader to "look with a fresh eye" at the powerful "manifestation" of these novel industrial machineries:

> If we forget for a moment that a steamship is a machine for transport and look at it with a fresh eye, we shall feel that we are facing an important

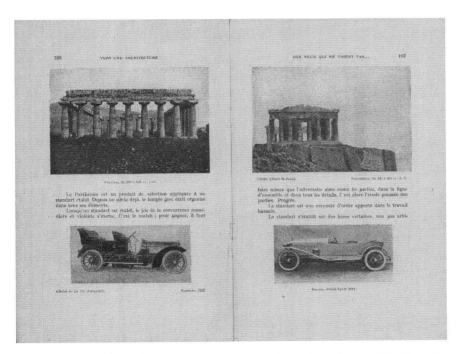

**FIGURE 3.4** Le Corbusier: *Comparison between Greek temples and automobiles*. From Le Corbusier. *Vers une Architecture*, 1923.

Courtesy of Fondation Le Corbusier/Artists Rights Society (ARS), New York, 2017.

manifestation of temerity, of discipline, or harmony of a beauty that is calm, vital and strong.[33]

In what would become the basis of a modern architectural lexicon, in 1914 Le Corbusier devised the system *Dom-ino*. Architecture, according to this scheme, could be reduced to its most essential components: bases, columns, stairs, and slabs (Figure 3.5). In his essay on "Rationalism," Alan Colquhoun relates Le Corbusier's *Maison Dom-ino* to the French *rational* and *a priori* tradition that goes back to Laugier and Durand:

> His drawing of the Dom-ino frame was the first demonstration of a dialectical principle that was to dominate all his subsequent work. Here, the concrete frame carries all the certainty of a Cartesian a priori. Within this frame, the volumes and equipment of the house can be independently arranged, according to practical needs.[34]

Le Corbusier's *Dom-ino* can be interpreted as the modern response to Laugier's primitive hut—two iconic images capable of synthesizing the fundamentals of a "new" architecture: one constituting a referential archetype to be endlessly imitated, the other becoming the precursor of modularity and industrialized

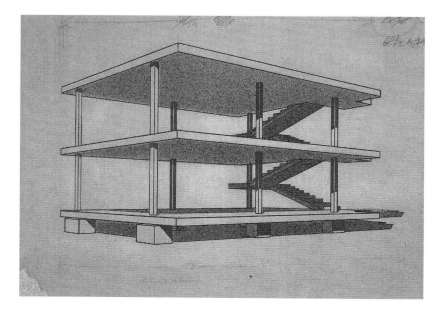

**FIGURE 3.5** Le Corbusier: *Maison Dom-ino*, 1914.

Courtesy of Fondation Le Corbusier/Artists Rights Society (ARS), New York, 2017.

construction, ultimate conditions for the development of modern architecture. As argued by Pier Vittorio Aureli, Le Corbusier brings into play something that was present in the rustic hut, though Laugier didn't elaborate on it—the free plan: "In this reinvented context, architecture becomes mere framework, and the most important consequence of this model—its success and diffusion in architecture are indisputable—is the elimination of walls and facade as fundamental creators of architectural space."[35]

In 1920, with the idea of integrating the problematics of social housing with the rigor of the automobile industry, Le Corbusier conceived the residential unit *Citrohan*[36] (Figure 3.6). The project can be understood as a new *specimen*, a hybridization of modernism's structural argument represented by the *Dom-ino* with the advantages of industrialized production.[37] As observed by Alan Colquhoun, the *Dom-ino* and *Citrohan* design processes mark a rearrangement of interests in Le Corbusier, going from the individual and the exceptional towards the general and the typical.[38] The construction process of the *Citrohan* is therefore analogous to the automobile industry—a mass-production assembly line making standardized parts to be assembled *in situ*. Just like any household object, the *Maison Citrohan* was devised as an industrial *prototype* (from the Greek *proto*: first, original),[39] capable of being indefinitely replicated. As Le Corbusier wrote,

> "Citrohan" (not to say Citroën). That is to say, a house like a motor-car, conceived and carried out like an omnibus or a ship's cabin. The actual needs of the dwelling can be formulated and demand their solution. We must fight against the old-world house, which made a bad use of space. We must look upon the house as a machine for living in or as a tool . . . As to beauty, there is always present when you have proportion; and proportion costs the landlord

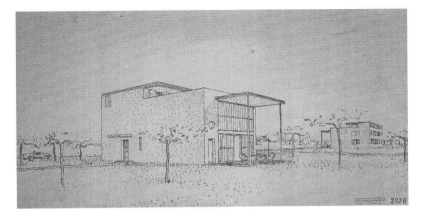

**FIGURE 3.6** Le Corbusier: *Maison Citrohan*, 1922.

Courtesy of Fondation Le Corbusier/Artists Rights Society (ARS), New York, 2017.

**62** Twentieth Century—Shifting Considerations

nothing, it is at the charge of the architect! The emotions will not be aroused unless reason is first satisfied, and this comes when calculation is employed. There is no shame in living in a house without a pointed roof, with walls as smooth as sheet iron, with windows like those of factories. And one can be proud of having a house as serviceable as a type-writer.[40]

By emulating industrial design, Le Corbusier redefines architecture as the art of creating and developing prototypes, some of which, after having been accepted by society, will evolve into established types. Thus, following a Darwinian process of "natural" selection, Le Corbusier argues that mass production demands a search for the "standard," and once it is established, through a process of trial and error, will lead towards perfection:

But there is another reason for the enduring quality and beauty of the standard. To create a standard you must satisfy completely economic criteria. You must find the exact, and not the approximate solution. And precision is the essence of beauty . . . Thanks to the machine, to the identification of what is typical, to the process of selection, to the establishment of a standard, a style will assert itself.[41]

It is interesting to note that Le Corbusier's conception of "standard" is reminiscent of Quatremère's notion of "type" as a mimetic evolutionary process: the identification of a precedent which is subsequently altered, modified, and adjusted with the ultimate goal of arriving at the most perfecting version of that formal idea.

Anthony Vidler coined modern architecture's prototypical design the "second typology,"[42] understood as the stage following Quatremère's "first typology," where the type-form is the antecedent and the point of departure from a design process substantiated in Aristotelian imitation. The "second typology" conveys a novel strategy for developing the architectural project where the individual components *and* the entire building can be generated through standardization and mass production. As posited by Vidler, "Buildings were to be no more and no less than machines themselves, serving and molding the needs of man according to economic criteria."[43] The procedure suggests a fusion of architecture (traditionally understood as unique work for a specific site) and industrial design, where a mold can be replicated in unlimited models. Soon after Vidler's essay, Moneo summed up correctly the problem when he wrote,

This new idea of type effectively denied the concept of type as it had been conceived in the past. The singularity of the architectural object which in the nineteenth century had permitted adaptability to site and flexibility for use within the framework of a structure was violently denied by the new architecture, committed to architecture as mass production.[44]

During the 1920s, Le Corbusier sustained a strong interest in developing residential units as industrial prototypes. Initially he conceived the *Immeuble-Villa* unit, an adaptation of the *Maison Citrohan* integrated into the large residential blocks of the *Ville Contemporaine* (1922), and later he explored variations of this idea in his urban proposals *Plan Voisin* and *Ville Radieuse*. However, the series of houses he designed during this period displays a very different compositional strategy: "the five points." As is further discussed in Chapter 5, the *pilotis*, the free plan, the free façade, the horizontal window, and the roof garden can be seen as both a continuity of building tradition and a transformation of classical types. Houses like the *Maison Cook*, the *Villa Savoye*, and the *Villa Stein* evidence a rechanneling of Le Corbusier's attraction to mechanistic and industrial precedents. Rather than deriving from mechanized systems of production, now those images of ships, airplanes, and automobiles transpire into his architecture as iconographic, poetic, and metaphorical references. "The Villa Savoye," summons Colin Rowe, was devised by Le Corbusier as a "floating palace, an emblem of the island and of the soul, and became also an emblem of efficiency and of the future."[45]

## Type, According to Gropius

While Le Corbusier gradually lost interest in developing an architecture devised upon industrial prototypes,[46] over the same decades Walter Gropius (1883–1969) was coming to grips with the subject. Gropius's trajectory—initially associated with the Werkbund and later becoming a leading figure of the Bauhaus—can be interpreted as a synthesis of the disparate (and somehow contradictory) ideals of the modern movement: while at some moments he presented agro-industrial constructions as formal and iconographic antecedents for modern architecture, at other points he expressed affinities with the most radical avant-garde groups, such as de Stijl. Particularly after migrating to the United States in 1937, Gropius's interests gravitated towards prefabrication and standardization of the architectural project, arguing that the profound technological changes occurring during the twentieth century demanded a full reassessment of the discipline.

In his book *Scope of Total Architecture* (1943),[47] Gropius states that architecture must be generated upon values such as economy, industrialization, and mass production, therefore limiting traditional craftsmanship and custom-made solutions:

> The machine certainly has not stopped at the threshold of building . . . In a gradual evolutionary procedure, the hand-building process of old is being transformed into an assembly process of ready-made industrial parts sent from the factory to the site.[48]

Among the principles of his "total architecture" is the notion of "standard," understood with a *Darwinian* connotation as a constructive component destined to be continuously perfected, or an item to be replaced by a superior iteration:

> The creation of standard types for everyday goods is a social necessity. The standard product is by no means an invention of our own era. It is only the methods of producing it which have changed. It still implies the highest level

**64** Twentieth Century—Shifting Considerations

> of civilization, the seeking out of the best, the separation of the essential and superpersonal from the personal and accidental. It is today more necessary than ever to understand the underlying significance of the conception "standard"—that is to say, as a cultural title of honor—and firmly to combat the shallow catchword propaganda which simply raises every industrial mass product to that high rank.[49]

Gropius's association of the notions of "standard" and "type" draws attention for various reasons. To begin with, there are notable similarities between his precisions and Durand's design methodologies developed more than a century before. As discussed in Chapter 1, Durand understood the architectural project as an assemblage and disposition of building parts and elements. Since those parts were the result of a (historical) distillation process, they should be accepted as they "are," without demanding alterations. When considering standardized building parts in the architectural project, Gropius adopts a similar criterion; the architect must accept the components delivered by the construction industry while focusing on the disposition and situation of each part. In both cases the designer is in charge of selecting—not redesigning—the parts; in one case the inventory derives from "history," in the other it is delivered by "industry." The correspondence between Durand's and Gropius's understandings of type, and by extension their similar conceptions of the architectural project, underlines the anticipatory qualities of Durand's theories, and their impact on certain facets of modern architecture.

Even more surprising in Gropius's text is the utilization of the word "type," a term that had virtually disappeared from the architectural discourse since the beginning of the twentieth century. As observed by Kenneth Frampton,[50] the single early modern architect expressing interest in type as an agent in the design process was Hermann Muthesius, who during the Congress of the *Deutsche Werkbund* of 1914 proposed the notion of *Typisierung* as a tool utilized to relate building's past forms to industrial production. Closing his argument, Muthesius declared, "Essentially, architecture tends towards the typical. The type discards the extraordinary and establishes order."[51] Henry van de Velde, one of the leaders of the association, refuted Muthesius's proposal, calling it a restriction of formal inventiveness: "So long as there are still artists in the Werkbund and so long as they exercise some influence on its destiny, they will protest against every suggestion for the establishment of a canon and for standardization."[52]

After Muthesius's unsuccessful argument, the term "type" was marginalized from modern architectural vocabulary, the most notable exceptions being Le Corbusier and Nikolaus Pevsner. In the late 1910s, together with his friend the artist Amédée Ozenfant, Le Corbusier advanced an art movement they coined "purism." In the movement's manifesto, *Après Le Cubisme* (1918), Le Corbusier and Ozenfant proposed incorporating into their artworks *objet-types*, domestic and mundane objects of industrial culture. In their view, the *objet-type* was an instrument that had become perfect after a Darwinian process of depuration of forms, such as pipes, bottles, or chairs. Those objects transcend authorship, time period, and culture—similar ones

Modern Architecture's Uncertain Consideration of Type **65**

could be found on any continent. For Le Corbusier, the presence of standardized and repetitive objects suggests a connection between a timeless past—expressed in the tradition of the folk artisan—and modernity,[53] conveyed by mass production and mechanization. As suggested by Alina Payne, during the 1920s and 1930s Le Corbusier translated those interests in his search for the ideal "house-type," an architectural project capable of conveying a similar level of perfection as the *objet-type*.[54] His aim was to produce a functional architecture ("a house is a machine for living in")[55] capable of transpiring poetic qualities (it is worth remembering the illustration that closes *Vers une architecture* is a briar-pipe).[56]

Another modern utilization of the word "type" appears in Nikolaus Pevsner's *A History of Building Types* (1976),[57] where the term indicates the intended use of the building, such as "Library," "Museum," "Prison," or "Hotel." Surprisingly, Pevsner doesn't acknowledge that a single architectural form can host a variety of functions (as will be discussed in the following chapter, this was Argan's and Rossi's central argument against functionalism). As commented by Alan Colquhoun, Pevsner's text is particularly disappointing:

> In his brief introduction Dr. Pevsner makes no attempt to establish a theoretical framework for his study. He puts forward no theory of types, nor does he relate his study of types to any historical tradition. He simply accepts "typology" as found in the nineteenth century and uses its methods to guide us through architectural history.[58]

In short, Pevsner missed the extraordinary opportunity of elucidating the notion of type from modernism's point of view. Instead, he conveys a "pre-Durand" conception of type, assumed simply as cataloguing of building forms, without elaborating on the types' genealogy, meaning, or incidence in the design process.

Besides Le Corbusier and Pevsner, the vast majority of modern architects and historians, from Mies and Wright to Giedion and Hitchcock, consistently *avoided using the term type*. Conceivably the concept appeared too associated with the programs at the *École des Beaux-Arts*, where the long shadows of Quatremère and Durand and the contemporary leadership of Julien Guadet appeared contrarian to the agenda of modernism.[59]

It is difficult to say if Gropius was fully aware of the underlying meanings and connotations of a term and a concept so clearly associated with nineteenth-century academic tradition. Given his linguistic and cultural background, he likely considered the term similar to Muthesius's *Typisierung*, which in German can be interpreted as both "type" and "standard."[60] This interweaving of meanings results in an expression that offers a connection simultaneously with the distant past (as discussed in Chapter 1, the word "type" derives from the ancient Greek word *typos*) and with the ongoing process of normalization and standardization of the construction's industry.

These questions introduce a defining aspect of modern architecture: the tension between originality and typicality in the architectural project. On the one

**66** Twentieth Century—Shifting Considerations

hand, many of modernism's most renowned buildings, such as the chapel of *Notre Dame du Haut* in Ronchamp by Le Corbusier and the *Guggenheim Museum* by Frank Lloyd Wright, have been celebrated for their sheer singularity, a condition of uniqueness that cannot be reduced to any obvious categorization. On the other hand, various contemporary critics have drawn attention to how many of the most celebrated modern buildings were conceived advancing typologically driven mechanisms. Such is the case with Jean Castex's analysis of the *Prairie Houses* by Frank Lloyd Wright,[61] Demetri Porphyrios's essay "Alvar Aalto's Typological Conception of Design,"[62] Pier Vittorio Aureli on Mies van de Rohe's use of the plinth as a recurrent "motif,"[63] and studies of Le Corbusier's consideration of type in design process by Stanislaus von Moos,[64] Kenneth Frampton,[65] and Alan Colquhoun.[66]

## Modernism's Misconstruction of Urbanity

In the last portion of *Scope of Total Architecture*, Walter Gropius focuses on urban-related topics. He starts discussing the selection of the most appropriate building type in relation to its urban conditions. The chapter titled "Houses, Walk-ups or High-Rise Apartment Blocks?"[67] is indicative of his criteria, where each building form is considered as a *given*, a predefined model that should be accepted *as is* (it is interesting to note that Gropius's consideration of building precedent in the realization of the architectural project presents clear affinities to Durand's design methodologies discussed in Chapter 1). According to this scenario, the architect's task is selecting the appropriate housing type by considering its adequate height, the correlation between footprint and lot size, and specific zoning regulations. The notions of standardization and duplication, previously assumed as tactics for manufacturing building parts and units, now dictate both architecture and urban planning. Long gone is the early modern's determination of creating new forms or prototypical invention.

At no point does Gropius discuss issues such as the quality of urban spaces, the relationship between buildings and their context, the historical lineages of types, or the influence of society and culture in shaping the city. This highlights how many of the principal modern architects disregarded the vital qualities of the urban experience and the incidence of architecture in defining the city. Much has been said about the radical nature of Le Corbusier's urban proposals, Wright's "disappearing city,"[68] or identifying Mies van der Rohe's ITT campus as an example of "anti-space."[69] It can be defined only as *paradoxical*, the fact that the principal architects of the twentieth century, many of them with extraordinary artistic talents, so strenuously failed in their urban conceptions—as if the historical bond relating architecture and urban design was inexorably broken. This paradox is confirmed by the city of Brasilia, where three exceptionally creative designers, Lucio Costa, Oscar Niemeyer, and Burle Marx, guided by CIAM's urban doctrines, delivered a city that cancels the pedestrian experience and can be appreciated only through an automobile's (or an airplane's) window. As will be discussed in the following chapter, the reconsideration of the concept of type as an instrument for analyzing the urban

## Modern Architecture's Uncertain Consideration of Type 67

environment as well as a mechanism for generating the architectural project will foster a renovated relationship between architecture and history, and also between architecture and the city.

## Notes

1 Banham, Reyner, *A Concrete Atlantis: U.S. Industrial Building and European Modern Architecture 1900–1925*. Cambridge, MA: MIT Press, 1989, 20.
2 For an analysis of the controversies generated around the notion of style throughout the nineteenth century, see Hübsch, Heinrich, *In What Style Should We Build?: The German Debate on Architectural Style*. Santa Monica, CA: Getty Center for the History of Art and the Humanities, 1992.
3 Guadet, Julien, and N. Clifford Ricker. *Elements and Theory of Architecture*. Urbana, IL: University of Illinois, 1916.
4 As noted by Jürgen Habermas, "[t]he term 'modern' has a long history . . . in its Latin form 'modernus' was used for the first time in the late fifth century in order to distinguish the present, which had become officially Christian, from the Roman and pagan past. With varying content, the term 'modern' again and again expresses the consciousness of an epoch that relates itself to the past of antiquity, in order to view itself as the result of a transition from the old to the new" Habermas, Jürgen, "Modernity—An Incomplete Project." In Foster, Hal (ed.), *The Anti-Aesthetic: Essays on Postmodern Culture*. Port Townsend, WA: Bay Press, 1983, 3.
5 Semper, Gottfried, and Mallgrave, Harry Francis, *The Four Elements of Architecture: And Other Writings*. Cambridge: Cambridge University Press, 1989. See the chapter "Science, Industry and Art," 130–167.
6 See Benjamin, Walter, *The Arcades Project*. Cambridge: Harvard University Press, 2002.
7 Modern architecture displayed various approximations towards the presence of type in the architectural project, such as the notion of typological invention, modern consideration of vernacular precedents (discussed in Frampton, Kenneth, *Le Corbusier*. London: Thames & Hudson, 2001, 131–149), and the consideration of classical typologies by the Italian fascists (Richard Etlin, *Modernism in Italian Architecture, 1809–1940*. Cambridge, MA: MIT Press, 1991).
8 Cited in Aiello, Thomas, "Head-First Through the Hole in the Zero: Malevich's Suprematism, Khlebnikov's Futurism, and the Development of a Deconstructive Aesthetic, 1908–1919." *E-maj Journal on Line 1*, July–December 2005, http://emajartjournal.com. Accessed November 20, 2014.
9 Malevich's associating the ambition of restarting art (history) with the number (or "ground") zero is present in Rosalind Krauss's depiction of the avant-garde: "More than a rejection or dissolution of the past, avant-garde originality is conceived as a literal origin, a beginning from ground zero, a birth." Later she added, "The self as origin is the way an absolute distinction can be made between a present experienced de novo and a tradition-laden past." Rosalind E. Krauss, "The Originality of the Avant-Garde: A Postmodernist Repetition." *October, Vol. 18* (Autumn, 1981). Cambridge, MA: MIT Press, 53–54.
10 Theo van Doesburg, "Towards a Plastic Architecture," (1924). In Conrads, Ulrich (ed.), *Programs and Manifestoes on 20th-Century Architecture*. Cambridge, MA: MIT Press, 1970, 78.
11 Van Doesburg, "Towards a Plastic Architecture," 78.
12 Van Doesburg, "Towards a Plastic Architecture," 78 (italics in original).
13 Part of the descriptions of the house follows those in Mallgrave, Harry Francis, *Modern Architectural Theory. A Historical Survey, 1673–1968*. Cambridge, MA: Cambridge University Press, 2005, 244.
14 In his essay "Rationalism" Alan Colquhoun stressed avant-garde's sliding interests from formal explorations to social responsibility and mass production: "In the 1920s most

## 68   Twentieth Century—Shifting Considerations

of the avant-garde architects began to accept the replacement of craft by the machine as the price architecture had to pay in order to tackle the urgent social tasks presented to it." This transition, adds Colquhoun, was particularly noticeable in the works of the architects associated with the Bauhaus, "such as Hannes Meyer, Ernst May, Mart Starn, and Hans Schmidt, among others." See Colquhoun, Alan, "Rationalism: A Philosophical Concept in Architecture." In *Modernity and the Classical Tradition: Architectural Essays 1980–1987*. Cambridge, MA: MIT Press, 1989, 67.

15   Banham, *A Concrete Atlantis*, 3.

16   Gropius's 1913 text is cited in Cohen, Jean-Louis, *Scenes of the World to Come—European Architecture and the American Challenge 1893–1960*. Paris: Flammarion and the Canadian Centre for Architecture, 1995, 64.

17   Cohen, *Scenes of the World to Come*, 63.

18   Gropius's expression the "Motherland of Industry" is the title of a chapter in Cohen's book discussing the impact of industrial construction on European architects. See Cohen, *Scenes of the World to Come*.

19   Mendelsohn, Erich, *Amerika*. New York: Dover, 1993.

20   Mendelsohn, *Amerika*, 47.

21   Cited by Banham, *A Concrete Atlantis*, 6.

22   Observed by Banham, *A Concrete Atlantis*, 11.

23   Le Corbusier, *Towards a New Architecture*. New York: Dover, 1986, 41. A better translation of Le Corbusier's seminal book, with an introductory comment by Jean-Louis Cohen, can be found in Le Corbusier, Jean-Louis Cohen, and John Goodman. *Toward an Architecture*. Los Angeles, CA: Getty Research Institute, 2007.

24   Le Corbusier, *Towards a New Architecture*, 29.

25   Le Corbusier, *Towards a New Architecture*, 26.

26   Le Corbusier, *Towards a New Architecture*, 26–29. Capitalization and italics in original.

27   Le Corbusier, *Towards a New Architecture*, 25–26.

28   As discussed by Mallgrave, the interest of German modern architects in the relationship between industry, design, and architecture was influenced by the thinking of Gottfried Semper, particularly his essay *Wissenschaft, Industrie und Kunst* ("Science, Industry and Art," 1852). See Malgrave, *Modern Architectural Theory*, 135.

29   The quote is from the "Manifesto dell'Architettura Futurista" (1914) by Filippo Marinetti and Antonio Sant'Elia. In Conrads, Ulrich, *Programs and Manifestoes on 20th-Century Architecture*. Cambridge, MA: MIT Press, 1994, 36.

30   Alan Colquhoun discusses Le Corbusier's conception of the opposite (though symmetrical) figures of architect and engineer: "While the works of the engineer are needed to reflect the underlying mathematical order of the universe, the engineer is also seen as representing the blind forces of history and as a working toward the solution of practical problems. His works constitute the highest collective achievement of mankind and tend toward the rational organization of society. On the other hand, it is precisely the fact that the engineer is not consciously concerned with values and is free from ideology that makes it impossible for him to replace the artist-architect, whose task is to satisfy a longing for images of the idea. It is thus that Le Corbusier justifies the role of the artist-architect in an industrial society and establishes the work of architecture as simultaneously a work of technology and a work of art." See "The Significance of Le Corbusier." In Colquhoun, *Modernity and the Classical Tradition*, 168.

31   Le Corbusier, *Towards a New Architecture*, 41.

32   Le Corbusier, *Towards a New Architecture*, 85–148.

33   Le Corbusier, *Towards a New Architecture*, 102.

34   Colquhoun, Alan, "Rationalism: A Philosophical Concept in Architecture." In *Modernity and the Classical Tradition. Architectural Essays 1980–1987*. Cambridge: MIT Press, 1989, 77.

35   Aureli, Pier Vittorio, "The Theology of Tabula Rasa: Walter Benjamin and Architecture in The Age of Precarity," *Anyone*, Log, No. 27 (Winter/Spring 2013), 127.

36   As stated by Le Corbusier, the term "Citrohan" derives from the French car factory *Citroën*. See Le Corbusier, *Towards a New Architecture*, 240.

Modern Architecture's Uncertain Consideration of Type **69**

37  According to Kenneth Frampton, "the name 'Dom-ino' seems to derive from contacting and combining the words *domicile* and *innovation.*" Frampton, *Le Corbusier*, 21.

38  "We have now," says Le Corbusier, "arrived at the fateful moment in the historical cycle when our sentimental urges must be seen as identical to the rule of reason. The general, the typical, and the common appeal to us more than the individual and the exceptional." Cited in Colquhoun, Alan, "Architecture and Engineering: Le Corbusier and the Paradox of Reason," from Colquhoun, *Modernity and the Classical Tradition*. 1989, 100.

39  For the etymology of the word prototype, see Online Etymology Dictionary, www.etymonline.com/index.php?term=prototype. Accessed November 5, 2016.

40  Le Corbusier, *Towards a New Architecture*, 240.

41  Le Corbusier, "Mass-Produced Buildings" (1924), from *Architecture and Design, 1890–1939: An International Anthology of Original Articles*, New York: Whitney Library of Design, 1975, 134.

42  Vidler, Anthony, "The Third Typology." In Michel K. Hays (ed.), *Architectural Theory Since 1968*. Cambridge, MA: MIT Press, 1998, 288–294.

43  "Buildings were to be no more and no less than machines themselves, serving and molding the needs of man according to economic criteria." Vidler, "The Third Typology," 291.

44  Moneo, Rafael, "On Typology," *Oppositions 13*. Cambridge, MA: MIT Press, 1978, 33.

45  Rowe, Colin, *The Architecture of Good Intentions: Towards a Possible Retrospect*. London: Academy, 1994, 59.

46  Colquhoun relates Le Corbusier's signs of disinterest in mechanical production during the 1930s to his disillusion with European governments' policies towards housing and urban planning: "Le Corbusier's loss of faith in the application of industrial techniques in architecture dates from considerably before the war and seems to have been the result of his own failure to interest either the government or industrial management in the mass production of housing." From "The Significance of Le Corbusier," in Colquhoun, *Modernity and the Classical Tradition*, 178.

47  Gropius, Walter, *Scope of Total Architecture*. New York: Collier Books, 1962.

48  Gropius, *Scope of Total Architecture*, 76.

49  Gropius, *Scope of Total Architecture*, 26.

50  Frampton, Kenneth, *Modern Architecture: A Critical History*. London: Thames and Hudson, 1992. See the chapter dedicated to the Werkbund, 109–115.

51  Frampton, *Modern Architecture*, 112.

52  Conrads, *Programs and Manifestoes*, 29.

53  The notion of *objet-type* can be traced to Le Corbusier's trip to Greece and Turkey in 1911, an experience later recounted in his autobiographical memoir. At various points Le Corbusier conveys his admiration for vernacular architecture and traditional craftsmanship, as when he observes, "Considered from a certain point of view, folk art outlives the highest of civilizations. It remains a norm, a sort of measure whose standard is man's ancestor—the savage, if you will." See Le Corbusier and Ivan Žaknić, *Journey to the East*. Cambridge, MA: MIT Press, 1987, 16.

54  In this very interesting and provocative text, Alina Payne argues that in modern architecture "objects" (from furniture to household) acquired the iconographic power of traditional ornamentation. Payne, Alina, *From Ornament to Object: Genealogies of Architectural Modernism*. New Haven: Yale University Press, 2012. 251–252.

55  Le Corbusier, *Towards a New Architecture*, 95.

56  It remains an enigmatic subject that the last illustration of *Vers une architecture* is a tobacco pipe, bearing no relationship with the often quoted pair of sentences closing the book: "Architecture or revolution. Revolution can be avoided." It is interesting to note that six years later, Magritte would paint a similar pipe titled "The Treachery of Images," with the inscription "*Ceci n'est pas une pipe*" ("This is not a pipe"). Le Corbusier, *Towards a New Architecture*, 289.

57  Pevsner, Nikolaus, *A History of Building Types*. Princeton: Princeton University Press, 1976.

**70** Twentieth Century—Shifting Considerations

58 Colquhoun, Alan, "Frame to Frameworks." In *Essays in Architectural Criticism. Modern Architecture and Historical Change*. Cambridge, MA: Opposition Books, MIT Press, 126.

59 The figure of Julien Guadet, author of *Eléments et théorie de l'architecture* and professor at the *École des Beaux-Arts* in Paris, constitutes a complex figure regarding the origins and early developments of modern architecture. During his tenure at the *École*, Guadet was openly repudiated by most modern architects. However, as observed by Reyner Banham, his theories, particularly regarding "composition," were quite influential in early modern theory and practice. See Banham, Reyner, *Theory and Design in the First Machine Age*. Cambridge, MA: MIT Press, 1992, 14–22.

60 In his essay "Type" Adrian Forty discusses the meanings and connotations of the German word "Typisierung," which has in the past been translated as "standardization," but which according to present consensus would be best translated as "type." See Forty, Adrian, "Type." In *Words and Buildings: A Vocabulary of Modern Architecture*. New York: Thames & Hudson, 2000, 307.

61 Castex, Jean, *Le printemps de la Prairie House*. Brussels: Pierre Mardaga, 1987.

62 Porphyrios, Demetri, "The Retrieval of Memory: Alvar Aalto's Typological Conception of Design." *Oppositions 22* (Fall, 1980), 55–73. Alan Colquhoun also examined the presence of type in Aalto's projects; see "Alvar Aalto: Type Versus Function," *Essays in Architectural Criticism*, 75–80.

63 Aureli observes that the use of the plinth is a recurrent "motif" in most of Mies's projects: "From his early suburban houses in Germany to his corporate office complexes in the United Sates, the simple, bounded form of the plinth (which can be interpreted as an abstract version of the Greek stylobate) is the precondition of nearly all of Mies's designs." Aureli, Pier Vittorio, *The Project of Autonomy: Politics and Architecture Within and Against Capitalism*. Princeton: Princeton Architectural Press, 2008, 36–37.

64 Moos, Stanislaus Von, *Le Corbusier, Elements of a Synthesis*. Cambridge, MA: MIT Press, 1979.

65 Frampton, Kenneth, *Le Corbusier*. Thames & Hudson, 2001.

66 "Displacement of Concepts in Le Corbusier." In Colquhoun, Alan, *Essays in Architectural Criticism*, 51–66.

67 Gropius, *Scope of Total Architecture*, 103–115.

68 Wright, Frank Lloyd, *The Disappearing City*. New York: W. F. Payson, 1932. *The Disappearing City* is Wright's principal urban manifesto, where he presents his project "Broadacre city." Wright's vision is based on a complete rejection of the traditional city, proposing instead a network of agrarian communities connected through highways, the car becoming the principal mean of transportation.

69 Steven Peterson's article "Space and Anti-space" assumes two opposite conceptions of space. On the one hand, "anti-space" is the representation of "modern space," defined by Peterson as "conceived to be a free element in nature, a found resource. It is thought to be transcendental, abstract, continuous, vast, and with no form." According to Peterson, Mies van der Rohe's architecture epitomizes anti-space. The counter-notion is "space," which is structured around two conditions: *positive space* and *negative space*. While *positive space* is the created and perceived space, *negative space* is the walls and solids what configure that space. See Peterson, Steven Kent, "Space and Anti-space." *Harvard Architecture Review, vol. 1*. Cambridge, MA: MIT Press, 1980, 89–113.

# 4

# TYPOLOGY RECONSIDERED

> *I am referring rather to familiar objects, whose form and position are already fixed, but whose meanings may be changed. Barns, stables, sheds, workshops, etc. Archetypal objects whose common emotional appeal reveals timeless concerns. Such objects are situated between inventory and memory.*
>
> —Aldo Rossi[1]

## Chapter 4—List of Contents

| | |
|---|---|
| *Antecedents* | 71 |
| *Italians "Rediscovering" the Concept of Type* | 73 |
| *Aymonino and Rossi* | 75 |
| *Type, According to Rossi* | 77 |
| *What Will Be Has Always Been* | 80 |
| *Colquhoun—Expansions of the Concept* | 83 |
| *Vidler's Third Typology* | 85 |
| *The Redeemed Relationship Between Type and City* | 87 |

## Antecedents

In the 1960s, Europe and the Americas experienced remarkable cultural, political and social changes. In the social sciences, those changes manifested with the surge of *structuralism*. The theoretical premises of structuralism were initially advanced by French anthropologist Claude Lévi-Strauss,[2] who, inspired by the linguistics and semiological studies of Ferdinand de Saussure (*Course in General Linguistics*, 1916), developed an epistemological approach capable of identifying the inner structure and relationships between fundamental elements. Lévi-Strauss argued that human behavior is defined not by what is perceived but by the "structures" that underlie

**72** Twentieth Century—Shifting Considerations

those actions. Because of its transdisciplinary qualities, structuralist methodology became very influential in the works of diverse thinkers, such as Roland Barthes (literary criticism), Jacques Lacan (psychoanalysis), Michel Foucault (critical history), and Louis Althusser (Marxist theory). As noted by Alan Colquhoun,[3] structuralism suggested a novel understanding of architecture, where meaning doesn't arise from appearance, but from the latent and intangible "structures" present in any particular system.

The 1960s "revolutionary" climate was also evident in the world of art; while the first great cycle of modern art began showing signs of fatigue, new radical forms of expression started emerging. In a process reminiscent of the eruption of European avant-garde during the beginning of the twentieth century, many of the 1960s groups started exploring paths fundamentally different from their predecessors. This state of affairs was rapidly interpreted by Octavio Paz, who by the end of the decade noted that "the avant-garde of 1967 repeats the deeds and gestures of those of 1917. We are experiencing the end of the idea of modern art."[4] While the early modern avant-garde groups proposed a break from the past and an unrelenting tendency towards abstraction, since the early 1960s, artists like Jasper Johns, Robert Rauschenberg, Andy Warhol, and Edward Kienholz in America, and Richard Hamilton, Jean Tinguely, Yves Klein, and Joseph Beuys in Europe, started diverting from abstract expressionism by introducing imageries drawn from mass media and popular culture. Inspired by the works and ideas of Marcel Duchamp,[5] this group of artists challenged the distinction between "high" and "low" art, celebrating the incorporation into their artworks of all kinds of images, forms, iconographies, and commonplace objects.

The architecture of the period experienced a similar process, with a new generation of architects and thinkers articulating intense criticisms of many of the ideals of the modern movement. Principles such as functionalism, elimination of ornamentation, and dismissal of historical forms, virtually undisputed for the previous generations, started to be intensively questioned. Rather than considering traditional and historical forms with suspicion, many young designers and critics started viewing history as a source for understanding the present, and a necessary factor for the development of the architectural project.

It is within this historical context that we can better understand the "rediscovery" of the concept of type within the architectural discourse. The emergence of the term during this period signaled a remarkable situation: it went from being ignored or rejected by most modern architects and critics (most likely associating it with the Beaux-Arts tradition) to becoming one of the principal theoretical and design subjects. The central focus of this chapter is to reconstruct the various definitions and interpretations of type since the 1960s, which can be characterized by two distinctive attitudes. In the first approach, type is understood as an instrument for classifying architecture, often used interchangeably with the term "typology." The second approach assumes type as a mechanism for the production of architecture—the process of selecting a precedent and subjecting it to various alteration tactics. In sum, while some considered type a strategy for developing a

## Italians "Rediscovering" the Concept of Type

better understanding of the built environment, for others it became an instrument for transforming it.

Particularly in Italy, where modernism's relationship with history was more intense than among Northern European countries, starting in the 1960s type was repositioned as a fundamental theoretical and analytical concept. One of the first architects to consider the notion of type was Saverio Muratori (1910–1973), who in his book *Studi per un'operante storia urbana di Venezia* (*Study for an Operational Urban History of Venice*, 1959) developed an extensive analysis of the evolution of the urban forms of Venice. Based on research initiated in 1950, *Studi per un'operante storia urbana* examined the evolution of built forms through history, and their impact in the development of the city. "Type," posited Muratori, is "formed through a process of reducing complex of formal variants to a common root form,"[6] demonstrating the continuity of architectural forms while establishing a connection with society and culture. There is, then, an inevitable link between the three scales defining the urban experience: type, urban fabric, and urban organism. To understand the type requires the identification of the urban fabric, and the consideration of the urban fabric demands its examination in relation to the encompassing urban organism. The city, according to his view, is an integral network which included architectural typologies, plots, monuments, urban spaces, and the urban region.[7]

Contemporary to Muratori, in his seminal article titled "Sul concetto di tipología architettonica" ("On the Typology of Architecture," 1962), Giulio Carlo Argan (1909–1992) introduced the notion of type in the contemporary theoretical discourse. For a preliminary definition of the term, Argan retrieved the precisions developed by Quatremère de Quincy a century and a half earlier. As discussed in Chapter 1, Quatremère defined type as a concept that encompasses various and contrasting meanings. It is therefore revealing that Argan singled out Quatremère's characterization of type as an "idea,"[8] as if its understanding as an abstract and metaphysical concept takes away the possibility of relating it with stylistic vocabularies or other nineteenth-century tendencies.

Already in the opening sentence, Argan establishes a dialectical dispute with modern thinkers: "Most modern critics who depend ultimately on some form of idealistic philosophy would deny that an architectural typology could in any way be valid."[9] Argan recognizes that the notion of type as a collective construct disputes the principal canons of modern architecture, such as the emphasis on the individual over the collective, originality over influence, and invention over imitation. The impossibility of "inventing" a type resumes its difficult stance against modern dogma—rather than being created by single artist, type is the result of a communal and cultural process developed over time. As posited by Argan, "The notion of the vagueness or generality of the 'type' . . . also explains its generation, the way in which a 'type' is formed. It is never formulated a priori but always deduced from a series of instances."[10] The distancing between type and modern architecture becomes

**74** Twentieth Century—Shifting Considerations

more evident when he discusses typology's "indifference" towards function, one of modernism's fundamental principles: "Type," posits Argan, "is independent of the functions, sometimes complex, which such buildings must fulfill."[11]

While Argan conveys explicit or implicit criticism towards modern architecture, in other passages he adopts a more conciliatory tone, as if trying to convey (to modern architects and critics) the advantages of developing the design process under the spectrum of type. He starts by reminding the reader about the influence of agro-industrial typologies during the early stages of the modern movement: "Industrial architecture which deals with altogether new demands has created new 'types' which have, in many cases, great importance for the later development of architecture."[12] The underlying message is that although never acknowledged, type was a factor in the origins and evolution of modernism. Then, Argan presents one of the essay's main arguments, the consideration of type as a vital and creative mechanism:

> The conclusion must be that the typological and the inventive aspect of the creative process are continuous and interlaced—the inventive aspect being merely that of dealing with the demands of the actual historical situation by criticizing and overcoming past solutions deposited and synthesized schematically in the "type."[13]

As demonstrated by the previous statement, Argan develops a detailed description of a design process under the domain of type. Although—as discussed in Chapter 1—Quatremère anticipated this question by equating typological artistic process with Aristotelian imitation, he didn't offer specific examples. In turn, Argan articulates a very precise account of a typologically driven process, using Bramante's design for the *Tempietto di San Pietro in Montorio* in Rome (Figure 4.1) as an example.[14] According to Argan, Bramante's first decision was identifying the type he would work with: the "circular peripteral temple." Following, he compiles and analyzes various typological precedents, such as the temple of Sibyl at Tivoli and Vitruvius's description of round temples. In the following step, according to Argan, Bramante conceives a "synthesis" of the chosen type by identifying its most salient and recurrent features: circular plan, perimetral colonnade, and semi-spherical dome. It is only after these steps that Bramante finally initiates what Argan refers to as the "aspect of formal definition"[15]—that is to say, the architectural design *per se*. Summarizing, the typological design process described by Argan is developed in four instances: (1) the selection of the type; (2) the elaboration of an inventory based on typological precedents; (3) a synthesis of the type's fundamental features; and (4) the process of formal manipulation and definition, thus creating a new typological instance.

With his brief essay Argan conveys three fundamental subjects. First, he recovers Quatremère's conception of type, relating his definitions with the notions of "idea," classification, and imitation. Second, he argues for the continual validity of type in the development of the design process, implicitly highlighting modern

**FIGURE 4.1** Bramante: *Tempietto di San Pietro in Montorio*, 1502.
Photograph courtesy of Catherine Vollmer.

architecture's difficulty with the subject. And third, he demonstrates that the concept of type is absolutely unrelated to stylistic or ornamental considerations, and it should be therefore considered an "acceptable" factor for modernism.

## Aymonino and Rossi

The ideas of Muratori and Argan had an enormous influence in contemporary academic circles, particularly at Italy's leading school of architecture, the *Istituto Universitario di Architettura di Venezia* (IUAV). In the early 1960s, a group of young teachers coincided at the IUAV who would later become influential architects and scholars, such Carlo Aymonino, Vittorio Gregotti, Manfredo Tafuri, Giorgio Grassi, Aldo Rossi, Giuseppe Samonà, and Giaungo Polesello.[16] Several of those figures were also collaborating with the magazine *Casabella Continuità* under the influence

**76** Twentieth Century—Shifting Considerations

of its director, Ernesto Rogers. Two of the principal teachers of the IUAV, also active writers at *Casabella Continuità*, were Carlo Aymonino (1926–2010) and Aldo Rossi (1931–1997), who later both became members of the group known as *La Tendenza*.

Between 1964 and 1965 Aymonino published three very influential books that directly or indirectly discussed the notion of type: *La città territorio* (The urban territory, 1964), *La formazione del concetto di tipologia edilizia* (The formation of concept of building typology, 1965), and *Origini e sviluppo della città moderna* (Origin and development of the modern city, 1965). Like Muratori, Aymonino articulated his theories around the relationship between the notions of city, architecture, history, and the concept of type. In his essay "Type and Typology,"[17] Aymonino avoids establishing a fixed definition of type; he refers to it as "an instrument and not a category," adding, "in our case it is one of the instruments needed to be able to carry out studies on urban phenomena."[18] Therefore he understands typology as an evolving discipline that needs to be continually reassessed depending on particular urban conditions.

The principal instrument for understanding the city, according to Aymonino, is "typology," which is

> the study of the artificial organizational and structural elements (meaning not only buildings but also walls, avenues, gardens etc.—the whole built fabric of the city) with the aim of classifying them in relation to the urban form of a specific historical period (or a particular urban form, which is the same thing).[19]

Typological classification, according to this idea, implies a process of identifying the common features within a certain group of buildings. Therefore a building (or a type) makes sense when considered part of an urban context, and as such, its meaning arises in relation to the city.

The beginning of Aldo Rossi's academic career is closely linked to Carlo Aymonino. In 1955, while completing his studies as the *Politecnico di Milano*, Rossi met Aymonino at the magazine *Casabella Continuità*. Shortly thereafter, Rossi was invited to join the faculty at the IAUV, where initially Aymonino was his supervisor. In 1965 Rossi published an essay titled "The Concept of Type," arguing that the most relevant architectural debate of their time was the relationship between the city and the concept of type. He developed many of the ideas presented in that article further in his influential book *L'architettura della città* (*The Architecture of the City*, 1966). *L'architettura*'s main thesis was the restructuring of an "urban science" around the relationship between the city, its history, and its architecture. The two main components of the city, states Rossi, are the "primary elements," monuments and landmarks constituting the collective memory of the city, and the "secondary elements," which occupy the realm of the residential and private, of the anonymous and the generic.

It can be inferred from those definitions that Rossi was describing the fundamentals of the *traditional city*, composed of streets, squares, blocks, urban fabric, typologies, and monuments. According to Rossi, the idea of the city as a collective construct had been threatened by the modern movement's urban model. It is from this dichotomy (modern *versus* historical) that Rossi develops an intense critique of modern "planning," which implied the disposition of urban zones according to their intended function. Rossi challenges not only the ideals of the modern city but also one of the fundamental principles of modern architecture: the correspondence between form and function. At this point, the Milanese architect "doubles the stake," arguing that architecture is absolutely *indifferent* to function; in other words, a building form is independent of the activities it may host. To convey this idea, Rossi refers to the *Palazzo della Ragione* in Padua, a building which has served multiple functions over the centuries, and still acts as a vital urban landmark:

> When one visits a monument of this type . . . one is always surprised by a series of questions intimately associated with it. In particular, one is struck by the multiplicity of functions that a building of this type can contain over time and how these functions are entirely independent of the form. At the same time, it is precisely the form that impresses us; we live it and experience it, and in turn it structures the city.[20]

Similarly to Argan, Rossi had a conflictive and at moments contradictory consideration of modern architecture. While he dismisses functionalism's design strategies and favors a historical understanding of architecture and the city—notions contrarian to modernism—he conveyed a notable fascination for the paradigmatic modern works of Adolf Loos, Ludwig Hilberseimer, and Le Corbusier.[21] Therefore Rossi's "trouble" with modernism is neither formal nor stylistic, but methodological—how architecture is examined and created.

## Type, According to Rossi

In the third section of the first chapter of *L'architettura della città*, Rossi introduces the concept of *type*,[22] a term that over the years became strongly associated with his *persona*. Like Argan, for an initial definition Rossi resorts to Quatremère's description of type as an "idea," thus corroborating the distinction between conceptualization and materialization of architecture. In other passages, though, Rossi relies on Muratori's descriptions, which assumed it as an instrument for classifying and categorizing the built environment. Muratori's influence becomes apparent in Rossi's depiction of a specific type, the *house with a loggia*, "an old scheme; a corridor that gives access to rooms is necessary in plan and present in any number of urban houses."[23] Type is, therefore, a metonymic representation of architecture:

> Thus typology presents itself as the study of types of elements that cannot be further reduced, elements of a city as well as of an architecture . . . The process of reduction is a necessary, logical operation, and it is impossible to talk about problems of form without this presupposition. In this sense all architectural

theories are also theories of typology, and in an actual design it is difficult to distinguish the two moments.[24]

For Rossi, type is both an instrument for understanding architecture and a mechanism for developing the architectural project. The architectural project, according to this idea, implies a process of *typological distillation*: a persistent removal of ornamentation, texture, and color until the type is reduced to its most minimal and essential expression. This approach is observed in his housing project *Gallaratese* (Figure 4.2), located in the outskirts of Milan, where the most prominent architectural form is the loggia, among the city's most conspicuous typologies. The loggia at *Gallaratese* is defined by few architectural elements appearing absolutely *bare*: a succession of rectangular columns defining a space where the single temporal reference is the projection of shades of those elements. By removing the superfluous and the incidental, the essential is revealed. While its smooth and white surfaces are reminiscent of the 1910s and 1920s buildings by Loos and Le Corbusier, the spatial structure denotes one of the most ancient building types: the *stoa*. The space becomes both familiar and desolated, bringing to mind Rossi's definition of type as "the very idea of architecture, that which is closest to its essence."[25]

**FIGURE 4.2** Aldo Rossi: *Gallaratese*, 1969–74.

© Luigi Ghirri, courtesy of Fondazione Aldo Rossi.

Typology Reconsidered **79**

In 1976 Rossi presented his collage *Città Analoga* (*The Analogous City*), a project that repositioned the role of type in the design process under the domain of analogy (Figure 4.3). This idea was later developed in the essay "An Analogical Architecture,"[26] where type and object are assumed as anonymous *apparatus* embedded in the collective unconscious of society. If with *Gallaratese* Rossi saw type as the process of condensing past forms until driving architecture to its most essential condition, with "Analogical Architecture" he equated type with the solitary condition of objects. Within this context, domestic objects, such as cups, coffeepots, and pencils, concur with architectural elements, such as beach cabins, chimneys, and domes.

While initially Rossi understood type as a permanent and logical presence, the architectural process was assumed to be a continual process of typological reaffirmation; after the introduction of analogy, the notions of type and object appear integrated. Rather than synthesis and abstraction, the predominant tactics became fragmentation, alteration of scale, and displacement. By equating the concepts of type and object, Rossi is diverging from Quatremère's canonical definition of type

**FIGURE 4.3**   Aldo Rossi: *Città Analoga*, 1976.

Courtesy Fondazione Aldo Rossi.

**80** Twentieth Century—Shifting Considerations

(discussed in Chapter 1), particularly his distinction between "type" and "model" (interestingly, a subject Rossi never fully addressed). As will be discussed in Chapter 6, the correspondence between the notions of type and object is perhaps the most pressing question towards a contemporary understanding of the concept of type in the architectural project.

## What Will Be Has Always Been

Similar to what Italy was experiencing, in the 1960s, modern architecture (which after the MOMA exhibit of 1932 began to be known as the *International Style*) in the US started showing signs of fatigue. It is within this historical context that can be better understood the emergence of Louis Kahn (1901–1974), who with his architectural projects as well as with academic activities began expressing a renewed consideration of historical forms in the development of architecture.

Kahn's trajectory was marked by his architectural studies at the University of Pennsylvania, and years later by his residency at the American Academy in Rome.[27] During the 1920s, the school of architecture at Penn was led by French professor Paul Cret (1876–1945), a graduate from the *École des Beaux-Arts* in Paris under the direction of Jean-Luis Pascal and Julien Guadet. After moving to Philadelphia, Cret established one of the most successful architectural practices in the US, responsible for projects such as the Organization of American States in Washington, DC, the Rodin Museum in Philadelphia, and the master plan and main buildings for the University of Texas campus in Austin. During Cret's tenure, the University of Pennsylvania was considered among the American institutions that most faithfully observed the rigors of academic doctrine.[28] In his design studios, Cret exposed students to a wide range of concepts and ideas; while instilling an appreciation of the classical tradition, he emphasized that the designer's priority should be the interpretation of the client's needs.[29] As commented on by David Brownlee and David De Long, Cret also displayed a sense of openness to new ideas and trends—as demonstrated by his 1927 positive review of Le Corbusier's recent translated *Vers une architecture*.[30]

In 1950, Louis Kahn was awarded a fellowship at the American Academy in Rome. During the next year he had the opportunity to travel though Italy, Egypt, and Greece,[31] taking an interest in past forms—particularly ancient Roman—an issue that would deeply influence his future development as architect and thinker. Kahn's ideological evolution is attested by his questioning of functionalism, certainly one the fundamental principles of modern architecture. While discussing Roman Baths, he commented on the preponderance of form and space over "merely" functional considerations: "It is ever a wonder when man aspires to go beyond the functional. Here was the will to build a vaulted structure 100 feet high in which men could bathe. Eight feet would have sufficed. Now, even as a ruin, it is a marvel."[32]

Upon his return to Philadelphia, and evidently marked by his European experience, Kahn began developing a distinctively different formal vocabulary than before his travels. His new projects were populated with ancient typologies, such as arches, loggias, barrel vaults, bell towers, cloisters, and pyramids (Figures 4.4 and 4.5). As Vincent Scully wrote, "Kahn discovered late in life how to transform the ruins

**FIGURE 4.4** Louis Kahn: *Kimbell Art Museum*, 1972.
Courtesy of Roberto Passini.

**FIGURE 4.5** Louis Kahn: *Suhrawardy Hospital*, 1974.
Courtesy of Naquib Hossain.

of ancient Rome into modern buildings."[33] Kahn's connection with tradition can also be appreciated in his utilization of materials such as brick, stone, wood, and concrete (originally used by the Romans), allowing the continual practicing of ancestral construction techniques. Another feature in his architecture is the recurrent presence of primary geometrical figures. Scully[34] relates Kahn's attraction for geometry and math to the long lineage of architectural thinkers, ranging from Vitruvius to Leonardo, who were influenced by the correspondence between architecture and mathematical proportions.[35] Both in the shaping of rooms and in the designs of the façades, Kahn explores a novel figurativism defined by the persistent presence of squares, triangles, and circles (Figure 4.6). While those pure geometrical forms suggest a relationship with humanity's first intellectual and scientific developments, they also establish an understanding of the universe as *mathema*.

Like most architects and critics associated with modernism, Kahn displayed an uncertain position towards the term "type."[36] It is clear that Kahn's use of historical

**FIGURE 4.6** Louis Kahn: *National Assembly Building of Bangladesh*, 1974.
Courtesy of Naquib Hossain.

Typology Reconsidered **83**

types, a notion largely avoided by most modern architects, became an emblem of his architecture. His approximation to the notion of type is also evident in many of his writings. For instance, his famous soliloquy that became the title of one of his most celebrated texts, *What Will Be Has Always Been*,[37] establishes a relationship between the past, the permanent forms, and the future of architecture, thus suggesting a clear association with the concept of type. In his text "Monumentality," Kahn discussed the recurrent forms through architectural history:

> The influence of the Roman vault, the dome, the arch, has etched itself in deep furrows across the pages of architectural history. Through Romanesque, Gothic, Renaissance, and today, its basic forms and structural ideas have been felt. They will continue to reappear.[38]

Again, the expression presents clear echoes of the notion of type. It should be noted, however, that while type has been a persistent presence in Kahn's projects and ideas, neither in his writings, nor in recordings of his teachings, nor in his interviews did he use the term.

This topic brings back a question raised in the previous chapter, which is the dismissal of the word "type" in modern architectural discourse. In the case of Kahn, the term could appear too closely associated with his academic education at the University of Pennsylvania, where under the spell of Paul Cret "type" was considered one of the fundamental design and theoretical principles.[39] While Kahn recurrently expressed admiration and gratitude for his teacher Cret, it is plausible that as an aspiring (and then established) "modern architect," he would rather not be associated with the *Beaux-Arts* tradition; while still a strong force in American architecture, most progressive minds regarded the institution as regressive and reactionary.

## Colquhoun—Expansions of the Concept

As earlier discussed, at the beginning of the 1960s, both sides of the Atlantic experienced a sense of discontent with many postulates of modern architecture. For many architects and critics, a necessary development for overcoming modernism's crisis was establishing a renewed consideration of historical precedents. This situation was discussed by Vincent Scully[40] while examining the parallels between the formal and theoretical explorations of the Italian neo-rationalists and Louis Kahn's works. Both sides, argues Scully, coincided in the need for an improved appreciation of historical heritage; while the Italians focused on the conditions of the traditional city, Kahn's projects gravitated towards an assimilation of historical forms. While the word "type" was emblematic of the neo-rationalists' discourse, in Kahn's case it remained a latent presence.

The first critic to introduce the concept of type to the English-speaking world was Alan Colquhoun, who in his 1967 essay "Typology and Design Method"[41] examined the impact of typology on the architectural project. In what became a constant for many theoretical essays of the period, Colquhoun started outlining a critique of the modern movement by highlighting its inability to articulate

**84** Twentieth Century—Shifting Considerations

transmittable design mechanisms. According to Colquhoun, modern architecture offered two (deficient) design methodologies. The first was based on expressionism's belief that "the freedom of intuition" could become a strategy for all artistic creations. This theory, he noted, proposed discarding "all historical manifestations of art, just as modern architectural theory rejected all historical forms of architecture."[42] The second methodology derived from the functionalist doctrine, defined by Colquhoun as "biotechnical determinism," where "Form was merely the result of a logical process by which the operational needs and the operational techniques were brought together."[43] In Colquhoun's view, the "scientific methods of analysis" were incapable of determining architectural form, thus refuting the dogma establishing a correspondence between form and function.

Given modernism's inability to propose viable design methodologies, Colquhoun argued it should contemplate typologically driven design mechanisms. To frame the discussion, he reviewed a lecture by modern theoretician Tomas Maldonado at Princeton University. In his presentation, Maldonado conveys an ambivalent consideration of type. While he initially rejects the presence of type in the architectural project, calling it "a cancer in the body of the solution,"[44] he later concedes that it may be a "provisional solution"—until modernism develops new design methodologies. Detecting a sense of vacillation in Maldonado's words, Colquhoun contends on the (almost) inevitable presence of type in the realization of architectural projects:

> In mentioning typology, Maldonado is suggesting something quite new and something which has been rejected again and again by modern theorists. He is suggesting that the area of pure intuition must be based on a knowledge of past solutions applied to related problems, and that creation is a process of adapting forms derived either from past needs or from past aesthetic ideologies to the needs of the present. Although he regards this as a provisional solution—"a cancer in the body of the solution"—he nonetheless recognizes that this is the actual procedure which designers follow.[45]

Two questions emerge from Colquhoun's essay. On the one hand, he confirms that the modern movement was undergoing a sense of exhaustion, as if the insistence on continuously attaining original solutions and forms, or considering the project as a result of programmatic analysis, became impossible strategies to sustain. On the other hand, by citing a thinker firmly aligned with modern principles, such as Tomas Maldonado, Colquhoun underlines an issue that has been hovering for decades but virtually never manifested—that is, modernism's dismissal of the concept of type.

By referencing contemporary explorations in the visual arts, Colquhoun stresses that modern architecture should consider traditional forms as points of departure for the development of the architectural project. "My purpose in stressing this fact," he states,

> is not to advocate a reversion to an architecture which accepts tradition unthinkingly . . . if we look at the allied fields of painting and music, we can see that in the work of a Kandinsky or a [Arnold] Schoenberg, traditional

formal devices were not completely abandoned but were transformed and given a new emphasis by the exclusion of ideologically repulsive iconic elements.[46]

Within the realm of architecture, those precedents can derive from conventional architectural lineage, or they can be "borrowed from other disciplines, such as space engineering or Pop Art."[47] As examples of this approach, he refers to the works by the Russian constructivists, Le Corbusier, and recent projects by Archigram, "who borrowed the forms" of engineering inventions.[48]

On closer inspection, Colquhoun is approximating type to the notion of *mimetic precedent*, which comprises not only traditional architectural forms (or types) but also a wide range of elements outside the conventional boundaries of architecture, such as industrial machineries, artistic manifestations, and natural forms. According to this view, rather than a disciplinary construct, the fundamental attribute of type lies in its repeatability, a subject to be further discussed in Chapter 6.

## Vidler's Third Typology

A central question raised by Rossi, Aymonino, and other members of *La Tendenza* was the unequivocal relationship between building type and the traditional city— concepts that have been rejected or ignored by modern architecture. A thinker who most intensely discussed the connection between type and city was Anthony Vidler (1941). Vidler's biographical details follow the pattern of many English theoreticians and historians established in the United States, such as Colin Rowe, Alan Colquhoun, Reyner Banham, and Kenneth Frampton. After completing his studies in Cambridge and obtaining his doctorate at the University of Delft, in 1965 Vidler moved to the US to work as a professor of theory at Princeton University. His main area of research has been eighteenth-century architecture in France, which, as previously discussed, was a crucial historical moment regarding the origins and evolution of the concept of type.

Vidler wrote two essential essays on the concept of type, both published in 1977. The first was "The Idea of Type: The Transformation of an Academic Ideal, 1750–1830,"[49] where he identifies the origins of type as a phenomenon characteristic of the epistemological evolution during the eighteenth century, highlighting European society's interest in the origins of man-made things. It is from this background that Vidler examines Quatremère's definition of type and its influence on his contemporaries. Vidler's second essay, entitled "The Third Typology,"[50] was a proposal for understanding type in relation to the contemporary city. He starts by identifying three conceptions of type, each one associated with a particular historical phase. The "first typology" refers to Quatremère's late eighteenth-century definition, where type is assumed in relation to origin, classification, and imitation of forms. The "second typology" derives from the nineteenth century's industrial revolution and the implementation of new industrial methodologies, such as mass production and standardization, where "buildings were to be no more and no less than machines themselves, serving and molding the needs of man according to economic criteria."[51]

**86** Twentieth Century—Shifting Considerations

Following, Vidler introduces the "third typology," which is the central subject of the essay. The third typology, he argues, was conceived as a reaction against the postulates of the modern city:

> This new typology is explicitly critical of the Modern Movement; it utilizes the clarity of the eighteenth-century city to rebuke the fragmentation, decentralization, and formal disintegration introduced into contemporary urban life by the zoning techniques and technological advances of the twenties.[52]

This argument conveys notable affinities with Rossi's description of the city as a cultural construct. To this end, Vidler deduces that the city must be reinterpreted as a "new ontology," a collective construction that is developed over time:

> This concept of the city as the site of a new typology is evidently born of a desire to stress the continuity of form and history against the fragmentation produced by the elemental, institutional, and mechanistic typologies of the recent past.[53]

The fundamental strategy of this "new typology" is typological transformation: "The technique or rather the fundamental compositional method suggested by the Rationalists is the transformation of selected types—partial or whole—into entirely new entities that draw their communicative power and potential criteria from the understanding of this transformation."[54] "For this typology," he adds,

> there is no clear set of rules for the transformations and their objects, nor any polemically defined set of historical precedents. Nor, perhaps, should there be; the continued vitality of this architectural practice rests in its essential engagement with the precise demands of the present and not in any holistic mythicization of the past.[55]

With the "third typology," Vidler proposes reestablishing the bond between architecture and the city, an idea that echoes Alberti's famous analogy relating the house and the city, or, relating architecture and urbanism. Thus, just like a building typology comprises several elements or "subtypes," such as columns, walls, and roofs, the third typology is defined by the constituents of the city: building types, urban spaces, urban fabric, and monuments. According to this position, the notion of the isolated and self-referential architectural object, which became the paradigm of modernity, is replaced by the urban type, which by definition is a collective creation and its meaning evolves through its relation to the city.

The idea of installing the relationship between type and city as a central theoretical debate inevitably leads to underlining the concept of type as an agent of urban transformation. To analyze architecture, Vidler argues, we must first examine the city, and for that we must consider the typological question. The correspondences between "the city and its typology," Vidler concludes, "are reasserted as the only possible bases for the restoration of a critical role to public architecture otherwise assassinated by the apparently endless cycle of production and consumption."[56]

## The Redeemed Relationship Between Type and City

A consequence of the essays by Aymonino, Rossi, Colquhoun, and Vidler (which in turn represented a continuation of the writings of Muratori and Argan) was the realization that while type was a constituent present in all cities, each one contains its particular and idiosyncratic typologies. Therefore, in the 1980s a peculiar phenomenon began to appear: a large number of architects and scholars began identifying and studying each city's distinctive types—a matter mostly ignored by previous generations of architects. What was initially perceived as an eminently "Italian" subject was now regarded as a concept of universal repercussions. Therefore, a large number of towns, cities, and regions became interested in developing their own identification and analysis of local typologies. Reminiscent of archaeology, architectural and urban studies aimed at understanding and interpreting the realizations of culture through time.

As a result of this process, numerous studies were dedicated to examining the role of type in the development of cities. Jean Castex,[57] for instance, carried out an extensive research on the impact of Haussmann's urban intervention in Paris, describing the variable relationships between plot, urban fabric, and building typology. In Barcelona, Oriol Bohigas[58] and Ignasi Solà-Morales[59] adopted a similar strategy by examining the impact of building typologies in shaping the street, the public square, the city block, and the urban fabric. In Philadelphia, John Blatteau and Paul Hirshorn[60] performed extensive research on the row-house typology, identifying its permanent features as well as variations according to plots lengths (Figure 4.7). For his part, Steven Holl[61] developed an inventory of North American

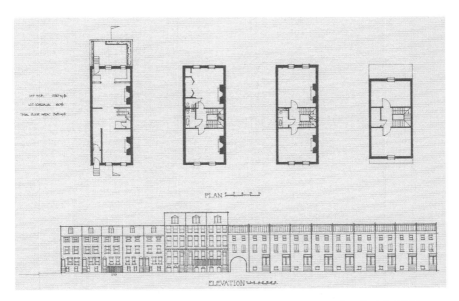

**FIGURE 4.7** John Blatteau and Paul Hirshorn: *Comparative study of Philadelphia row houses*. Collection, Architectural Archives, University of Pennsylvania.

## 88 Twentieth Century—Shifting Considerations

urban and rural types, identifying the most recurrent morphological structures (Figure 4.8). With a more ambitious agenda, the founders of *new urbanism*—Andrés Duany and Elizabeth Plater-Zyberk[62]—examined the urban and building typologies of American towns, highlighting the contrast between traditional urbanism and *suburban sprawl*.[63]

One of the most original studies on the relationship between type and city was developed by Argentine critic Fernando Diez, who analyzed the role of typology in the urban transformation of Buenos Aires. Influenced by Carlo Aymonino's understanding of type,[64] Diez distinguishes between the notions of type and

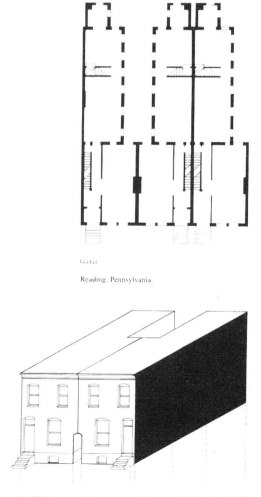

**FIGURE 4.8** Steven Holl: *Passages between row houses in Reading, PA.*
Courtesy of Steven Holl Architects.

typological series while examining the relationship between building type, plot, and city block (Figure 4.9).[65] Particularly illustrative is his analysis of the origins of the "casa chorizo" (or "half patio house"), the most traditional residential type in Buenos Aires. Diez deduces that the "casa chorizo" derives from the "colonial house," in turn a descendant of the "Mediterranean courtyard house" imported by Spanish and Italian immigrants. The origins of the "casa chorizo," according to Diez, responded to speculative reasons: towards the beginning of the nineteenth century and as a result of the valorization of the urban plot, several houses were split in half by inserting a transversal party wall (Figure 4.10). Therefore, each property originally 17 meters wide was "replaced" by two symmetrical houses of about 8.50 meters in width. Soon after, the "casa chorizo" started being replicated as a new construction, thus consolidating the emergence of a new building type. As a consequence of this process, in new urban developments—such as the 1882 master plan for the city of La Plata—the plots were dimensioned to accommodate the emerging type. The urban normative, in other words, was adapted to contemplate the presence of a new typology.

The studies by Diez, Duany, Holl, Castex, Blatteau, and Bohigas, among others, demonstrate the relevance of typological studies over the course of these last decades. Type, in this context, is understood as an instrument that allows a profound understanding of the built environment. Because of its particular characteristics,

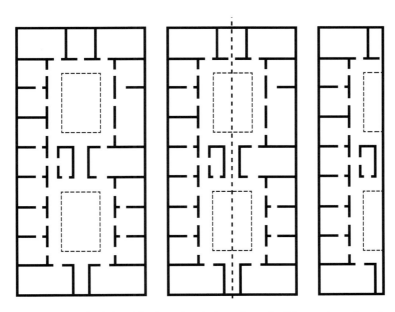

**FIGURE 4.9**  Fernando Diez: *Typological evolution—from the "Roman house" to the "casa chorizo."*

Redrawn by Abby Freed.

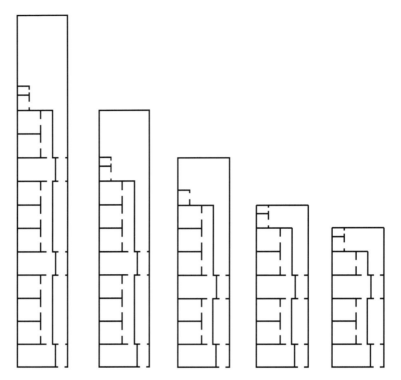

**FIGURE 4.10**  Fernando Diez: *Variations "casa chorizo" according to the lot dimensions.* Redrawn by Abby Freed.

it confirms the inexorable relationship between architecture and the city, in turn establishing links with a place's culture and history. The following chapters will lay out how type can become an agent in the development of the design process, certainly a more contentious subject.

## Notes

1 Rossi, Aldo, "An Analogical Architecture." In Nesbitt, Kate (ed.), *Theorizing a New Agenda for Architecture: An Anthology of Architectural Theory, 1965–1995.* New York: Princeton Architectural, 1996, 349.
2 Two key texts by Lévi-Strauss discussing structuralism are: Lévi-Strauss, Claude, *The Structural Anthropology*, New York: Basic Books, Aug 5, 2008 (originally published in 1958); and *Totemism*, Boston: Beacon Press, 1963 (originally published in 1962).
3 Colquhoun, "Postmodernism and Structuralism: A Retrospective Glance," 243–254.
4 Cited in Habermas, Jürgen, "Modernity—An Incomplete Project." In Foster, Hal (ed.), *The Anti-aesthetic: Essays on Postmodern Culture.* Port Townsend, WA: Bay Press, 1987, 3.
5 The influence of Duchamp in contemporary art is discussed in Dorothy Kosinski, *Dialogues: Duchamp, Cornell, Johns, Rauschenberg.* New Haven, CT: Yale University Press, 2005.

6 Argan, Giulio Carlo, "On the Typology of Architecture." In Nesbitt, Kate (ed.), *Theorizing a New Agenda for Architecture: An Anthology of Architectural Theory, 1965–1995*. New York: Princeton Architectural, 1996, 243.

7 For a thorough discussion of Muratori's book and theories, see Oliveira, Vítor, *Urban Morphology: An Introduction to the Study of the Physical Form of Cities*. Berlin: Springer, 2016, 88.

8 Argan quotes Quatremère's entry discussed in Chapter 1, whereby type "does not present so much an image of something to be copied or imitated exactly as the idea of an element which should itself serve as a rule for the model." See Argan, "On the Typology of Architecture," 243.

9 Argan, "On the Typology of Architecture," 242.

10 Argan, "On the Typology of Architecture," 242.

11 Argan, "On the Typology of Architecture," 244.

12 Argan, "On the Typology of Architecture," 246.

13 Argan, "On the Typology of Architecture," 246.

14 Argan, "On the Typology of Architecture," 245.

15 Argan, "On the Typology of Architecture," 245.

16 For a brief review of the principal professors and scholars at IAUV during the 1960s and 1970s, see Semerani, Luciano (ed.), *The School of Venice*. London: Architectural Design, 1985.

17 Aymonino, Carlo, "Type and Typology," in Semerani, Luciano (ed.), *The School of Venice*, 49–51.

18 Aymonino, "Type and Typology," 50.

19 Aymonino, "Type and Typology," 49.

20 Rossi, Aldo, *The Architecture of the City*. Cambridge, MA: MIT Press, 1982, 29.

21 For discussion on Rossi's consideration of modern architecture, see Aureli, Pier Vittorio, *The Project of Autonomy: Politics and Architecture Within and Against Capitalism*. Princeton: Princeton Architectural Press, 2008, 57–58.

22 Rossi, *The Architecture of the City*, 35–45.

23 Rossi, *The Architecture of the City*, 41.

24 Rossi, *The Architecture of the City*, 41.

25 Rossi, *The Architecture of the City*, 68.

26 Rossi, "An Analogical Architecture," 348–352.

27 Most of the biographical notes on Kahn were taken from Brownlee, David H., and De Long, David Gilson, *Louis I. Kahn: In the Realm of Architecture*. Los Angeles, CA: Universe, 1997.

28 Brownlee and De Long, *Louis I. Kahn*, 13.

29 Brownlee and De Long, *Louis I. Kahn*, 14.

30 Brownlee and De Long, *Louis I. Kahn*, 14.

31 For an overview of Kahn's experience during his fellowship at the American Academy of Rome, see Vincent Scully, "Louis I. Kahn and the Ruins of Rome." *Engineering and Science*, vol. 56, no. 2, Winter 1993, 3–13.

32 Cited in Brownlee and De Long, *Louis I. Kahn*, 51.

33 Brownlee and De Long, *Louis I. Kahn*, 9.

34 Scully, "Louis I. Kahn and the Ruins of Rome," 7.

35 Kahn's interest in mathematical proportions was probably accentuated after his meeting with Rudolph Wittkower, author of the seminal treatise *Architectural Principles*, where he analyzed Palladio's implementation of mathematical proportions in the design of his villas. In addition, in 1950 Kahn had a "prolonged conversation" with Colin Rowe, Wittkower's most important disciple and later author of the influential essay "Mathematics of the Ideal Villa." Within a few weeks after their meeting Rowe sent Kahn a new edition of Wittkower's book. Commented on in Brownlee and De Long, *Louis I. Kahn*, 69.

36 During the preparation of this book I consulted about Kahn's consideration of the term "type" with William Whitaker, curator and collections manager of the Architectural Archives of the University of Pennsylvania, home of the Louis Kahn Archives. Whitaker stated that "Kahn did not use the term type, preferring form or character as a generator of shape." William Whitaker, e-mail message to author, June 21, 2017.

**92** Twentieth Century—Shifting Considerations

37 Kahn, Louis I., and Richard Saul Wurman, *What Will Be Has Always Been: The Words of Louis I. Kahn*. New York: Access, 1986.

38 Louis Kahn, "Monumentality," *The New Architecture and City Planning*, in Zucker, ed., 578–579. Cited in Frampton, Kenneth, and John Cava, *Studies in Tectonic Culture: The Poetics of Construction in Nineteenth and Twentieth Century Architecture*. Cambridge, MA: MIT, 1995, 210.

39 For an extended discussion of the adaptation of the concept of type from the French *Beaux-Arts* tradition into the American schools of architecture during the first part of the twentieth century, see Hyungmin Pai, *The Portfolio and the Diagram: Architecture, Discourse, and Modernity in America*. Cambridge, MA: MIT Press, 2002.

40 "Introduction" by Vincent Scully, in Brownlee and De Long, *Louis I. Kahn*, P 9.

41 Colquhoun, Alan, "Typology and Design Method." In Nesbitt, Kate (ed.), *Theorizing a New Agenda for Architecture: An Anthology of Architectural Theory, 1965–1995*. New York: Princeton Architectural, 1996, 250–257.

42 Colquhoun, "Typology and Design Method," 255.

43 Colquhoun, "Typology and Design Method," 252.

44 Colquhoun, "Typology and Design Method," 254.

45 Colquhoun, "Typology and Design Method," 254.

46 Colquhoun, "Typology and Design Method," 257.

47 Colquhoun, "Typology and Design Method," 257.

48 Colquhoun, "Typology and Design Method," 257.

49 Vidler, Anthony, "The Idea of Type: The Transformation of the Academic Ideal, 1750–1830." *Oppositions 8*. Cambridge, MA: MIT Press, 1977.

50 Vidler, Anthony, "The Third Typology." In Michel K. Hays (ed.), *Architectural Theory Since 1968*. Cambridge, MA: MIT Press. 1998, 288–294.

51 Vidler, "The Third Typology," 291.

52 Vidler, "The Third Typology," 293.

53 Vidler, "The Third Typology," 292.

54 Vidler, "The Third Typology," 293.

55 Vidler, "The Third Typology," 293.

56 Vidler, "The Third Typology," 294.

57 Panerai, Philippe, Jean Castex, Jean-Charles Depaule, and Ivor Samuels, *Urban Forms: Death and Life of the Urban Block*. Oxford: Architectural, 2004.

58 Bohigas, Oriol, *En Contra una arquitectura adjetivada*, particularly the chapter "Metodología y Tipología." Barcelona: Seix Barral, 1969.

59 De Solà-Morales i Rubió, Manuel, *Las Formas de Crecimiento Urbano*. Ediciones UPC, 1997.

60 Between 1979 and 1981 John Blatteau and Paul Hirshhorn developed a research about the row house typology entitled "A Comparative Study of Philadelphia Rowhouses." Accessed November 12, 2014, www.brynmawr.edu/iconog/rowhse/frontpage.html.

61 Holl, Steven, *Rural & Urban House Types in North America*. New York: Pamphlet Architecture 9, 1982.

62 Some publications by Duany y Plater-Zyberk are: Duany, Andres, Elizabeth Plater-Zyberk, Alex Kreiger, and William R. Lennertz: *Towns and Town-Making Principles*. Cambridge, MA: Harvard University Graduate School of Design, 1991. Also Duany, Andres, Elizabeth Plater-Zyberk, and Robert Alminana, *The New Civic Art: Elements of Town Planning*. New York: Rizzoli, 2003.

63 Duany, Andres, Elizabeth Plater-Zyberk, and Jeff Speck, *Suburban Nation: The Rise of Sprawl and the Decline of the American Dream*. New York: North Point, 2000.

64 Fernando Diez refers to Carlo Aymonino's understanding of type as an "instrument, rather than a category." Diez, Fernando, *Buenos Aires y algunas constantes en las transformaciones urbanas*. Buenos Aires: Editorial de Belgrano, 1996, 21.

65 See Diez, *Buenos Aires y algunas constantes en las transformaciones urbanas*, 46–52.

# PART 3

# Type and Project— Alteration Tactics

# 5

# TYPOLOGICAL ALTERATIONS

*Art (the definition might run) is a suggested improvement on nature: an imitation that conceals within it a demonstration [of what the original should be]. In other words, art is a perfecting mimesis.*

—Walter Benjamin[1]

## Chapter 5—List of Contents

| | |
|---|---|
| *Antecedents* | *95* |
| *Type as a Design Process—Moneo* | *96* |
| *The Elasticity of the Type—Michelangelo and Gaudí* | *97* |
| *The Magnification of Types—Boullée and Oldenburg* | *102* |
| *Abstraction, Juxtaposition, and Assemblage—Ledoux and Libera* | *107* |
| *Typological Substitutions—Le Corbusier* | *112* |
| *Subtle Transformations—Álvaro Siza* | *114* |

## Antecedents

As discussed in Chapter 4, in the early 1960s, Saverio Muratori[2] and Giulio Carlo Argan[3] reintroduced the notion of type into the architectural discourse. Muratori became attracted to the subject after his analysis of traditional Venetian housing, while Argan developed a reinterpretation of Quatremère's theories by focusing on the "idea" of type, and its relationship to the notion of imitation. The contrast between Muratori and Argan would become more pronounced with the positions assumed by the "next generation" of Italian architects and thinkers—namely, the members of the so-called *School of Venice*. Carlo Aymonino adopted a stance that presented clear echoes of Muratori's ideas—an understanding of type as a classification tool.[4] Instead, Gianugo Polesello developed a position closer to Argan's,

**96** Type and Project—Alteration Tactics

stating that while "given types have their origins in history; they may also be the product of invention."[5] The evolution of Aldo Rossi's thought can be interpreted as a synthesis of this duality: in his first period—mainly identified with his book *L'architettura della città*[6]—he refers to type as a tool for the analysis of architectural and urban inventory; in his later texts, such as "An Analogical Architecture"[7] and *Autobiografia Scientifica*,[8] he understands type as a fundamentally poetic notion, a precept capable of evoking analogic associations.

## Type as a Design Process—Moneo

In his 1978 article "On Typology,"[9] Rafael Moneo developed a historical and theoretical overview of the concept of type, focusing on the typological design process. Echoing Argan's essay, Moneo describes the typological design as a two-step process: first the architect selects or "identifies his work with a precise type," and then he develops a mechanism with which he "can destroy it, transform it or respect it."[10] A notable feature of Moneo's text is its level of specificity, its ability to list and describe the possibilities and potentials of typological transformation:

> In this continuous process of transformation, the architect can extrapolate from the type, changing its use; he can distort the type by means of a transformation of scale; he can overlap different types to produce new ones. He can use formal quotations of a known type in a different context, as well as create new types by a radical change in the techniques already employed. The list of different mechanisms is extensive—it is a function of the inventiveness of architects.[11]

Moneo understands a typological process as the selection of a preexisting formal idea, which can be extrapolated, distorted, superimposed, distorted, fragmented, or inserted in an unforeseen context. When the new resolution maintains certain features of the adopted type, the result is a new iteration of that type. Otherwise, if the transformation is too extreme, its new form may no longer be recognized as "belonging" within the original typological range.

Moneo continues by introducing an *expansive* interpretation of the typological precedent. According to this idea, the concept of type should not be confined to the field of architecture since it can be applied to all man-made objects: "a work of architecture, a construction, a house-like a boat, a cup, a helmet can be defined through formal features."[12] Influenced by the anthropological theories of George Kubler,[13] Moneo's definition of type extends beyond the conventional category of "building typology," so that all reproducible objects that populate the world, such as tools, instruments, objects, architectural elements, and building components, are referred to as "types." This interpretation displays clear affinities with the comments of Quatremère, who, towards the end of his rubric on "Type," wrote that "no one is unaware that a multitude of pieces of furniture, tools, seats, and clothes have their necessary type."[14]

In his essay, Moneo introduces two interrelated issues. On the one hand, architecture may no longer be assumed as a *cohesive unit*, where the parts must be conceived in relation to the whole; now every element or detail can be considered and defined separately. On the other hand, he proposes to dissolve the distinction between the *architectural element* and the *object*, as he considers both conditions as types. Type, in this view, may be active through repetition or imitation—which implies a varied range of morphological alterations and deviations. Thus, the work of the architect may be presumed as analogous to the industrial designer, the ceramist, or the cabinetmaker—the essence of their works lies in repeatability. The distinction between those disciplines is dependent not on the scale of the intervention but on the intention that fuels each one of those processes.

## The Elasticity of the Type—Michelangelo and Gaudí

While Moneo didn't offer concrete examples of the typological transformation mechanisms he describes, following his guidelines this study proposes a *diachronic* examination of projects that may illustrate those tactics. Various historians have identified the work of Michelangelo as among the best examples of conceiving architecture as an assemblage of typological elements bound to be transformed independently. In his biographical study, John Summers pointed out that a defining quality of Michelangelo's design is the intensity and originality of his formal manipulations: "inversion, rotation, interlacing, as well as combination and transformation ... could not be more striking."[15] James Ackerman in turn draws an analogy between Michelangelo's architectural projects and his consideration of the human figure, which is no longer assumed as an integral and harmonious figure but as an assemblage of "members" subject to various transformation processes. "By thinking of buildings as organisms," writes Ackerman, Michelangelo "changed the concept of architectural design from the static one produced by a system or predetermined proportions to a dynamic one in which members would be integrated by the suggestion of muscular power."[16] This principle assumes a drastic departure from the canons derived from Vitruvius that established an analogic relationship between architecture the human body, provided that the proportions of the building components must correspond to the whole.[17]

As a point of departure, Michelangelo adopts a range of elements that derive from the classical vocabulary, which he subjects to an intense process of transformation that makes all the parts, ornaments, and even spaces capable of being distorted or disfigured. Despite the intensity of those transformations, Ackerman notes that Michelangelo "invariably retained essential features from the ancient models in order to force the observer to recollect the source while enjoying the innovations."[18] In other words, while the new iteration appears remarkably innovative and unique, its forms remain associated with the original type.

The vestibule of the Laurentian Library in Florence is an example of typological transformation, where every component has been vigorously transfixed. The tabernacles display a trapezoidal shape—an unusual geometrical figure at the time—and

**98** Type and Project—Alteration Tactics

convert the "negative" space of the niche into a trapezoid form (Figure 5.1). The brackets that hold the tabernacles stand out for their magnified scale; they also pose a sharp contrast with the relatively small door. A pair of columns (or pilasters?) seems uncomfortably compressed, as if the scale of the opening where they stand is "too

**FIGURE 5.1** Michelangelo Buonarroti: *Vestibule of Laurentian Library*, c. 1525.
Photograph courtesy of Fernando Diez.

small." The four walls that surround the chamber resemble an unexpected *assembly* or *collage*, and each of the architectural elements is recognizable as such, though in an ostensibly altered fashion. The overall effect is of tension and unity by coexistence.

David Leatherbarrow refers to the architecture of Michelangelo as "elastic geometry,"[19] a process that comprises various transformation strategies, such as "mutation, fusion, reverberation [or] undulation."[20] According to Leatherbarrow, "It is a modification of canonical proportions (canons Michelangelo knew very well) that indicates the peculiar virtue or essential character of the figure—its life force, temper, or mixture of passions."[21] This notion can be appreciated in the resolution of the staircase of the vestibule. Through the design and study of its dimensioning, shape, situation in space, and relationship with other architectural elements of the vestibule and the reading room, Michelangelo got closer to the notion of transforming a type up to the point of proposing a novel typological creation (Figure 5.2). The fact that the steps can provoke so many analogical associations—lava, cascade, slope of a mountain, a tongue—hints at the semantic condition the staircase exposes: the *metaphor* (the capacity to suggest simultaneity of secondary meanings).

The notion of understanding the project as a coexistence of types subject to being transformed can also be detected in the architecture of Antoni Gaudí, conceived as a reconsideration of "familiar" typologies, such as *loggias*, domes, columns, and towers, all of which are subjected to persistent and occasional radical distortion processes. Unlike Michelangelo, who assumed the classical vocabulary as a point of departure, the range of types and ornamentations considered by Gaudí is much more eclectic and diverse, with his buildings displaying elements of classical, Gothic, Romanesque, and Moorish architecture.

The parallels between the architecture of Michelangelo and Gaudí can also be appreciated for their mutual interest in the notion of *metaphorical transformation* by which the type is distorted up to the point of *transforming* into a creation foreign to architectural conventions. Just as the staircase of the vestibule of the Laurentian Library is capable of insinuating a copious list of analogies and metaphors, critic Carlos Eduardo Comas has observed the metaphorical associations present in Gaudí's works evoking images of dragons, swords, masks, or swirls.[22] In these cases the original types have been transformed up to the point of departing away from the iconographic conventions of architecture, transforming into figurative sculpture.

The moment that most clearly illustrates Gaudí's notion of typological transformation is the *loggia* at Park Güell in Barcelona. What first draws the attention of this project is the distortion of the type "column"—its shaft and capital seemed to have merged into a single helical form (Figure 5.3). Due to its unusual shape, the column resembles a swirl, suggesting a metaphor that contradicts the conventional function of a structural component: instead of transmitting the weight from above to the ground, the aerobic forces seem to ascend. In addition, because of the columns' inclined disposition the space defined by the *loggia* appears remarkably distorted (Figure 5.4). With this work, Gaudí raises one of the fundamental questions posed by the notion of typological transformation, which is up to what point it is possible to distort a given type so that the new iteration will continue to be considered within the margins of that specific typological territory.

**FIGURE 5.2** Michelangelo Buonarroti: *Detail of staircase at Vestibule of Laurentian Library*, c. 1525.

Photograph courtesy of Fernando Diez.

**FIGURE 5.3** Antoni Gaudí: *Park Güell*, 1900.
Photograph courtesy of Marc Llimargas Casas.

**FIGURE 5.4** Antoni Gaudí: *Park Güell*, 1900.
Photograph courtesy of Marc Llimargas Casas.

## The Magnification of Types—Boullée and Oldenburg

The scale of a building (or an object) may be considered according to the *real* scale and the *relative* scale. The *real* scale relates to measurement, the actual dimensions of a certain element. The *relative* scale derives from the relationship between an element and the context within which it is inserted. One of the reasons the staircase of the Laurentian Library appears so extraordinary is the relationship between its dimensions and the space it is located. The surprising factor is its *relative* scale, since it appears "too large" for that room. Another example of alteration of relative scale in the work of Michelangelo is the "colossal" pilasters of the *Palazzo dei Conservatori* facing the *Piazza del Campidoglio* (Figure 5.5). Because of their double height, the

**FIGURE 5.5** Michelangelo Buonarroti: *Colossal Order at Palazzo Nuovo*, c. 1545.
Photograph courtesy of Catherine Vollmer.

pilasters display a monumental proportion in relation to the building in which they are housed. Thanks to this operation, Michelangelo conceived a new occurrence of the architectural element, which ceases to be a decorative element of the façade and becomes an instrument that helps define the urban proposal. According to Alois Riegl,[23] with this project Michelangelo inaugurated a new conception of the pilaster, which will be later imitated by the following generation of Baroque architects.

The strategy of intensively magnifying traditional types is the main characteristic of the work of Étienne-Louis Boullée (1728–1799). Assuming as a point of departure classical forms such as domes, vaults, or pyramids, Boullée alters the *relative scale* of those types up to the point of shifting the meaning of those forms. An example of this process is his project for the *Bibliothèque Nationale* (Figure 5.6), where he conceives an "Immense Basilique"[24] crowned at each end with "triumphal arches," paying homage to the most characteristic typologies of ancient Rome. Boullée describes the project as a "gigantic amphitheater . . . a magnificent spectacle of books."[25] His particular interest in the ancient world becomes more evident for his references to the mural *The School of Athens* by Rafael Sanzio, a rendering of history's most famous philosophers, which—just like *Bibliothèque*—displays a great vault open to the elements.[26]

The *Cénotaphe à Newton* of 1784 (Figure 5.7) perhaps best illustrates the notion of re-signifying a type after its variation of scale. In an approach similar to the *Bibliothèque Nationale*, Boullée adopts a type of Roman origins—in this case, the dome—and proceeds to magnify it in an extraordinary fashion. Boullée's idea becomes apparent in the renderings, where the scattered persons indicate the relative scale of

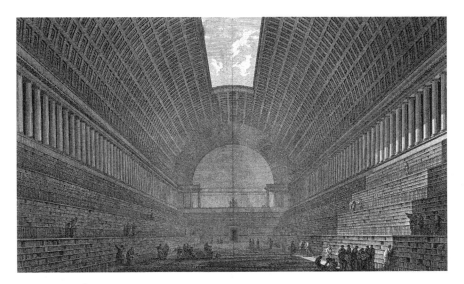

**FIGURE 5.6**   Étienne-Louis Boullée: *Bibliothèque Nationale*, 1785.

Bibliothèque Nationale de France.

**FIGURE 5.7** Étienne-Louis Boullée: *Cénotaphe à Newton*, 1784. Bibliothèque Nationale de France.

the colossal dome. According to Boullée, the adoption of a perfect sphere as a fulfillment of the dome becomes the appropriate tribute to Isaac Newton, the greatest scientist of his time, an issue poetically described in his *Essai*:

> The unique advantage of this form is that from whichever side we look at it … we see only a continuous surface which has neither beginning nor end and the more we look at it, the larger it appears. This form has never been utilized and it is the only one appropriate to this monument.[27]

The section of the *Cénotaphe* highlights what appears to be an unprecedented typological operation: the dome, traditionally conceived as a half-sphere, is completed to comprise a full sphere. The mechanism can be interpreted either as the daring transformation of a traditional building type, or as the inauguration of a new and distinctive type. Seemingly inspired by the *Cénotaphe*, Boullée's contemporaries Ledoux (*House of the Agricultural Guards* in Chaux) and Lequeu (*Temple de la Terre*) adopted this form in some of their projects, suggesting the consolidation of a new type. However, throughout the nineteenth and twentieth centuries, the solution was abandoned; instead the preferred form continued to be the half-sphere dome. Therefore, rather than the irruption of a new type, the visionaries' utilization of the "sphere" should be interpreted as an oddity, an exceptional case. The circumstance of singular and extraordinary moments that fall short of becoming consolidated types was discussed by George Kubler, positing that "An invention may appear to meet the edge of possibility, but if it exceeds the penumbra, it remains a curious toy or it disappears into fantasy."[28]

★

The notion of altering the anticipated size of building components has only occasionally been discussed in architectural theory.[29] In his thesis dedicated to the subject, Aníbal Parodi Rebella[30] analyzes how this issue (both magnifying and minimizing) becomes a defining issue in the works of Adolf Loos, Le Corbusier, Carlo Scarpa, Ettore Sottsas, and Frank Gehry, among others. According to Parodi Rebella, "modifying substantially the perceived scale of a volumetric-spatial entity is to completely change its relationship with the environment, thus affecting the entity's meaning."[31]

The tactic of changing the meaning of objects through their extreme magnification has defined the work of artist Claes Oldenburg (1929). The work of Oldenburg, occasionally together with his wife, Coosje van Bruggen, proposes the intersection of figurative sculpture, architecture, and urban moments, where everyday and "banal" objects, such as spoons, baseball bats, buttons, or plugins, are magnified up to the point of becoming urban edifices. The fusion between architecture, urban monument, and figurative sculpture devised by Oldenburg is especially evident in his sporadic collaborations with Frank Gehry, such as the *Chiat/Day* building in Los Angeles (1985), where binoculars of colossal dimensions becomes the entrance portico of the complex (Figure 5.8). In Oldenburg's universe, sculpture, architecture, and urban moment converge onto an indivisible unit at which none of

**FIGURE 5.8** Frank Gehry and Claes Oldenburg: *Chiat/Day* building, 1985.

Photograph courtesy of Leonardo Finotti.

the disciplines prevail. This approach is substantiated in Oldenburg's writings when he expresses an interest in transdisciplinary parameters, such as the curious notion of classifying forms in horizontal or vertical dispositions.[32]

One of the works that characterize Oldenburg's artistic approach is the urban sculpture *Clothespin*, the silhouette of an ordinary and mundane device represented with colossal dimensions (Figure 5.9). As noted by Joseph Mascheck,[33] Oldenburg

**FIGURE 5.9** Claes Oldenburg: *Clothespin*, 1976.

Photograph Pablo Meninato.

conceived this piece as a sort of parodic homage to Brancusi's celebrated sculpture *The Kiss* (1908), a block of stone that abstractly displays a man and a woman embracing into a seemingly eternal kiss (the initial title of the piece was *Proposal for a Colossal Structure in the Form of a Clothespin—Compared to Brancusi's KISS*). Oldenburg substitutes Brancusi's iconic silhouette for a utilitarian device resembling a pair of "humanoids" engaging in a lasting amorous act. With this work, Oldenburg seems to have discovered in everyday domestic objects secret and surreptitious existences.

*Clothespin*'s initial conception curiously intersects the narrative of architectural historiography. In 1967 Oldenburg submitted the proposal as a fictitious "latter entry" for the historic 1922 Chicago Tribune competition.[34] This gesture exposes a twofold irony: on the one hand it presumes a placement of an everyday object instead of an office tower, therefore embodying an "architectural" work which in fact is not. At the same time, Oldenburg ensures that his name will be associated with other renowned modern architects whose projects were rejected in that competition, such as Walter Gropius, Eliel Saarinen, and Adolf Loos. In 1976, almost ten years after it conception, *Clothespin* was installed not in Chicago but at the Centre Square plaza in Philadelphia, right across from the City Hall (Figure 5.8). Fifty-six feet high, the work shows the delicate correspondence between the mundane object, the figurative sculpture, and the building type.

## Abstraction, Juxtaposition, and Assemblage—Ledoux and Libera

Michelangelo's explorations demonstrated a conception of architecture as a set of independent parts, which could be individually altered and/or reassembled in different fashions. Among the most notable examples of this strategy are the projects of the late eighteenth-century architect Claude-Nicholas Ledoux (1736–1806), one of the "three revolutionary architects."[35] In his biographical essay, Anthony Vidler[36] identifies parallels between the architecture of Ledoux and the human body, a notion reminiscent of James Ackerman's analysis of Michelangelo.[37] According to Vidler, Ledoux's design techniques should be understood as anatomical analogies; his projects seem to be

> literally to be dismembering the organic, classical body of architecture—itself founded on the proportional principles of the human form—and, having dispensed with all anthropomorphic relations, to be playing a fantastic game of "heads, bodies, and legs" to give birth to some proto-Frankensteinian monster.[38]

Ledoux's design methodology could be broken down into a three-step process. First he proceeds to "disarticulate" architecture into independent parts, then he removes the ornamentation (of those parts), and finally he recombines them according to an unusual logic (or syntax). This strategy was utilized in his project for the *Barrières* in Paris (1783–91), a series of pavilions designed with the purpose

**108** Type and Project—Alteration Tactics

of taxing the merchandise entering the city. The program required a succession of freestanding, clearly identifiable buildings in various areas of Paris. As Vidler points out,[39] while the purpose of the *barrière* was to house administrative activities, it was also (or mainly) to have a symbolic function, an identifiable and memorable urban element that would become the "Propylaeas" (from the Greek, *Propylaea*, meaning "entrance") to the city.

Ledoux's[40] urban plan was intimately related to its architectural forms. Each *barrière* was conceived as a unique and singular object, though simultaneously he encouraged the observer to detect the resemblances and variations among the pavilions. As observed by Vidler, "Ledoux obviously used the commission for the barriers as a kind of experimental laboratory of type form and their combinations."[41] Most of the typological explorations consisted of volumetric alterations and variations, usually utilizing as a point of departure the Greek cross plan, the peripteral plan, or the "Palladian Villa Rotonda," which were subsequently subject to various processes of rotation, reassembling, and/or juxtaposition (Figure 5.10).

Ledoux continued exploring the strategy of typological dismantling, abstraction, and reassembling in his various proposals for the salt manufacturing village of *Chaux*, in the region of *Arc-et-Senans*. This project was conducted in two stages, each one characterized by quite different circumstances. In its first phase (1771–1789) as *Commissaire des Salines*, Ledoux was in charge of both the urban plan and the architectural design, which included a number of administrative, residential, and factory shops. In 1790, as a consequence of the revolution the whole project was halted.

But then something curious happened: Ledoux decided to continue working *a motu proprio* in what he referred to as the "Ideal City of Chaux." The new master plan initially mirrored the semicircle, thus creating a circular figure, which is then transformed into an oval shape (Ledoux justifies this geometry as a "tribute to the elliptical path of the earth around the sun").[42] For this new iteration he added a number of pavilions to be situated at various locations throughout the region (Figure 5.11).

During this period Ledoux developed a strong interest in the relationship between ancestral production methods and the shaping of the architectural forms that house those activities.[43] An example of this concern is his "House and Workshop for the Charcoal Burners," for which he initially gathers information about the trade's traditional constructions and working methods.[44] Based on this investigation, Ledoux detects a *recurrent charcoal workshop type*: a conical or pyramidal volume with an opening at the top that allows the exit of fumes. Founded on this precedent, Ledoux proposes a "pyramid" that rests on a four-sided pedestal; in each side he places a gate with *Palladian* motifs. Ledoux comments that this project "refers to the first ideas" because of its relationship with vernacular forms and its reference to the "ancient" Egyptian pyramids.[45] In other words, the process consists in the identification of a traditional typology that relates to the origins of architecture and to the

**FIGURE 5.10** Claude-Nicolas Ledoux: *Axonometric study of the Barrières*, 1785. Drawings by Malvina Lampietti and Lorissa Kimm. Courtesy of Anthony Vidler.

**FIGURE 5.11** Claude-Nicolas Ledoux: *Vue perspective de la ville idéale de Chaux*, 1804. Bibliothèque Nationale de France.

*charcoal workshop buildings' evolution*. The adopted type is subsequently transformed, thus creating a form that results in both the familiar and unexpected.

The relationship between a person's profession and the architectural forms he inhabits was also explored in his proposal for a "House for the Surveyor of the Loue River." In this case, Ledoux assumes the occupant will be the prefect of the river,[46] whose main task would be monitoring the water levels in relation to the intensity of the water currents. The proposal could be described as a *bridge-house amalgamation*, or a colossal storm drain tube that guides the continuous running of water. Like most of Ledoux's designs, the idea of the project is captured in the perspective (Figure 5.12), which displays the juxtaposition of two dissimilar volumes: the base is an extruded square with staggered flanks, overlapped by a huge elongated ellipse disposed horizontally. The project can be interpreted as an assembly of various typological components (stairs, base, bridge, barrel vault)[47] articulated by an unpredictable syntax.

★

Ledoux introduces a more *ludic* approach towards the combination and assembly of types—as if their historical and symbolic lineages have been temporarily suspended. Once reassembled, each of those typologies, such as the barrel vault, the pyramid, or the dome, recovers (at least partially) its meanings. With his *Casa Malaparte* (1942), Adalberto Libera revisits many of the themes Ledoux developed nearly two centuries earlier. Just like Ledoux's explorations, the project by Libera starts with the selection of a reduced catalog of typological components, which are then combined, assembled, or juxtaposed in surprising ways (Figure 5.13).

Libera "strips" each of the selected typologies (the *cubic shelter*, the *terrace*, and the *staircase-amphitheater*) until obtaining their most abstract and essential versions.

**FIGURE 5.12**  Ledoux: *House and office of Inspector of Loue River*. Bibliothèque N. de France.

**FIGURE 5.13**   Adalberto Libera: *Casa Malaparte*, 1942.
Photograph courtesy of Irma de Arrascaeta.

He then engages in a process of repositioning, juxtaposing, and integrating those components into a new ensemble, creating a "place" that looks both familiar and strange. The project does not stand out for its formal alterations, but for the delicate attention to the integration of the different components. *Casa Malaparte* could be described as an unusual combination of ancestral typologies facing an extraordinarily overwhelming landscape and seascape. A visit to the place translates into an experience that, according to John Hejduk,

> serves a double purpose: it is access to the vision of sky and sea, and upon one's descent, going back, the stair acts as the seating for a theater, setting the imaginary audience's backs to the horizontal horizon line of the sea.[48]

With *Casa Malaparte*, Libera develops a process of disciplinary and formal hybridization. The house integrates and dissolves the differentiation of architecture and landscape, and the "staircase type" appears, though not becoming an amphitheater; the complex can be interpreted as both figurative and abstract. Libera's project demonstrates that types, even in their most abstract and fragmented condition, can convey a multiplicity of meanings.

## Typological Substitutions—Le Corbusier

One objective of this study is to develop a reconsideration of modern architecture's attitude towards the concept of type and the typological design process. The modern movement has shown ambivalent positions towards type: while in various cases the concept was dismissed or rejected, at the same time many of the most celebrated modern architects actively engaged in typological design processes. As stated earlier, recent studies have thoroughly examined this issue by identifying and analyzing the presence of typological-driven mechanisms in the works of Frank Lloyd Wright,[49] Le Corbusier,[50] Mies van de Rohe, Alvar Alto,[51] and Louis Kahn.[52]

A distinctive feature in the work of Le Corbusier (1887–1965) was his recurrent interest in preexisting forms and iconographies, and the ways those precedents can be integrated into the language of modern architecture. As argued by Alan Colquhoun,[53] Le Corbusier consistently adopted typologies inherited from classicism in order to replace them with their modern equivalences. While in some cases he proposed substituting classical forms for those derived from industrial, agrarian, or vernacular constructions (a subject examined in Chapter 4), in other situations he developed alternative typological solutions. His conception of the "Five Points," for instance, can be interpreted as a variation of this approach; he replaces the conventional typologies of classical architecture with their modern equivalents (or at least his interpretation of what should be the modern vocabulary).

The type "column," the architectural element more associated with classical vocabulary, is redefined by Le Corbusier by proposing a total removal of its ornaments and subdivisions (base, shaft, and capital). The architectural element, therefore, is determined after considering its primordial structural function—that is, a vertical "vector" (Figure 5.14). The conception of the *pilotis* (note that the type's transformation includes its relabeling) is also reminiscent of early modern abstract painting (e.g., the work of Malevich or Kandinsky), where the final image is the result of successive waning of figurative traits.

Another case of typological substitution advanced by Le Corbusier was the "pitched roof," one of the most characteristic and iconic forms of European domestic architecture. In this case the process involves a partial elimination of construction components, since instead of two inclined planes he proposes a single flat one. This typological reconversion also carries spatial implications. It eliminates the "attic" (the space between the inclined roofs) and at the same time it creates a new outdoor space (Figure 5.15). Just as in the case of the column, the redefinition of the type contemplates its relabeling: the "roof-terrace."

The "window" is probably the typological substitution that posed a more lasting impact in the vocabulary of modern architecture.[54] Le Corbusier simultaneously developed two alternate though related proposals for reassessing the window type.[55] First of all, he proposed "the horizontal window," an operation that may be interpreted as a simple rotation of the vertical (or French) window. This option, observes Colquhoun, retains the notion of "the traditional isolated window, at the same time transforming it from a repetitive to a unique element"[56] (Figure 5.16). The

**FIGURE 5.14**  Le Corbusier: *Ville Savoye—detail of pilotis*.

Courtesy of Fondation Le Corbusier/Artists Rights Society (ARS), New York, 2017.

**FIGURE 5.15**  Le Corbusier: *Ville Savoye—detail of roof garden*.

Courtesy of Fondation Le Corbusier/Artists Rights Society (ARS), New York, 2017.

**FIGURE 5.16** Le Corbusier: *Ville Savoye—detail of horizontal window.*
Courtesy of Fondation Le Corbusier/Artists Rights Society (ARS), New York, 2017.

second alternative appears as a deformation of the previous one, since the opening runs through the whole façade. In other words, Le Corbusier proposes a *continuous horizontal ribbon window* ("la fenêtre en bandeau"), which slices the full extent of the exterior wall. This proposal is partially a consequence of the conception of the "Free Façade" (another of the five points), where by removing the structural function from the outer wall the whole volume becomes a nonstructural "envelope."

While not listed among the "five points," the proposal of the "ramp" as an alternate for the "staircase" constitutes another recurring strategy in the architecture of Le Corbusier. Unlike previous examples, where the reassessment of traditional forms involved *typological substitutions*, Le Corbusier considered the ramp as an *alternative* to the conventional staircase. Although several of his houses display a coexistence of ramp and staircase (e.g., the Villa Savoye or the Casa Curutchet), it is clear that Le Corbusier relegates the staircase to a secondary role, while the ramp becomes a major spatial and formal protagonist (Figure 5.17).

It could be argued that the listed operations are not *genuine* typological inventions, as each one of the types redefined by Le Corbusier was preexistent. Le Corbusier does not "invent" the *pilotis*, the horizontal window, or the flat roof; his innovations reside in the *idea* of replacing those traditional types with unusual solutions that became part of the formal lexicon of modern architecture. Alan Colquhoun describes these procedures as "displacement of concepts,"[57] summarized by their variation of meaning through dislocations and/or formal alterations. Ultimately, the *pilotis* is a simple cylinder, but once it is designated as a "column" it acquires a new meaning. These tactics present similarities with other proposals developed by Le Corbusier, such as the introduction of maritime or automobile iconography into the design of his houses, or his consideration of vernacular and industrial typologies. In Colquhoun's words, Le Corbusier's proposal "consists not of transformations of the themes of 'high' architecture but of the assimilation into architecture of elements outside this tradition."[58]

## Subtle Transformations—Álvaro Siza

The cases discussed so far demonstrate the possibilities offered by the various tactics of typological abstraction, alteration, and substitution. The projects reviewed

**FIGURE 5.17** Le Corbusier: *Casa Curutchet—detail of ramp.*
Photograph courtesy of Maite Iriarte.

constitute *exceptional moments*, however; they are the result of *extra*ordinary talents and circumstances, and should be considered as such. This phenomenon was examined by anthropologist George Kubler[59] in his analysis of society's reception of everyday objects. Kubler compares the irruption of extraordinary creations with "prime objects," the mathematical notion that refers to sporadic and unpredictable occurrences, "whose character as primes is not explained by their antecedents, and their order in history is enigmatic."[60] According to Kubler, due to their exceptional character, "prime objects" affect the evolutionary sequence of those objects, their appearances generate "entire system of replicas, reproductions, copies, reductions, transfers, and derivations, floating in the wake of an important work of art." "Their character as primes," he adds, "is not explained by their antecedents, and their order in history is enigmatic."[61]

A more thorough discussion of the typological process should also contemplate examples that propose a more subtle range of transformations, that stand out for their restraint and modesty rather than for their exceptionality. Such is the case of several projects by Álvaro Siza, whose typological transformations appear carefully calibrated and controlled. The work and thought of Álvaro Siza (1933) demonstrate a very personal approach to the question of type. Although he is only two years

**116** Type and Project—Alteration Tactics

younger than Rossi, he did not complete his architectural studies until 1965[62] (a year before the publication of *L'architettura della città*), so by the time Siza formally began his professional career many of the issues raised by the Milanese architect had been assimilated by most young European architects. According to Kenneth Frampton,[63] a key figure in development of Siza and the one who introduced him to issues related to the concept of type was his teacher and mentor Fernando Távora. While Siza was pursuing his studies at the *Escola Superior de Belas-Artes do Porto*, Távora was also involved in an extensive and ambitious project, the study and analysis of building typologies in Portugal, a work that culminated with the publication of *Arquitectura Popular em Portugal* (1961). Távora's project, which consisted of a documentation of Portuguese vernacular types, displayed clear affinities with the typological studies Muratori developed in Venice a few years earlier. In his writings, Távora distinguishes between the notions of type and style, defining typology as "something of the character of our people,"[64] which is to say, the result of what each culture generates.

It is out of this background that Siza's recurrent interest in the forms of the past—particularly those related to the Portuguese culture—can be better understood. These issues would converge in his personal and idiosyncratic consideration of type as a design process. Following the rise of the socialist government in 1974, Siza had the opportunity to explore a particular typological avenue: collective social housing. In the *São Victor* (1974) and *Saal da Bouça* (1977) communities Siza favored the adoption of already accepted typologies, such as the row house ("moradia geminada"), which allowed him to explore notions of sequence, rhythm, and repetition. Because of the serial character of Siza's approach, both projects appear restricted by the regulations imposed by the type; therefore the proposals focus on issues of economy, construction efficiency, and standardization of parts.

While working in the row-house communities, Siza had the opportunity to engage in other projects that allowed him to explore other typological avenues, such as the recurring use of the open "U" courtyard, a scheme he developed on at least a dozen occasions, such as the house *Beires-Póvoa de Varzim* (1976), the house *Carlos Siza* in Santo Tirso (1978), the *Faculdade de Arquitectura* in Porto (1984), the *Restaurante e Sala de Chá* in Malagueira (1992), and the *Rectorado* for the *Universidad de Alicante* (1998) (Figure 5.18). A notable aspect of these spatial schemes is that they constitute a kind of courtyard that contradicts one of the fundamental characteristics of the "patio type," which in all its variations, such as the Roman *atrium*, the *cortile*, or the *cloister*, is a space open to the sky though entirely enclosed by building components. Siza's U-shaped patio proposal can be understood as a variation of the conventional idea of a courtyard, and therefore expanding the limits of the typology.

The U-shaped courtyards developed by Siza propose a subtle tilt of their flanks, allowing the central space to adopt a trapezoidal shape. This particular geometrical figure creates a *theatrical perspective*, provoking in the observer the illusion that the

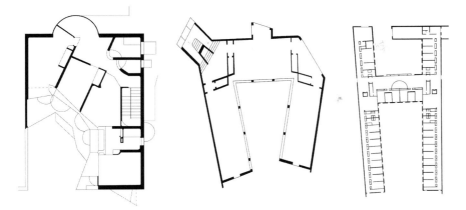

**FIGURE 5.18** Álvaro Siza: *Variations of U-shaped courtyards*. Left: *Casa Beires-Póvoa de Varzim*, 1976. Center: *Faculdade de Arquitectura da Universidade do Porto*, 1974. Right: *Rectorado para la Universidad de Alicante*, 1998.

Redrawn by Abigail Freed.

space appears larger or smaller than what it actually is. While the precedents of this spatial typology are the *Piazza del Campidoglio* by Michelangelo and the *Piazza San Pietro* by Bernini, Siza's proposals shy away from any suggestion of monumentality or grandeur; his courtyards draw attention for their nuances and slight asymmetries, realizing an *(un)monumentalized* version of that type. Siza's tactic recalls the musical formula "theme and variations," for which the theme is the principal melody (the trapezoidal courtyard), which is then developed as a sequence of deviations and iterations.

With his *open courtyards*, Siza introduces a new typological path, or perhaps, a *subtype*. All examples share the same formal idea and genealogic traits, though simultaneously each courtyard appears subtly special and unique. At first sight the typological alterations and variations may seem minimal, as if they have been carefully qualified and meted out. The dimensions of the components, the layout or height of the walls, the roof overhangs, and the degrees of transparency or opacity are some of the countless variables explored. As stated by Rafael Moneo,

> This is an architecture that is attentive to the slightest inflection, the smallest of slants. Alvaro Siza has always given importance to alignments. He knows that spaces change, both inside and out, when they defy orthogonality, and surely the slight obliqueness of this project has a definitive effect on the building's form.[65]

**118**  Type and Project—Alteration Tactics

Although Siza is not a prolific writer, his occasional texts represent a clear supplement to many of his design concerns. For instance, he expresses disdain for the extravagance in contemporary architecture, stating that "To begin [a design] and be obsessed with being original is to be uncultured and shallow."[66] His architecture is generated from his personal interpretation of context and the acceptance of traditional forms. Having internalized these concerns, Siza only then allows himself the freedom of distorting or altering some of those originating forms.

This dialectic between convention and originality, or between predictability and surprise, is present in the church of *Santa Maria* in Marco de Canaveses (1996). Again, Siza appeals to the U-shaped patio typology, in this case a subtle way of indicating the entrance to the temple (Figure 5.19). Because of its dimensions, proportions, and materiality, the church appears as a modest, humble, and reserved proposal. Instead of calling for attention, it stands out for its simplicity and austerity—a white symmetrical volume gently inserted in the urban context.

A careful examination of the temple reveals several alterations that only slightly transform the chosen scheme (or type). Among those distortions, the most striking are the extraordinary dimensions of the entry doorway (Figure 5.20). About ten meters high, the size of the two panels of wood defies the conventions of the "door-type"; if compared to the rest of the building they appear extraordinarily large. The design mechanism is reminiscent of the typological transformations by Michelangelo; though unlike the mannerist artist who sought to distort virtually all architectural elements, Siza undertakes a very careful selection of the parts he will distort, a process characterized by its restraint and discretion. While some alterations are barely noticeable, others, such the large entry door, are potent and forceful.

When discussing Ignasi de Solà-Morales's essay on "weak architecture," Michael Hays associates that condition with the works of Álvaro Siza.[67] Evolving from Gianni Vattimo's premise of "weak thought,"[68] Solà-Morales understands weakness as an enhancing of the senses, fostering an appreciation of "the small, the fragmented, the momentary."[69] In what may appear as an oxymoron, Solà-Morales argues that the fundamental characteristic of weak architecture lies in its *monumentality*.[70] But he doesn't understand monumental in a "classical" sense, or as he puts it, the *imago Dei* ("image of God"); instead he identifies the etymological link between the terms "monument" and "permanence,"[71] or between testimonial and remembrance. It is in this sense that the work of Álvaro Siza can be better understood as simultaneously weak *and* monumental, where attention to details and a delicate connection with the past assume a comprehensive prominence. "This is the strength of weakness," writes Solà-Morales, "that strength which art and architecture are capable of producing precisely when they adopt a posture that is not aggressive and dominating, but tangential and weak."[72]

With his church in Canaveses, Siza confirms the notion of implementing *weak and subtle typological transformations*. Rather than the spectacularity of the resolution,

**FIGURE 5.19**  Álvaro Siza: *Church of Santa Maria en Marco de Canaveses.*
Photograph courtesy of Leonardo Finotti.

the proposal's richness and originality lie in the particularized attention to the variables that define the type. The works of Siza convey a careful consideration of the program, the client's budget, and the urban and historical context where the building will stand. Once these considerations are resolved, Siza starts introducing surprising moments, which are usually subtle typological alterations. The architecture of Álvaro Siza displays a delicate balance. On the one hand, it conveys the attitude of the *architect-citizen*, of someone committed to the needs of the client and the culture and history of the place; on the other hand, there is the *architect-poet*, who

**FIGURE 5.20** Álvaro Siza: *Church of Santa Maria en Marco de Canaveses, interior.*
Photograph courtesy of Leonardo Finotti.

proposes those unexpected moments by demonstrating his willingness to experiment and take risks, even if in homeopathic doses.

## Notes

1 Benjamin, Walter, "The Significance of Beautiful Semblance." In Benjamin, Walter, Edmund Jephcott, Howard Eiland, and Michael W. Jennings, *Walter Benjamin Selected Writings: 1935–1938, Volume 3.* Cambridge MA: Harvard University Press, 2002, 137.
2 Muratori, Saverio, *Studi per una operante storia urbana di Venezia.* Instituto poligrafico dello Stato, Libreria dello Stato, 1959.
3 Argan, Giulio Carlo, "On the Typology of Architecture." In Nesbitt, Kate (ed.), *Theorizing a New Agenda for Architecture: An Anthology of Architectural Theory, 1965–1995.* New York: Princeton Architectural, 1996, 242–246.

Typological Alterations **121**

4 Aymonino, Carlo, "Type and Typology." Essay published in Semerani, Luciano (ed.), *The School of Venice*. London: Architectural Design, 1985, 49–51.
5 Gianugo Polesello, "Typology and Composition in Architecture." In *The School of Venice*, 43.
6 Rossi, Aldo, *The Architecture of the City*. Cambridge, MA: MIT Press, 1982.
7 Rossi, Aldo: "An Analogical Architecture." In Nesbitt, Kate (ed.), *Theorizing a New Agenda for Architecture: An Anthology of Architectural Theory, 1965–1995*. New York: Princeton Architectural, 1996, 348–352.
8 Rossi, Aldo, *A Scientific Autobiography*. Cambridge, MA: MIT Press, 1981.
9 Moneo, Jose Rafael, "On Typology." *Oppositions 13*. Cambridge, MA: MIT Press, 1978, 23.
10 Moneo, "On Typology," 23.
11 Moneo, "On Typology," 27.
12 Moneo, "On Typology," 23.
13 Kubler, George, *The Shape of Time: Remarks on the History of Things*. New Haven, CT: Yale University Press, 1962.
14 Quatremère, *The Historical Dictionary of Architecture*, 256.
15 Summers, David, *Michelangelo and the Language of Art*. New York: Princeton University Press, 1981, 150.
16 Ackerman, James, *The Architecture of Michelangelo*. Chicago: University of Chicago Press, 1986, 44.
17 In his Book 3, Chapter 1, Vitruvius discusses the correspondences between human body and architecture: "Without symmetry and proportion there can be no principles in the design of any temple; that is, if there is no precise relation between its members, as in the case of those of a well-shaped man." See Vitruvius, *The Ten Books of Architecture*. Translated by M.H. Morgan. Cambridge, MA: Harvard University Press, 1914, The Project Gutenberg EBook no. 20239. www.gutenberg.org. Release date 31 December 2006, 72.
18 In the chapter titled "Michelangelo's Theory of Architecture," James Ackerman discusses Michelangelo's ambition of conceptually integrating architecture and the human body. See Ackerman, *The Architecture of Michelangelo*, 280.
19 Leatherbarrow, David, *The Roots of Architectural Invention: Site, Enclosure, Materials*. Cambridge: Cambridge University Press, 1993.
20 Although Leatherbarrow is referring to Leo Steinberg's description of Borromini's work, the idea behind these lines is to highlight the influence of Michelangelo on Baroque architecture. See Leatherbarrow, *The Roots of Architectural Invention*, 116.
21 Leatherbarrow, *The Roots of Architectural Invention*, 111.
22 Several of the metaphoric associations suggested in the architecture of Gaudí are commented on in the essay by Carlos Eduardo Comas, "Gaudí e a Modernidade Arquitetônica brasileira." Arco WEB- O Portal da Revista PROJETO DESIGN. Originally published in PROJETO DESIGN, edição 268, junho 2002. Also available online: http://arcoweb.com.br/projetodesign/artigos/artigo-gaudi-e-a-modernidade-arquitetonica-brasileira-01-06-2002. Accessed June 12, 2016.
23 Riegl, Alois, *The Origins of Baroque Architecture in Rome*. Los Angeles: Getty Research Institute, 2010, 150.
24 Rosenau, Helen (ed.), Boullée, Etienne Louis, *Boullée & Visionary Architecture: Including Boullée's 'Architecture, Essay on Art.'* London: Academy Editions, 1976, 105.
25 Middleton, Robin (ed.), *The Beaux-Arts and Nineteenth-Century French Architecture*. Cambridge, MA: MIT Press, 1982, 225.
26 Boullée states, "I was deeply impressed by Raphael's sublime design for the School of Athens and I have tried to execute it; doubtless I owe what success I have had to this idea." Boullée, Etienne-Louis, *Architecture: Essai sur l'art*. J.M. Perouse de Montclos, 1968, 104.
27 Boullée, *Architecture, Essay on Art,* 107.
28 Kubler, *The Shape of Time*, 65.
29 I would like to mention two essays dedicated to the notion of scale: "Bigness and the Problem of Large," in Rem Koolhaas and Bruce Man, *S, M, L, XL*, New York: Monacelli Press, 1995, 494–516; and "The Superblock," in Colquhoun, Alan, *Essays in Architectural Criticism: Modern Architecture and Historical Change*. Opposition Books. Cambridge, MA: MIT Press, 1981, 83–127.

**122** Type and Project—Alteration Tactics

30 Parodi Rebella, Aníbal, *Escalas Alteradas: La manipulación de la escala como detonante del proceso de diseño*. Universidad Politécnica de Madrid (unpublished doctoral thesis), 2010. In his thesis, Parodi develops an exhaustive analysis of the notion of scale in architecture, design, and art.

31 Parodi Rebella, *Escalas Alteradas*, ix.

32 "The real art here is architecture, or anything really that stands up, making a perpendicular to the magnificent horizontal. Any chimney, any tree, any object (any fire plug)." Cited in Oldenburg, Claes, and Germano Celant, *Claes Oldenburg*. New York: Guggenheim Museum, 377.

33 Masheck also compares Oldenburg's *Clothespin* with Duchamp's silhouettes in his first *Cemetery of Uniforms and Liveries* (1913), a study for *The Bride Stripped Bare by Her Bachelors, Even (The Large Glass)* (1915–1923). See Masheck, Joseph (ed.), *Marcel Duchamp in Perspective*. New York: Da Capo Press, 2002, 12.

34 Cited in Parodi Rebella, *Escalas Alteradas*, 577.

35 Ledoux is together with Boullée and Lequeu one of the "three revolutionary architects," the title of Emil Kaufmann's seminal text that introduced this trio into contemporary historiography. See Kaufmann, Emil, *Three Revolutionary Architects*. Philadelphia: American Philosophical Society, 1952.

36 Vidler, Anthony, *Claude-Nicolas Ledoux: Architecture and Social Reform at the End of the Ancien Regime*. Cambridge, MA:: MIT Press, 1990, 251.

37 Ackerman, *The Architecture of Michelangelo*, 37–52.

38 See Vidler, *Ledoux*, 251. It should be noted that that Vidler assumes it is Quatremère who is making those comments about Ledoux's work.

39 See Vidler, *Ledoux*, 253.

40 See Vidler's comments about the urban conception of the *barrières*: "the gates were calculated to produce the effect of a chain of association, stimulated in the perception of an observer moving along the new boulevards that bounded the city." Vidler, *Ledoux*, 235.

41 Vidler, *Ledoux*, 230.

42 Vidler, *Ledoux*, 266.

43 Cited in Vidler, *Ledoux*, 302–306.

44 See Vidler, *Ledoux*, 312.

45 Regarding the considered image, Vidler assumes that the titles that appear in *L'Architecture* are probably wrong, since they are identified as "House and Workshop for the Woodcutters" instead of "House and Workshop for the Charcoal Burners." Vidler, *Ledoux*, 313–315.

46 Vidler develops an exhaustive description of the "House for the Inspectors of the River Loue," Vidler, *Ledoux*, 317.

47 Kaufmann writes that one of the compositional principles of Ledoux and Boullée was the tactic of "isolation of the parts," allowing the independent reconfiguration of each part (or element). See Kaufmann, *Boullée*, 212.

48 Hejduk, John, "Adalberto Libera's Villa Malaparte." Article originally published on Domus Magazine 605, April 1980, www.domusweb.it/en/from-the-archive/2012/07/21/adalberto-libera-s-villa-malaparte.html. Accessed December 16, 2014.

49 Castex, Jean, *Le printemps de la Prairie House*. Brussels: Pierre Mardaga, 1987.

50 There are various studies on Le Corbusier's consideration of typological mechanisms in his architectural projects. See Rowe, Colin, *The Mathematics of the Ideal Villa and Other Essays*. Cambridge, MA: MIT Press, 1976; Moos, Stanislaus Von, *Le Corbusier, Elements of a Synthesis*. Cambridge, MA: MIT Press, 1979; "Displacement of Concepts in Le Corbusier." In Colquhoun, Alan, *Essays in Architectural Criticism: Modern Architecture and Historical Change*. Opposition Books. Cambridge, MA: MIT Press, 1981, 51–66.

51 Porphyrios, Demitri, "The Retrieval of Memory: Alvar Aalto's Typological Conception of Design." *Oppositions 22*, 1980, 55–73.

52 In Chapter 4 I discussed the presence of type in many of Louis Kahn's projects.

53 See Colquhoun, "Displacement of Concepts in Le Corbusier," 51.

Typological Alterations **123**

54 As Beatriz Colomina and Jennifer Bloomer pointed out, August Perret and Le Corbusier engaged in a heated debate regarding the advantages of the vertical (favored by Perret) versus the horizontal (Le Corbusier's proposal) window. See Bloomer, Jennifer, and Beatriz Colomina. *Sexuality & Space*. New York: Princeton Architectural, 1992, 112–113.

55 It should be noted that modern architecture developed a third alternative of the type window: "the curtain wall" (a resolution less associated with Le Corbusier). This operation can be interpreted as a questioning of the limits of the type. On one hand the curtain wall can be understood as an extraordinary magnification of the "type window," to the point of extending through the whole building front. Or it can be interpreted as the reformulation of the "type wall."

56 Colquhoun, "Displacement of Concepts in Le Corbusier," 52.

57 See Colquhoun, "Displacement of Concepts in Le Corbusier," 51–66.

58 Colquhoun, "Displacement of Concepts in Le Corbusier," 57.

59 Kubler, *The Shape of Time*.

60 Kubler, *The Shape of Time*, 39.

61 Kubler, *The Shape of Time*, 39.

62 Frampton, Kenneth, *Alvaro Siza—Complete Works*. London: Phaidon Press, 2000, 12.

63 Frampton, *Alvaro Siza*, 12.

64 Comment by Robert Levit. http://alvarosizavieira.com/thoughts-on-his-style. Accessed November 23, 2014.

65 Moneo, José Rafael, *Theoretical Anxiety and Design Strategies in the Work of Eight Contemporary Architects*. Cambridge, MA: MIT, 2004, 211.

66 Moneo, *Theoretical Anxiety*, 203.

67 In his introduction to Ignasi de Solà-Morales's essay, Michael Hays identifies the work of Alvaro Siza as an example of "weak architecture." See Hays, K. Michael, *Architecture Theory Since 1968*. Cambridge, MA: MIT Press, 2015, 614.

68 For a discussion of Gianni Vattimo's "weak thought," see Rovatti, Pier Aldo, Gianni Vattimo, and Peter Carravetta, *Weak Thought*. Albany: State University of New York, 2012.

69 Hays, *Architecture Theory Since 1968*, 615.

70 Solà-Morales, Ignasi de, "Weak Architecture." In Hays, *Architecture Theory Since 1968*, 623.

71 Solà-Morales relates the term "permanence" to the theories of Aldo Rossi, who in *The Architecture of the City* employed "the term *monument* to signify permanence." Solà-Morales, "Weak Architecture," 623.

72 Solà-Morales, "Weak Architecture," 623.

# 6

# AFFINITIES

## Typological Displacement and Readymade

> Duchamp devises a strategic approach, one that "draws" on previous traditions, only to uncover within them new forms of artistic appropriation. He plays chess with art, using both sides of the board in order to redefine the game. In doing so he liberates the artist from the obligation of producing art objects, for plasticity now emerges as a function of the shifting strategies on the board, rather than as a feature of a particular object. Artistic creativity in this context takes on an entirely new meaning.
>
> —Dalia Judovitz[1]

## Chapter 6—List of Contents

| | |
|---|---:|
| *Antecedents* | *124* |
| *The Secret Life of Objects* | *125* |
| *The Fountain, the Maiden, and the Readymade* | *128* |
| *Type, Object, and the Question of Repetition* | *132* |
| *Doors and Windows* | *134* |
| *Unexpected Affinities—Lequeu and Duchamp* | *136* |
| *The Displaced Column—The Presumed Irony of Loos* | *141* |
| *In Praise of the Ordinary—Venturi and Rossi* | *145* |
| *Typological Riddles—Herzog & de Meuron* | *154* |

## Antecedents

The insertion of elements into unexpected contexts has been considered in the arts since ancient times. During the first years of the Christian era, Horace described this tactic in his *Ars Poetica*:

> If a painter should wish to unite a horse's neck to a human head . . . so that what is a beautiful woman in the upper part terminates unsightly in an ugly

fish below ... poets and painters (you will say) have ever had equal authority for attempting any thing.[2]

Historian John Summers defines the implementation of this tactic in the work of Michelangelo as "Scattered Beauty."[3] He introduces this notion by retelling the ancient story of the Greek painter Zeuxis, who,

> faced with the task of painting a Helen, gathered together a number of lovely maidens, from each of whom he took some single part, finally to display the beauty of his subject by combining all of the perfect parts into one perfect image.[4]

Michelangelo, who according to Summers was quite familiar Zeuxis's story, recurrently engaged in the practice of identifying and recombining fragments of diverse sources, frequently (dis)placing those parts in unexpected positions or settings.

David Leatherbarrow examined this effect in one of Michelangelo's most well-known sculptures, the *Pietà*, with the "the thirty-three-year-old body of the dead Christ on the lap of a woman who appears to be in her early twenties, perhaps late teens."[5] The two characters portrayed in the scene seem to belong to incompatible realities, a young lady appearing as the mother of an aged man. Many of Michelangelo's contemporaries criticized the inconsistency; some even considered it a blasphemy. Michelangelo's biographer Giorgio Vasari justified the poetic license by instrumenting a peculiar interpretation of the doctrine of the *Immaculate Conception*: "Because virgins are uncontaminated, they maintain their youthful appearance."[6] What Michelangelo demonstrated is that the meaning of each character (in this case Christ or Mary) depended on the positioning of the other. Certainly separate portraits of Christ as an aged man or of Mary as a youthful lady would not have sparked much controversy; it was their joint (and improbable) presence in a scene that provoked intense reactions.

## The Secret Life of Objects

One modern artist who more intensely explored the notion of displacement of elements into unexpected contexts was Marcel Duchamp (1887–1968). As discussed by his biographer Calvin Tomkins,[7] in order to understand Duchamp's artistic evolution it is necessary to consider the events that took place in the year 1912, when his career took a dramatic turn. In March of that year Duchamp submitted to the cubist exhibition at the *Salon des Indépendants* in Paris his painting *Nu Descendant un Escalier, no. 2* (*Nude Descending a Staircase*, No. 2, 1912) (Figure 6.1), which represents in a very abstract fashion a fragmented silhouette descending a staircase. Albert Gleizes and Jean Metzinger, curators of the exhibit, rejected the painting; they believed it did not quite follow the principles of cubist art. Many years later, Duchamp commented to Pierre Cabanne about his disappointment with this event and at the increasing dogmatism of the cubist movement:

> People like Gleizes ... who were, nevertheless, extremely intelligent, found this "Nude" wasn't in the line that they had predicted. Cubism had lasted two

**FIGURE 6.1** Marcel Duchamp: *Nu descendant un escalier*, 1912.
Courtesy of Philadelphia Museum of Art/Artists Rights Society (ARS), New York, 2017.

or three years, and they already had an absolutely clear, dogmatic line on it, foreseeing everything that might happen.[8]

The rejection of the *Nu Descendant* had a profound impact on Duchamp. Initially the incident caused his departure from cubism, and subsequently, his definitive abandonment of pictorial activity. Thanks to the intermediation of his friend Francis Picabia, soon after he accepted a rather dull job at the *Sainte Geneviève*

*Library*, where Picabia's uncle, Maurice Davanne, was the director.[9] The position at the library inaugurated a particularly reflective period of Duchamp's life, when he had the opportunity to read and take notes on artistic, scientific, and philosophical subjects. It was during this time that he became interested in establishing a full reconsideration of the creative act; instead of "retinal" and formal qualities, the accent was placed on the intellectual and conceptual aspects of the artistic process.

During this period Duchamp reflected on the artistic potential of ordinary objects, an issue he initially exposed in his paintings *Moulin a cafe* (*Coffee Grinder*, 1912) and *La Broyeuse de Chocolat Nr 1* (*Chocolate Grinder*, 1913) (Figure 6.2). A stark departure from cubism and other abstracting trends, these images could be interpreted as a return to figuratism, though rather than people, natural elements, or landscapes, Duchamp expresses interest in domestic artifacts of industrial production. It is interesting to note the differences between his attraction to machineries and similar interests expressed by the futurists, who developed their ideas and

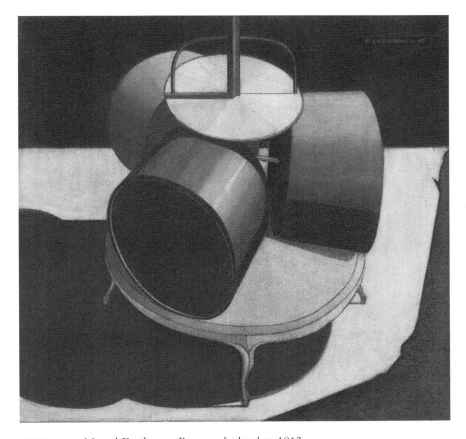

**FIGURE 6.2** Marcel Duchamp: *Broyeuse de chocolate*, 1913.

Courtesy of Philadelphia Museum of Art/Artists Rights Society (ARS), New York, 2017.

# 128 Type and Project—Alteration Tactics

*manifestos* during approximately the same years. While for the futurists, the *macchina* represented a cultural, technologic, and political aspiration, a point of departure towards a new and transcendental civilization, Duchamp was attracted to the hidden poetic quality of artifacts that go unnoticed.

Duchamp "discovered" in those objects subtle metaphorical associations, anatomical analogies and erotic insinuations, secretive readings to be interpreted and revealed. He was fascinated by their particular forms, the relationship between use and movement and their condition of "indifference."[10] He seemed to indicate that the world is already saturated by objects, of all types and forms, that the artist doesn't necessarily need to create new objects, but rather has the option of detecting or "discovering" the hidden qualities of those objects. This idea is illustrated in the well-known anecdote in which Duchamp, Brancusi, and Léger go to an aviation fair. Standing in front of an airplane, Duchamp asks them, "Painting has come to an end. Who can do anything better than this propeller? Can you?"[11] Duchamp would elaborate the answer to that question with his *Bicycle Wheel* (*Roue de bicyclette*, 1913) (Figure 6.3), a piece that reiterates his fascination for industrial artifacts. However, his attention now resides in the particular (dis)positioning of those objects: the wheel appears unexpectedly installed upside-down and bolted to a stool—therefore removed from its expected function.

## The Fountain, the Maiden, and the Readymade

In 1917 Duchamp moved to New York, where he conceived *Fountain* (1917), a work that would suppose a notable impact on Duchamp's trajectory as well as the development of twentieth-century art. The anecdotes that surrounded its conception, posterior rejection, misunderstandings, and the subsequent interpretations sum up the iconoclastic character of this work. The story is quite well known: the *Society of Independent Artists* organized an exhibition of contemporary art with the intention of disseminating new works by modern artists. The only requirement for participating in the show was paying a fee which allowed the artist to exhibit up to two works of art. An unknown artist submitted a standard porcelain urinal with the signature "*R. Mutt*" on one of its sides and titled *Fountain* (Figure 6.4), a proposal that shocked most members of the reception committee. A heated debate ensued within the committee about whether to accept the urinal (no different than one could find at any plumbing supply store), which would imply considering it an artistic work, or to reject it. The discussions lasted until shortly before the opening of the exhibition, and by a minimum margin, the committee decided to dismiss the work. The enormous irony was that Duchamp and Walter Arensberg (a philanthropist who would become Duchamp's main patron) were among the dissenting members of the committee that rejected the sculpture. A few days later, the magazine *The Blind Man*, codirected by Duchamp, included a sort of editorial describing the work presented by Mr. R. Mutt. Following is the full text.[12]

**FIGURE 6.3** Marcel Duchamp: *Roue de bicyclette*, 1913.

Courtesy of Philadelphia Museum of Art/Artists Rights Society (ARS), New York, 2017.

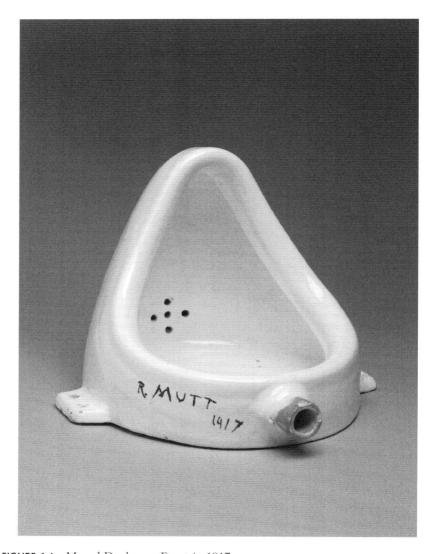

FIGURE 6.4   Marcel Duchamp: *Fountain*, 1917.
Courtesy of Philadelphia Museum of Art/Artists Rights Society (ARS), New York, 2017.

## The Case of Richard Mutt

They say any artist paying six dollars may exhibit.

> Mr. Richard Mutt sent in a fountain. Without discussion this article disappeared and never was exhibited.

What were the grounds for refusing Mr. Mutt's fountain:

1    Some contend it was immoral, vulgar.
2    Others, it was plagiarism, a plain piece of plumbing.

Now Mr. Mutt's fountain is not immoral, that is absurd, no more than a bathtub is immoral. It is a fixture that you see every day in a plumber's show windows.

Whether Mr. Mutt with his own hands made the fountain or not has no importance. He CHOSE it. He took an ordinary article of life, placed it so that its useful significance disappeared under the new title and point of view—created a new thought for that object.

As for plumbing, that is absurd. The only works of art America has given are her plumbing and her bridges.

What would not be known until several years later was that the "author" who sent the urinal signed under the pseudonym of "R. Mutt" was Marcel Duchamp, who at the time was sitting at the society's board of directors. Upon its reception, *Fountain* was perceived by most jurors as an absolutely banal plumbing fixture, an artifact of no artistic value. Consequently, this indecent bathroom appliance was "hidden" (or "suppressed," as stated by Duchamp)[13] for the rest of the exhibition, only to be retrieved later and delivered to Walter Arensberg, who lost the piece while it was in his possession. The single visual record of the original artifact is the often-reproduced photograph by the gallery owner and *marchand* Alfred Stieglitz.

A remarkable aspect of *Fountain* is the fact that despite the controversies and debates, with the exception of a single photograph and the "editorial" in *The Blind Man*, the "original" urinal seems to have barely existed—an oral tale impregnated with fabled orchestrations. As Dalia Judovitz points out, the posterior reproductions and iterations of *Fountain* by themselves generated a bizarre plot composed of a multiplicity of replicas, "signed originals," and "authorized" versions scattered in various museums around the world.[14] The irony of an artwork intending to challenge the notions of originality and authorship through duplication and reappropriation has been ceaselessly replicated. As will be discussed later in this chapter, rather than a conventional artwork, *Fountain* should be considered as an "idea," where the actual materiality of the object appears to be a secondary question.

Duchamp himself coined the idea of displacing an everyday object into an unforeseen context as "readymade." Because of its "ordinary" status, available and for sale in any hardware store, the readymade removes the most conventional condition expected in any artwork: it must be realized by the artist's hands.[15] The absence of craftsmanship in the making of the work of art suggests that the intervention must be understood as an intellectual operation. Despite its resemblance to sculpture, the readymade proposes leaving behind traditional means of artistic production by incorporating the mechanisms of repetition and dislocation.

**132**   Type and Project—Alteration Tactics

*Fountain* has been subject to multiple interpretations: some considered the whole operation a big irony, a denial of art, and others have deciphered sexual or erotic connotations. As put by Calvin Tomkins, "An object with female attributes that serves as receptacle for male fluid, thus becomes ... a symbol of the sexual comedy that underlies all of Duchamp's mature work."[16] In her study, Judovitz reinforces the piece's erotic and bodily insinuations:

> The shape of the urinal follows the dictates of anatomy, but in reverse order. Although it represents the quintessential male instrument, the adaptation of this receptacle to male anatomy generates the potential inscription of femininity, since its visual appearance is that of an oval receptacle. This effort to reproduce the male body by molding the urinal to its shape ironically generates the literal impression of femininity, its obverse.[17]

Hector Obalk has observed that the single definition of "readymade" published under the name of Marcel Duchamp is in André Breton and Paul Éluard's *Dictionnaire abrégé du Surréalisme*: "an ordinary object elevated to the dignity of a work of art by the mere choice of an artist."[18] The readymade, in other words, implies a redefinition of the artistic process, since the artist is no longer in charge of producing the work, but of "choosing" it. A remarkable aspect of Duchamp's initiative was that the "chosen" object was ostensibly dissociated from the "artistic universe"; it was only through its selection and relocation that it experienced a sort of "alchemic process," a conversion of an "ordinary" fixture or tool into a "work of art." As Joseph Kosuth pointed out, "With the ready-made, art changed its focus from the form of the language to what was being said."[19]

## Type, Object, and the Question of Repetition

Ultimately, the readymade is a displaced object. Therefore, it can be understood as an operation analogous to the displaced type, which can also be referred to as *typological displacement*. An examination of the affinities between readymade and typological displacement demands a preliminary analysis of the entities to be dislocated—namely, *type* and *object*. It is useful to revisit Quatremère's writings on the subject (as discussed in Chapter 1), and his distinction between "type" and "model." According to Quatremère, each of these mechanisms represents opposite artistic approaches: the "type," assumed to be a process of formal manipulation substantiated in the doctrine of *mimesis*, and the "model," understood as an exact replica, "an object that should be repeated as it is."[20] The design of a building following a typological process contemplates a series of variations and alterations of the initial typological reference; if designed as a model, the building is an exact copy of a previous one. In his essay *De l'imitation*,[21] Quatremère applied a similar argument to the fine arts, identifying two kinds of *resemblance*, "the one identical, being in fact only the repetition of a thing by the thing itself; the other imitative, being the repetition of a thing by some other which becomes the image of it."[22]

What can be deduced from Quatremère's comments is a correspondence between the architectural and the artistic processes; the notion of "model" in architecture is equivalent to the act of "repeating" in the fine arts, and therefore "imitation" in the visual arts equates the "typological process" in architecture.

The understanding of type as *imitation*, in contrast to "model" as *repetition*, persists through most of Quatremère's writings. However, as discussed in Chapter 1, towards the end of the rubric "*Type*," Quatremère appears to contradict his earlier statements contrasting the notions of type and object: "No one is unaware that a multitude of pieces of furniture, tools, seats, and clothes have their necessary type."[23] On closer inspection, Quatremère is presenting the concept of type as two distinctive (though supplementary) categories: within the realm of architecture, he insists that typological process must be developed under the domain of imitation; though when discussing mass-produced objects ("furniture, tools"), he accepts them as having "their necessary type," their fabrication therefore is produced under repetition. According to this thesis, repetition intersects imitation.

The correspondence between type and object was revisited by contemporary critics Rafael Moneo and Anthony Vidler. As discussed in Chapter 5, Moneo introduced an *expansive* interpretation of *typological precedent*.[24] Influenced by the thinking of anthropologist George Kubler,[25] Moneo argues that the concept of type should not be confined to the field of architecture; it can be extended to all manmade objects: "a work of architecture can also be seen as belonging to a class of repeated objects, characterized, like a class of tools or instruments, by some general attributes."[26] Moneo's argument is that objects, tools, or pieces of craftsmanship can be considered in a similar method as building types, dissolving the differences between architecture and industrial production. Anthony Vidler[27] pushed the argument further by conveying how Le Corbusier and other early twentieth-century architects assimilated an assortment of types and iconographies derived from the world of machine production to incorporate them into the modern architectural lexicon. This strategy, wherein "architecture was now equivalent to the range of mass-production objects,"[28] also stimulated what could be described as the amalgam of architecture and object: the *prototype*.

Following the assertions by Vidler and Moneo, one possible conclusion would be to consider type and object as equivalent concepts. Yet the issue could also be framed in a different manner—the *object* assumed *as particular typological design mechanism*: the *repetition*. With this idea, while conventional mimetic tactics, such as distortion, juxtaposition, or variation of scale, assume some sort of formal alteration, repetition aspires to the precise replication of an existing form. The different attitudes towards the notion of repetition for contemporary art and architecture are notable. With the exception of the prototype (which conveys unique economic and technological conditions and justifications), the notion of repetition in the architectural design process has been generally dismissed by architectural critics and designers, whereas in contemporary art, practices such as *assemblage*, *tableaux*, and *installation art* (all clearly inspired by Duchamp)[29] have discovered in repetition suggestive and poetic qualities.

**134** Type and Project—Alteration Tactics

In his book *Difference and Repetition* (1967), Gilles Deleuze analyzes the inherent complexities around the notion of repetition. He starts by tracing the pervasive negative attributes of repetition to Plato's notion of *simulacra*, or "degraded copy," by which "the model is supposed to enjoy an originary superior identity than the copy."[30] According to Deleuze, Plato's theory of *ideas* strives for marking differences "between the 'thing' itself and its images, the original and the copy, the model and the simulacrum."[31] Deleuze proposes a counter-argument to Plato by identifying the "positive power" of repetition:

> If we say of the simulacrum that it is a copy of a copy, an endlessly degraded icon, an infinitely slackened resemblance, we miss the essential point: the difference in nature between simulacrum and copy, the aspect through which they form the two halves of a division.[32]

Elsewhere Deleuze challenges the actual (or literal) meaning of repetition, stipulating that the act of repeating (i.e., of producing an exact replication) an object or any other entity constitutes an *impossibility*, since every instance presupposes a (minimal) variation from the original model. "Repetition," he argues, "disappears even as it occurs, how can we say 'the second', 'the third' and 'it is the same'? It has no in-itself. On the other hand, it does change something in the mind which contemplates it. This is the essence of modification."[33] Rather than morphological, ponders Deleuze, the question of repetition concerns perception and semantics.

The notion of repetition was central to Duchamp's artistic development; it could be argued that all his works after 1912 involved some kind of repetition. In the 1930s, he introduced a curious concept he coined *inframince* ("infra" suggesting being outside the range of human perception, such as *infra*red light, while *mince* in French translates as "extremely thin"). Throughout the following decades Duchamp occasionally returned to the notion of the *inframince*, his definitions always varying slightly. In one of his *Notes* he (re)defined the term as the "differences" or "liminal intervals (thus infinitesimals) between two almost identical entities, such as the almost imperceptibles differences between 'two twins that look like two drops of water.'"[34] As critic Marcus Boon commented on the *inframince*,

> even if both objects were created in a mass-production facility using the same mold . . . the time and place of their production must be slightly different, they cannot be composed of exactly the same physical matter—the molecules of which they are made are not the same.[35]

Duchamp's notion of *inframince*, therefore, seems to anticipate Deleuze's arguments on repetition: there are no "perfect replicas."

## Doors and Windows

The *element of architecture*[36] is the territory wherein the notions of type and object (or imitation and repetition) appear to intersect. The element of architecture can be seen as a type—subject to be transformed—or as an object—a predefined standardized component bound to be replicated. It was likely this semantic ambiguity that drew Duchamp's attention towards architectural elements—namely, *doors* and *windows*. On first impression, *Fresh Widow* (1920) appears to be a reduced-scale version of the traditional French window, hence the pun implied in the title. Instead of glass, however, the panels were made of wood and wrapped with black leather (a clear association with "the widow"), blocking the views. By removing its expected function (to see *through*) Duchamp deconstructs the meaning of the window; *it doesn't work as such*. Consequently, the title and the actual artifact constitute a sort of *oxymoron*—a combination of two opposite expressions in a single figure—or, if preferred, an "anti-window."

In what became one of his main artistic principles, Duchamp reflects his efforts to rethink the notion of artistic creativity as both a material and a conceptual mode of production.[37] This notion is clearly stated in his comments about "his windows," where rather than formal manipulations, they are understood as intellectual interventions. In an interview with Anne D'Harnoncourt, Duchamp referred to these pieces as abstract and intangible concepts, "ideas" susceptible to innumerable variations:

> I used the *idea* of the window to take a point of departure, as . . . I used a brush, or I used a form, a specific form of expression, the way oil paint is, a very specific term, specific conception. See, in other words, I could have made twenty windows with a different idea in each one, the windows being called "my windows" the way you say "my etchings."[38]

With this statement, Duchamp makes explicit his intention of divorcing the materialization from the conceptualization in the realization of the work of art. According to this view, the primordial aspect of the artistic operation is the intellectual intention, the "idea." In the case of his "windows," the artistic procedure lies in the *decision* of realizing a miniature version, an oversized one, one blocking the views, or altering its expected spatial placement. Certainly, his most celebrated "window" was *La Mariee mise a nu par ses celibataires, meme* (*The Bride Stripped Bare by Her Bachelors, Even*, 1923) (also known as *The Large Glass*), a work that can be understood as a tale of desires, tensions, and discoveries. Duchamp highlights the importance of balancing the literary and intellectual components of the piece, pondering that *The Bride*

> is not meant to be looked at (through esthetic eyes); it was to be accompanied by as amorphous a literary text as possible, which never took form; and the two features, glass for the eye and text for the ears and the understanding, were to complement each other and, above all, prevent the other from taking an esthetic-plastic or literary form.[39]

The other architectural element recurrently examined by Duchamp was the "door," which akin to "his windows" appears relocated with its functions canceled or fundamentally altered. At first sight, *Porte, 11 rue Larrey* (1927) looks like an

**136** Type and Project—Alteration Tactics

ordinary and standard door; after a closer look, a quite distinctive feature is revealed: *Porte* allows for the panel to be simultaneously open or closed at two adjacent openings. Because of its location and the type of hinge, the door opens towards one room while simultaneously closing towards the other. Like with most of Duchamp's work, *Porte* doesn't stand out for its *spectacularity*, but rather for its subtlety and irony. The originality does not lie with the door itself (it is a standard and conventional element), but with its corner location, and its particular swing and operation. With this simple procedure Duchamp achieved a seemingly impossible condition: a door that is simultaneously open and closed.

Duchamp's "architectural" *rectified readymades*[40] evidence and denounces—through irony—the complex relationship between a repeated element, its form, and its expected use. Once a window—or a door, or a bicycle wheel—is positioned in an exhibition space it is no longer a "real window." Rather than transforming the architectural element, Duchamp opts to resignify it by placing it in an unexpected location and canceling its conventional purpose. As will be discussed in the following sections, a similar phenomenon occurs with displaced architectural types: when positioned in unforeseen contexts they cancel their expected function, thus conveying new and unpredicted meanings.

## Unexpected Affinities—Lequeu and Duchamp

The final segment of this chapter is dedicated to examining the parallels between *typological displacement* and *readymade* under the spectrum of the architectural project. To this effect, this study presents four areas of analysis that help frame the affinities (and divergences) between those mechanisms. The first section describes certain *moments* of the work of Lequeu, one of the so-called visionary architects of the end of the eighteenth century, whose work anticipates in astonishing ways many of the themes Duchamp will introduce a century later. The second section examines the now "famous" project for a skyscraper-column by Adolf Loos, demonstrating how issues such as typological displacement and magnification intersect with the notions of style and readymade. The third section discusses particular aspects of the work of Venturi and Rossi, who examined the notion of the *ordinary* and the presence of everyday objects in architecture and art. The final area of analysis concentrates on the works of Herzog & de Meuron, which explore the intersections between the origins, type, archetype, and readymade. Distilled from these discussions are the inevitable correspondences and parallels between Duchamp's works and ideas and architecture.

★

It is fascinating when similarities and coincidences are detected between two artists whose lives took place centuries apart, but even more so when there is no certainty that the more contemporary one was familiar with his predecessor. As noted by historian Philippe Duboy,[41] such is the case with the works and ideas of Jean-Jacques Lequeu (1756–1826) and Marcel Duchamp. Throughout his career, Lequeu had a persistent fascination with words, misspellings, puns, and displacements. In many drawings he explored issues such as voyeurism, transvestism, and erotism (Figure 6.5), and he was labeled by some critics as a pornographer (his portfolio was censored until the twentieth century because of his erotic drawings).[42] Lequeu's "fantastic" architectural projects anticipate a conception of architecture in which mundane and ordinary objects become new and unexpected *mimetic precedents*,

**FIGURE 6.5**  Jean-Jacques Lequeu: *Et nous aussi, nous serons mères . . .*
Bibliothèque Nationale de France.

**138** Type and Project—Alteration Tactics

combining them in ways that suggest notable coincidences with contemporary artistic mechanisms, such as *assemblage* and *collage*. As observed by Duboy, each one of the listed themes that define Lequeu's work also epitomizes the trajectory of Duchamp.[43]

Despite the recent interest in his work, many facts of Lequeu's life are still a mystery; only limited biographical records convey his developments. It is known he was born in Rouen in 1756, and attended courses in architecture and art at the *École Gratuite de Dessin*. After completing his studies he won several architectural competitions, but his designs failed to be built. He spent most of his life working for other architects, including Jacques-Germain Soufflot, or as a draftsman at several governmental offices.[44] After the revolution of 1789 his employment status becomes increasingly precarious, and he devoted his spare time to developing a series of portfolios that included his architectural projects, anatomic and physiognomic studies, and a profuse collection of erotic drawings. Little is known about the last years of his life, and even the exact date of his death is not certain. A recently discovered anecdote suggests that Lequeu ended up living above a brothel, providing an even more literary twist to his already profligate life. Several historians have represented Lequeu as an eccentric and temperamental man; Anthony Vidler described him as a probably "paranoid and neurotic" character, drawing analogies between his personality and Marquis De Sade's.[45]

Only at the beginning of the twentieth century was Lequeu's work "rediscovered," mainly due to the research on the eighteenth-century architecture "visionary architects" by Viennese historian Emil Kaufmann. In his seminal text, Kaufmann praised the originality and creativity of Boullée, Ledoux, and Lequeu (he lists them in that order), to the point of considering them among precursors of modern architecture.[46] While he regarded Lequeu as the most "fantastic" of the three, he also criticized his "excesses," describing some of his architecture as an indiscriminate and exotic mixture of architectural styles.

Many of Lequeu's compositions go beyond the appropriation of ancient or foreign styles to generate an unprecedented ornamentation lexicon by utilizing zoological attributes (heads of deer, bears, and pigs) (Figure 6.6), natural elements (concrete clouds, egg-shaped domes, or storm drainages in the shape of wine bottles) (Figure 6.7), or everyday objects (locks, bowls of milk, accordions, or a building that looks like a giant urn). This design approach challenges not only the conventions of the classical language but also the concepts of style, order, and abstraction. Lequeu developed a new compositional approach closer to the contemporary tactics of *montage* or *collage*, a reassembling of elements from dissimilar origins that produce inventive and bizarre images. Vidler described how Lequeu, perhaps for the first time in history, "in so extensive a manner, constituted his buildings with non-architectural elements";[47] objects and elements from all kinds of origins and backgrounds begin to assume the role of conventional architectural types.

Lequeu's compositions could be defined as an *improbable coexistence of disparate elements*, a notion manifested in his project titled *Tomb for Porsenna* (Figure 6.8). In this architectural ensemble, Lequeu draws elements from different contexts, alters

**FIGURE 6.6** Jean-Jacques Lequeu: *La porte de la chasse du Prince et l'étable*. Bibliothèque Nationale de France.

their scales, and juxtaposes them in an unusual way. The bottom section of the building is a conventional classical temple placed on a plinth; on top stands what seems to be a *gigantic urn*. The juxtaposition of the temple and the artifact creates a bizarre arrangement of two elements that "belong" to different contexts, an operation that suggests clear parallels with the *montage*. With its altered scale and placement in an unexpected context, the *object* becomes a building component—it has been converted into "architecture."

**FIGURE 6.7** Jean-Jacques Lequeu: *Temple à la divination*.
Bibliothèque Nationale de France.

**FIGURE 6.8** Jean-Jacques Lequeu: *Tombeau de Porsenna, roi d'Étrurie*.
Bibliothèque Nationale de France.

**FIGURE 6.9** Jean-Jacques Lequeu: "*The Cow Byre faces south on the cool meadow.*"
Bibliothèque Nationale de France.

Lequeu revisited magnification and displacement tactics in his project for a *cowshed* (the note next to the drawing reads, "The Cow Byre faces south on the cool meadow").[48] In this case he proposes a building sculpted as a giant cow with a slight asymmetrical posture and the entrance located between its forelegs (Figure 6.9)—an unprecedented design approach that blurs the distinctions between architecture and figurative sculpture. The idea of making a building using the shape of an oversized animal is so blunt and eccentric that it may be interpreted as a monumental irony, as well as an extreme attempt to replace the ingrained conventions of typological precedent and architectural composition and vocabulary with less explored concepts, such as replication and dislocation.

## The Displaced Column—The Presumed Irony of Loos

In his projects Lequeu explored formal processes such as typological magnification and displacement, suggesting the substitution of conventional architectural vocabulary with figurative sculpture. In addition to those processes there is another latent aspect present in his work: a humorous condition—namely, the *irony*. The term "irony" is defined as a rhetorical statement wherein "words mean the opposite of what you really think."[49] Irony establishes a humorous communication between an author and the public. One of the main characteristics of Duchamp's work was his attention to irony; his designation of a urinal as a sculpture or his addition of a

**142** Type and Project—Alteration Tactics

moustache to the Gioconda can be interpreted only under the umbrella of irony. For those who don't "appreciate" that quality, the works are incomprehensible.

Several *moments* of the work of Adolf Loos (1870–1933) have been interpreted as improbable ironies. His most well-known and controversial project, the proposal for the *Chicago Tribune* competition of 1922 (Figure 6.10), has been considered by various critics and historians as a profoundly ironic proposal. The competition's conditions demanded that the architect "erect the most beautiful and distinctive office building in the world,"[50] a building type which at that time had virtually no antecedents. Loos's proposal consisted of a skyscraper with the shape of a Doric column, composed of a cubic *base* and a slender cylindrical *shaft* crowned with a prominent *capital*. The process had two supplementary mechanisms: first, the extreme magnification of the column, and second, the placement of the enhanced typological fragment into an unexpected (urban) context. The column has been "placed" in lieu of the building.

When the international competition was called, the notion of a large vertical building (later labeled a "skyscraper") implied the conception of a typology with no clear precedents.[51] The fundamental premise, according to Loos, was to identify the appropriate *archetype* that would serve as a precedent for this new typological stage. Because of its slender proportions, tectonic connotations, and association with the *perpetual*, Loos understood that "the Doric column" was the perfect precedent for the emerging "skyscraper type." He accompanied his project with an article titled "The Chicago Tribune Column,"[52] in which he explained and justified the reasoning behind his astounding proposal. In his text Loos anticipates two possible objections to the project. Firstly, rather than freestanding, columns are usually positioned aligned or in rows; the second reservation was that the proposed column doesn't fulfill its primary purpose, which is to sustain or transfer a building's weight. In his "rebuttal," Loos states that history shows multiple examples of freestanding columns without structural purposes: "The writer chose the form of the column for his project. The motif of the free-standing giant column was provided by tradition. Trajan's column already served as the prototype of Napoleon's in the Place Vendome."[53]

The magnitude of Loos's proposal is reminiscent of previously discussed projects by Boullée, though rather than assuming a building or spatial typology, Loos adopts as a point of departure what is generally considered a minor architectural element. For his conversion into a building, Loos "respects" the conventional proportions of the Doric column with its tripartite subdivision of base, shaft, and capital, though its dimensions appear extraordinarily enlarged.[54] In the supplementary text Loos explains that the main portion of the building would be the "shaft," a twenty-two-story structure, covered with polished black granite, hosting administrative and journalist activities.

Loos's "column" has provoked many contrasting comments and interpretations. While some considered it a serious plan, others labeled it a gigantic irony. Aldo Rossi didn't believe that the project should be taken seriously, describing it as "only a game, a Viennese *divertissement*."[55] Manfredo Tafuri was extremely critical of the

**FIGURE 6.10** Adolf Loos: *Chicago Tribune competition*, 1922.

Courtesy of the Library of Congress, reproduction number: LC-DIG-ppmsca-51972.

**144** Type and Project—Alteration Tactics

proposal, describing it as "pathetic . . . a last effort to communicate an exhortation to the eternity of values."[56] In turn, Joseph Rykwert thought that Loos's column was an absolutely logical and rational idea, commenting that "some critics have bypassed the scheme as a prank, but no one seriously interested in Loos and his work could ever maintain such a view."[57] The mere fact that a project can provoke such eliciting and antagonistic comments demonstrates its remarkable singularity.

An issue intensely debated by historians and critics has been to determine whether Loos's proposal should be seen as a serious project or a *naïf* adventure, or if the whole affair was a *gigantic irony*. Joseph Masheck is absolutely certain: "It would be impossible to maintain that the Chicago Tribune Tower was without irony, at least with a straight face, i.e., impossible without thereby indulging in irony oneself."[58] It is hard to believe that one of the most important architects and intellectuals of his time, who was in contact with the main avant-garde trends, would not foresee the provocative nature of his proposal. The project may also be interpreted as a massive paradox, just as the trajectory of the Viennese architect was defined for its various paradoxical positions.[59] Loos is known as the author of the manifesto *Ornament and Crime* (1908),[60] one of the seminal texts of modern thought known for its rejection of ornamental decoration, but many of his works, such as *Villa Karma* (1906) or *Goldman & Salatsch Store* (1910), reveal the presence of classic elements. This apparent contradiction is evident in the design of his houses, which feature stripped and unornamented façades (occasionally compared with the most radical explorations of abstract art)[61] contrasting with rich interiors profusely decorated with marble, onyx, and *boiserie*.

Many of the issues that define the trajectory of Loos, such as the conspicuous presence of irony and humor, or his recurrent adoption of contradictory positions, were permanent features in the works and ideas of Duchamp. Although there is no certainty the two had a personal relationship, they both moved in similar cultural circles, such as the group *Dada*, among the most provocative artistic movements of the early twentieth century. As stated earlier, after the rejection of his painting *Nude Descendant* Duchamp became reluctant to join or associate with any artistic group;[62] still, *Dadaism* became one of the few movements with which he maintained a certain affinity, even participating in several of their meetings and exhibitions. Loos had a personal relationship with several *Dada* artists, such as Georges Besson and Paul Dermée,[63] and he was the architect of the celebrated Tristan Tzara house (1926), one of the leading members of Dadaism. In retrospect, Loos and Duchamp adopted similar positions on many issues, such as installing within the spectator doubts about the seriousness or the ironic intent of their proposals and their provocative stand in opposition to some of the most fundamental modernist dogma. Like Duchamp, Loos challenged one of the most fundamental modern canons by proclaiming in favor of *repetition*: "The best form is already available and no one should be afraid to use it, even though it may come from another source. Enough of original geniuses! Let us repeat ourselves endlessly!"[64]

This insistence on promoting repetition of past forms can be interpreted in several ways: as a great irony, as a challenge to modernism, or as an apology of figurativism, aspects that also define Duchamp's work. Joseph Masheck has observed that Loos and Duchamp share a "difficult classification" within modernism, up to the point that they were labeled as "anti-modern."[65] Notably, they both promote a very conscious questioning of the creative process, no longer assumed according to artistic conventions (i.e., as manipulation of forms), but as a provocative selection of objects (or types) subject to being altered and/or displaced. The Viennese architect concludes his memorandum for the competition with a rather prophetic statement, declaring that the project is ultimately understood as a *concept*:

> The great Greek Doric column must be built.
> If nor in Chicago, then in some other town.
> If nor for the "Chicago Tribune" then for someone else.
> If not by me, then by some other architect.[66]

With this statement Loos defined his "Doric column" as an intellectual process, independent from the context, the client, and even the architect. From this perspective, originality emerges as the illusion of multiple authorship. The magnification and displacement of a type, according to this premise, are fundamentally an *idea*, whereas the essential attributes of architecture are not physical or formal but rather conceptual and representational. The incorporeal quality Loos identifies in the architectural project suggests remarkable coincidences with both Quatremère's notion of type and Duchamp's understanding of readymade. As commented in Chapter 1, Quatremère repeatedly referred to type as an abstract and intangible concept, "less the image of a thing to copy or imitate completely, than the idea of an element."[67] In turn, one of Duchamp's main contributions was his introduction of "conceptual art" by emphasizing the intellectual and symbolic over the material and "retinal." In this regard, it is worth recalling his reflection in an interview with James Johnson Sweeney: "I was interested in ideas—not merely visual products. I wanted to put painting once again in the service of the mind."[68]

## In Praise of the Ordinary—Venturi and Rossi

While much of contemporary historiography has emphasized the theoretical and design differences between Robert Venturi and Aldo Rossi, their careers present considerable parallels. In 1966, the two most influential architectural books of the second half of the twentieth century, *The Architecture of the City*[69] and *Complexity and Contradiction in Architecture*, were published.[70] In their writings, both architects coincide in their criticism of the functionalist trend of the modern movement while proposing a reconsideration of past forms. Whereas Rossi understands architecture as a process of decanting the superfluous towards a maturation of forms and types, Venturi sees architecture as a diachronic *collage*, an extensive assemble of various mannerist moments.

The career of Venturi (1926) is symptomatic of the rearrangement of interests in architectural theory and practice during the second half of the twentieth century

**146** Type and Project—Alteration Tactics

(an issue discussed in Chapter 5). A key moment of Venturi's development was his residence at the *American Academy of Rome*, the city that sparked his interest in sixteenth-century mannerist architecture, particularly the work of Michelangelo.[71] As previously discussed, one of the premises of mannerism was the transgression of classical norms and the appeal to mechanisms such as transformation, distortion, and displacement. Venturi developed a personal interpretation of mannerism; rather than a historical period he understood it as an *attitude*, common in

> the sixteenth century in Italy or the Hellenistic period in Classical art, and is also a continuous strain seen in such diverse architects as Michelangelo, Palladio, Borromini, Vanbrugh, Hawksmoor, Soane, Ledoux, Furness, Lutyens ... and recently, Le Corbusier, Aalto, Kahn, and others.[72]

These ideas were reflected in his book *Complexity and Contradiction*, and they also became a palpable influence in many of his projects, such as *Mother's House* (1962–64), which he would later label "Mannerist House,"[73] and his *Guild House* (1963).

Together with mannerism, another issue that drew Venturi's attention was the notion of the *ordinary* (from Latin *ordinarius*: customary, regular, usual).[74] In a passage from *Complexity and Contradiction*, Venturi refers to the hidden quality of ordinary objects that usually go unnoticed:

> I do not refer to the sophisticated products of industrial design, which are usually beautiful, but to the vast accumulation of standard, anonymously designed products connected with architecture and construction, and also to commercial display elements which are positively banal or vulgar in themselves and are seldom associated with architecture.[75]

Venturi's notion of the ordinary, therefore, covers a wide spectrum: standard building components, doors, and windows listed in catalogs, vernacular structures, and the iconography of manufacturing and commercial constructions. In his view, architecture, art, and design need the ordinary; it is from the acceptance of the ordinary and its consensus that the *extra*-ordinary can be identified and created.

Venturi's appreciation of the *ordinary* relates to his interest in *pop art*, and by extension, the works and ideas of Duchamp. It should be noted that the vast majority of pop artists—Richard Hamilton, Andy Warhol, Robert Rauschenberg, Claes Oldenburg, and Jasper Johns[76] among them—have recognized Duchamp's influence in their work. This *genealogical lineage* between Duchamp and pop art is suggested by Venturi. "Pop Art," he writes, "celebrates the Ordinary ... with its depictions of everyday objects made special via modifications of medium, scale, and context."[77] This idea is explored in several of the architectural projects he developed together with his partner and wife, Denise Scott Brown, such as the "Mickey Mouse column" (Figure 6.11), located in the addition to the Allen Memorial Art Museum at Oberlin College (1976). The column may be interpreted as an amalgamation of Venturi and Scott Brown's two main influences, mannerism and pop art. In the first place, the "Ionian column" has been subjected to a process of *typological distortion* (the diameter appears disproportionally

**FIGURE 6.11** Venturi, Scott Brown and Associates (Principal: Robert Venturi with Denise Scott Brown), *Ironic Column*, Allen Memorial Art Museum, Oberlin College, 1973–1977.

Photograph by Tom Bernard, courtesy of Venturi, Scott Brown and Associates, Inc.

"fat" in relation to its height), a mechanism reminiscent of mannerism's transformation of "classical" architectural elements. The image also highlights the *iconographic* power of pop art, as the column's "Ionic capital" resembles the ears of the celebrated comic strip mouse—an ironic homage to the icon of the Disney empire.

Venturi and Scott Brown understand that one of the primary purposes of architecture is to convey meaning. To frame this issue they appeal to a simple but effective metaphor, which is the distinction between the "duck," identified as a

**148** Type and Project—Alteration Tactics

formalistic and sculptural building, and the "decorated shed," a generic structure for which the façade (or *billboard*) assumes the communicational role.[78] When describing the "duck," Venturi and Scott Brown accept that the architect, like the sculptor, has the ability to create buildings of virtually any form, whether figurative, abstract, or expressionistic, which will have the capacity to convey their use. In contrast, the "decorated shed" is a *generic* structure with a purpose identifiable only by signage and/or other applied ornamentation. While the "decorated shed" *requires* applied symbolism, the "duck" *is* the symbol.

For their 1984 proposal for *Times Square* (Figure 6.12), Venturi and Scott Brown developed their own "duck," allowing figurative sculpture to take over architecture. The project consisted of an "apple" with colossal dimensions crowning a generic building in one of New York City's most renowned areas. While the allusion is quite straightforward (since the 1950s New York has been known as *The Big Apple*), the image of a gigantic fruit suspended in the heart of Manhattan proposes a striking spectacle. For Venturi and Scott Brown, the apple holds a recognizable relation to Oldenburg's large-scale sculptures:

> this design proposes a Big Apple for Times Square: a piece of representational sculpture which is bold in form yet rich in symbolism . . . realism with a

**FIGURE 6.12** Venturi, Scott Brown and Associates (Frederic Schwartz, draftsman), *The Big Apple at Times Square Center*, 1984. Photograph by Will Brown.

Courtesy of Venturi, Scott Brown and Associates, Inc.

diversity of association. It is popular and esoteric—a Big Apple symbolizing New York City and a surrealist object evoking Rene Magritte or a Pop-art monument in the manner of Claes Oldenburg.[79]

Venturi and Scott Brown's urban-scale proposal suggests a nod to both Lequeu's *Cowshed*, in which figurative sculpture adopts the role of architecture, and Claes Oldenburg's works, always aspiring to participate in the urban dialog. Venturi and Scott Brown's "apple" can also be interpreted as an urban-scale readymade, a lasting presence *a bite away* from paradise.

★

Like Venturi, over the years Rossi became increasingly interested in the world of domestic and "ordinary" objects, though in his case he relates them to the concept of type. Rossi's consideration of type can be categorized in two stages. In the first stage, epitomized by *L'architettura della città*, Rossi sees type as the tool for recognizing the originating condition of architecture. Once (re)discovered, type is bound to be *purified* and become an instrument for reestablishing a link with beginnings of time. Rossi's second stage is defined by the notion of *analogy*, which implies the improbable (and poetical) correspondence between types and objects.

As discussed in Chapter 4, Rossi's notion of analogy as an urban instrument was first introduced with the collage *Città Analoga* (*The Analogous City*), which together with Eraldo Consolascio, Bruno Reichlin and Fabio Reinhart presented at the 1976 Venice Biennale of Architecture. *Città Analoga* is an ensemble of images containing Rossi's own projects, such as San Rocco and Gallaratese, intercalated with urban and architectural fragments, from Piranesi's Campo Marzio to drawings by Francesco Milizia and Le Corbusier. The composition also contains moments of Rossi's personal and lyrical world, such as mannerist painter Tanzio da Varallo's image of David pointing towards the center of the project and the shade of a man looking through a square window. If *L'architettura della città* proposed a unifying idea for the city, *Città Analoga* conveyed an urban and poetic landscape where fragments of maps, slices of projects, and personal memoires coexist by approximation.

Later Rossi translated many of the ideas present in *Città Analoga* into the architectural domain with his essay "An Analogical Architecture."[80] In Rossi's view, analogy is "mainly a matter of a logical-formal operation that could be translated as a design method";[81] later he added, "Today I see my architecture within the context and limits of a wide range of associations, correspondences, and analogies."[82] Analogy for Rossi involves the establishing of relationships or associations between dissimilar elements that correspond to different contexts. As he wrote,

> The question of things themselves, whether as compositions or components— drawings, buildings, models, or descriptions—appears to me increasingly more suggestive and convincing. But this is not to be interpreted in the sense of "vers une architecture" nor as a new architecture. I am referring rather to familiar objects, whose form and position are already fixed, but whose

**150** Type and Project—Alteration Tactics

meanings may be changed. Barns, stables, sheds, workshops, etc. Archetypal objects whose common emotional appeal reveals timeless concerns.[83]

These ideas are represented in his drawings of desolated *piazzas*, galleries, beach boxes, and bell towers, which appear next to his *ogetti d'afezione*, such as coffeepots, teacups, clocks, or saints. Rossi's images evince the influence of Giorgio De Chirico and his "metaphysical surrealism," a universe of familiar objects and figures that appear displaced or decontextualized in an almost imperceptibly fashion. Like De Chirico, Rossi alludes to a world of dreams where fragments of antiquity coexist with trains and deep green skies. Gradually, he began to "discover" the logic behind the displacement of those objects, the semantic possibilities awakened by the alteration of scale, the poetic metamorphosis of architectural forms:

> I particularly loved the strange shapes of the coffeepots enameled blue, green, red; they were miniatures of the fantastic architectures that I would encounter later. Today I still love to draw these large coffeepots, which I liken to brick walls, and which I think of as structures that can be entered.[84]

The meaning of the object, just like the significance of a type, depends on variables such as its location and expected scale (Figure 6.13). A "coffeepot," envisions Rossi, once magnified can became a building, just as a dome or a tower can provide a source of inspiration for the design of a teapot. In his introduction to *The Architecture of the City*, Peter Eisenman comments about Rossi's interest in issues such as displacement and variation of scale of buildings and objects, observing that "the subversive analogues proposed in Rossi's work involve two kinds of transformation. One is the dislocation of place, the other the dissolution of scale."[85] According to Eisenman, Rossi's interests are related to the famous analogy drawn by Alberti: "The city is like a great house, and the house is in turn like some small city." The work of Rossi, he adds, expands Alberti's metaphor by incorporating the scale of the objects' universe. "The object," Eisenman concludes, "represents a dialectic between the giant collective house of the city and its individual, specific houses, the city's artifacts."[86]

Rossi's sliding of interests is confirmed with the publication of his second book, *Autobiografia Scientifica*[87] (*A Scientific Autobiography*, 1981). With a decidedly lyrical tone, the book's format resembles an exercise of memory, an indeterminate and ambiguous thread without chapters or sections, only thoughts and recollections. In *Autobiografia Scientifica* Rossi discusses his increased interest in the universe of objects, initially as signs of his childhood memories, later coexisting with images of architecture and the city:

> In my interest for objects, I must admit that I have always managed to confuse the thing itself with the word through a kind of ignorance, or prejudice, or even through the suspension that this could give to the meaning of a statement or a drawing.[88]

A feature of Rossi's analogical thinking is that his ideas and projects seem to be articulated from memories, from which the personal and the collective evocations

Affinities **151**

**FIGURE 6.13** Aldo Rossi: *Teatro Faro, Toronto*, 1988–1989.
© Eredi Aldo Rossi, courtesy of Fondazione Aldo Rossi.

appear intertwined. A passing comment in his *Scientific Autobiography* would later become a *leitmotif* of his posterior projects. Rossi recalls how

> one morning, as I was passing through the Grand Canal in Venice on a *vaporetto*, someone suddenly pointed out to me Filarete's column and the Vicolo del Duca and the humble houses constructed where the ambitious palace of

this Milanese lord was to have been. I always observe this column and its base, this column that is both a beginning and an end.[89]

He is referring to the freestanding corner column of a fifteenth-century *palazzo* attributed to Filarete (Figure 6.14). While the *architectural moment* suggested by Rossi is not mentioned in the rest of the book, the image continues to resonate in his memory, and reappear many years later converted into repeated architectural assemblies.

The *Friedrichstasse* in Berlin (1981) (Figure 6.15) and the Civic Center in Perugia (1984) seem like magnified versions of Filarete's column. By replicating a mostly unnoticed architectural fragment Rossi incorporates its presence into society's collective memory. Both the *Friedrichstasse* and the Perugia Civic Center convey a sense of semantic ambiguity; they can be interpreted as a gigantic column strangely dominating a city's corner, or an oversized cylinder with uncertain structural or architectural functions. The idea behind both projects is reminiscent of Loos's Chicago Tribune Column, a conventional architectural element extraordinarily magnified and positioned in an unexpected context. However, Rossi's "pieces" appear more like a personal "discovery" of a forgotten moment, *objet trouvés* destined to be shared with the rest of society. Just like with his "objects," Rossi is interested in translating the incidental into the monumental, an analogic operation that conveys the effects of typological displacement on an urban scale.

**FIGURE 6.14** Filarete: *Ca' del duca Palace*, c. 1469.

Photograph courtesy of Nicola Goretti.

**FIGURE 6.15**  Aldo Rossi: *Friedrichstasse*, 1981.

Photograph courtesy of Andres Nicolini.

**154** Type and Project—Alteration Tactics

## Typological Riddles—Herzog & de Meuron

The careful consideration of the multiple typological processes is a subject that also appears at various moments in the architecture of Jacques Herzog (1950) and Pierre de Meuron (1950). The two studied architecture at the *Eidgenössische Technische Hochschule* (commonly known as ETH) in Zurich, the same school Gottfried Semper inaugurated and directed a century before. In addition, during their years at the ETH, Herzog and de Meuron had the opportunity to study under the direction of Aldo Rossi.[90] It is an educational history that points to the architects' interest and familiarity with the concepts of origins and type, issues that would recurrently appear in their thoughts and projects.

Critic Kurt Foster[91] reviews the architects' interest in the potential links between vernacular typologies and the origins of architecture, an issue initially considered by Quatremère de Quincy in his theory of the "three original types," and later by Semper with his notion of the "Caribbean hut." Towards the end of the nineteenth century, particularly in Switzerland, the question of the origins regained some interest thanks to the research directed by historian and archaeologist Jakob Hunziker, who sought to establish a lineage between the original settlements of mankind and the traditional building typologies of the Swiss cantons. According to Foster, Semper's and Hunziker's interests in the forms of the past, coupled with the influence of Rossi during their college days, generated in Herzog and de Meuron a persistent interest in the corresponding nature between the concept of type and the origins of architecture.

In many of their works, Herzog & de Meuron explored the notion of adopting the precedent of the archetypal house as a point of departure, such as the *Blue House* (1979) in Oberwil, Switzerland, *VitraHaus* (2009) in Germany, the *Parrish Art Museum* (2012) in Long Island, and the *Feltrinelli Porta Volta* in Milan (2013). Although gable-roof structures are inevitably associated with the traditional image of the house, none of these projects are residential. *Feltrinelli Porta Volta* assumed as precedent the archetype of the Northern Italian rural house, confirming the architects' fixation with this typology (Figure 6.16). However, in this case, the type conveys urban and historical dimensions: the symbolic recuperation of the *Mura Spagnole*, the ancient sixteenth-century city walls which were the last of a series of fortifications that since Roman times have defined the city's growing boundaries. The longitudinally extruded gabled roof forms, therefore, can be interpreted as the most recent materialization of those ancient boundaries, though instead of massive walls, they are concrete skeletons of glass and glass paneling. Rather than hosting a single function, the gabled roof structure allow a continual multistoried sequence of cafes, restaurants, shops, galleries, and office spaces. According to Herzog & de Meuron, "The new buildings are inspired by the long, linear Cascina buildings of traditional rural architecture in Lombardy, which already were an important reference in Aldo Rossi's work, for instance his residential building in Gallaratese."[92] The suggestive perseverance of the type is described as "an elongated and narrow architecture which in a vaguely figurative way introduces a roof which melts into the facades."[93] The result is an *extreme magnification and dislocation* of the traditional rural house, which in its urban disposition conveys unforeseen meanings and associations.

**FIGURE 6.16**   Herzog & de Meuron: *Porta Volta* in Milan, 2014.
Photograph courtesy of Nicola Goretti.

In the commented projects, the architects assume the task of "distilling" the most iconic and literal features that constitute the *archetypal* idea of the house: gable roof, chimney, and side windows. Those features *literally* constitute their proposal for the *Rudin house* in Leymen (1997) (Figure 6.17). At first glance, the project may appear predictable and banal, the infinitely repeated image of *la petite maison* (the

**FIGURE 6.17**  Herzog & de Meuron: *House Rudin in Leymen*, 1998

"little house") drawn by children from around globe, an image so embedded in the collective unconscious that it was described by Jacques Derrida as a "metaphor of a metaphor."[94] However, a closer look at the residence reveals a series of anomalies that contradict this presumption. For example, the house is not lying on the ground (as expected in a traditional setting) but on a platform that in turn rests on *pilotis*, a solution reminiscent of the *Corbusian Dom-ino*. Another issue that appears "misleading" is the exterior reinforced concrete walls, a material dissociated from the canons of the rural house. Furthermore, the proportions of the openings seem somewhat puzzling, on the same plane a vertical window (iconic component of traditional architecture) coexisting with a horizontal one (one of the architectural elements more associated with modern architecture). The project suggests at least two possible readings: the stereotypical image of the rural house, which appears as a universal presence; or a purported irony: a giant *objet trouvé* presented as *a doll's house* that was "found" (or "forgotten"?) on a green slope of the French countryside.

Kurt Forster discusses the presence of typological processes in many works by Herzog & de Meuron, who "reveal themselves to be avid students of a type of building that has continued to fascinate for centuries without ever yielding a definite clue about its interest."[95] He adds that "a key to Herzog & de Meuron's handling of *typological riddles* can perhaps be found in their ability to rethink the programmatic purposes of a building instead of rushing to meet them"[96] (italics added). The specific tactics of these "typological riddles" vary depending on the project. While the Feltrinelli Porta Volta expresses the *urban dimension of the type*, the Rudin house proposes the notion of typological displacement, a sort of *readymade* that revolves around the *idea* of "*la petite maison*." Discussing these issues, Jacques Herzog commented that "what we like about this typology is that it is open for many different functions, places and cultures. Each time this simple, almost banal form has become something very specific, precise and also fresh"[97]—a statement reminiscent of the thinking of their former teacher, Aldo Rossi.

The explorations of Herzog & de Meuron display particular examples of typological repetition and variation. Rather than focusing on the alterations of forms, their interest lay in detecting the effects of slightly deviating and relocating selected types. It is in this regard that their projects, as well as the others discussed in this chapter, convey a renewed consideration of the notion of typological precedent in the design process, where the emphasis is no longer placed in the effects of formal manipulation; instead, the variation of meaning is achieved through deviation, substitution, and displacement.

## Notes

1  Judovitz, Dalia, *Unpacking Duchamp: Art in Transit*. Berkeley: University of California Press, 1998, 241.
2  Horatius, "Ars Poetica." Cited in Harmon, William: *Classic Writings on Poetry*. New York: Columbia University Press, 2003, 73.
3  See the chapter "Scattered Beauty" in Summers, David, *Michelangelo and the Language of Art*. Princeton: Princeton University Press, 1981, 186–199.
4  Summers, *Michelangelo and the Language of Art*, 186.
5  Leatherbarrow, David, *The Roots of Architectural Invention: Site, Enclosure, Materials*. Cambridge: Cambridge University Press, 1993, 107.
6  Leatherbarrow, *The Roots of Architectural Invention*, 108.
7  Tomkins, Calvin, *Duchamp: A Biography*. New York: H. Holt, 1996, 75–84.
8  Cabanne, Pierre, and Marcel Duchamp, *Dialogues With Marcel Duchamp*. New York: Da Capo, 1987, 17.
9  Tomkins, *Duchamp: A Biography*, 114.
10  Cabanne, *Dialogues*, 41.
11  Cited in Tomkins, *Duchamp: A Biography*, 137.
12  Cited in Tomkins, *Duchamp: A Biography*, 185.
13  Judovitz, *Unpacking Duchamp*, 124.
14  Judovitz, *Unpacking Duchamp*, 128.
15  As noted by Dalia Judovitz, "The ready-mades redefine the notion of artistic creativity, since they do not involve the manual production of objects but their intellectual reproduction. Duchamp's intervention consists in redefining their status, both as objects and as representations, for the objective character of the ready-mades affirms their special status as reproductions that comment upon and question the representational function of art." Judovitz, *Unpacking Duchamp*, 76.
16  Tomkins, *Duchamp: A Biography*, 186.
17  Judovitz, *Unpacking Duchamp*, 129–130.
18  Obalk, Hector, "The Unfindable Readymade." In *Tout-fait the Marcel Duchamp Studies Online Journal*. www.toutfait.com/issues/issue_2/Articles/obalk.html. Accessed November 16, 2014.

**158** Type and Project—Alteration Tactics

19  Kosuth, Joseph, "Art After Philosophy." In *Art After Philosophy and After: Collected Writings, 1966–1990*. Cambridge, MA: MIT Press, 1991, 18.

20  Quatremère De Quincy, and Samir Younés, *The Historical Dictionary of Architecture of Quatremère De Quincy*. London: Andreas Papadakis, 1999, 254–255.

21  Quatremère de Quincy, *An Essay on the Nature, the End, and the Means of Imitation in the Fine Arts*. London: Smith, Elder, Cornhill, 1837, (original print 1823). Here referred as *De l'imitation*.

22  Quatremère, *De l'imitation*, 31.

23  Quatremère, *The Historical Dictionary*, 256.

24  Moneo, Rafael, "On Typology." *Oppositions 13*. Cambridge, MA: MIT Press, 1978.

25  Kubler George, *The Shape of Time: Remarks on the History of Things*. New Haven: Yale University Press, 1962.

26  Moneo, "On Typology," 23.

27  Vidler, Anthony, "The Third Typology." In Michel K. Hays (ed.), *Architectural Theory Since 1968*. Cambridge, MA: Cambridge: MIT Press. 1998, 288–294, (originally published in *Oppositions 7*, 1976).

28  Vidler, "The Third Typology," 291.

29  Regarding Duchamp's influence in contemporary art, Calvin Tomkins stated he "has come to be considered a forerunner of Conceptual Art, as well as Pop art, Minimal art, Performance art, Process art, Kinetic art, Anti-form and Multimedia art, and virtually every postmodern tendency; the great anti-retinal thinker who supposedly abandoned art for chess has turned out, in fact, to have had a more lasting and far-reaching effect on the art of our time than either Picasso or Matisse." Tomkins: *Duchamp A Biography*, 12.

30  Deleuze, Gilles, *Difference and Repetition*. New York: Columbia University Press, 1994. 70.

31  Deleuze, Gilles, "Plato and the Simulacrum." *October, Vol. 27*. Cambridge, MA: MIT Press, 1983, 45.

32  Deleuze, "Plato and the Simulacrum," 48.

33  Deleuze, *Difference and Repetition*, 70.

34  Cited in Ades, Dawn, Neil Cox, and David Hopkins, *Marcel Duchamp*. New York: Thames and Hudson, 1999, 184.

35  Boon, Marcus, *In Praise of Copying*. Cambridge, MA: Harvard University Press, 2011, 193.

36  *Element of architecture* is a term derived from Durand's *Précis*. See Durand, Jean-Nicolas-Louis, *Précis of the Lectures on Architecture; With, Graphic Portion of the Lectures on Architecture*. Los Angeles: Getty Research Institute, 2000, Vol. 1 (Ed. Orig. 1802).

37  The conception of the readymade as an "intellectual intervention" is elaborated in Judovitz, *Unpacking Duchamp*, 76.

38  Quoted in D'Harnoncourt, Anne and Kynaston McShine (editors), Marcel *Duchamp*, New York, Museum of Modern Art, 1973, 295.

39  Tomkins, *Duchamp: A Biography*, 3.

40  For an extensive description of the "rectified readymade," see Judovitz, *Unpacking Duchamp*, 137–138.

41  Duboy, Philippe, *Lequeu, An Architectural Enigma*. Cambridge, MA: MIT Press, 1987.

42  Observed in Duboy, *Lequeu*, 14.

43  It is worth commenting that there are no records of Duchamp acknowledging any familiarity with the works by Lequeu. However, based on his historical findings, Philippe Duboy has commented that Duchamp and his friend Francis Picabia (whose uncle was at the time director of the Bibliothèque Sainte-Geneviève) must have had unrestricted access to the "censored" material stored in the library, including, of course, Lequeu's "forbidden portfolios."

44  Kaufmann, Emil, *Three Revolutionary Architects: Boullée, Ledoux and Lequeu*. Philadelphia: American Philosophical Society, 1952, 538.

45  Vidler, Anthony, *The Writing of the Walls*, Princeton: Princeton Architecture Press, 1987, 103.

46  Kaufmann, Emil, *Von Ledoux Bis Le Corbusier*. Vienna: Verlag Dr. Rolf Passer, 1933. Kaufmann's was among the first texts that analyzed the relationship between eighteenth-century French architects and modern architecture.

47 Vidler commented that "while Boullée and Ledoux worked with all the apparatus of classicism," Lequeu developed a personal vocabulary "constituted with nonarchitectural elements." See Vidler, *The Writing of the Walls*, 122.

48 See the section "Figures et architecture" in Duboy, *Lequeu*, 303–346.

49 Definition of "Irony" from *Merriam-Webster Online Dictionary*, www.merriam-webster.com/dictionary/irony. Accessed March 2, 2016.

50 Rykwert, Joseph, *The Dancing Column: On Order in Architecture*. Cambridge, MA: MIT Press, 1996, 19.

51 Alan Colquhoun later defined the skyscraper as the type that epitomized the twentieth century's architecture. See the chapter "The Superblock." In Colquhoun, Alan, *Essays in Architectural Criticism: Modern Architecture and Historical Change*. Cambridge, MA: Opposition Books, MIT Press, 1981, 102.

52 Cited in Taisto, Mäkelä H., "Modernity and the Historical Perspectivism of Nietzsche and Loos." *Journal of Architectural Education*, Vol. 44, No. 3, 1991, 140.

53 Cited in Rykwert, *The Dancing Column*, 23.

54 Rykwert suggests that Loos's idea of extrapolating the skyscraper type from the Doric column may have been influenced by Louis Sullivan's text *The Tall Office Building Artistically Considered*, 1896. See Rykwert, *The Dancing Column*, 22.

55 Cited in Masheck, Joseph, *Adolf Loos: The Art of Architecture*. London: I.B. Tauris, 2013, 167.

56 Essay by Manfredo Tafuri, "The Disenchanted Mountain: The Skyscraper and the City." In Ciucci, Giorgio, *The American City: From the Civil War to the New Deal*. Cambridge, MA: MIT Press, 1979, 173.

57 Cited in Rykwert, *The Dancing Column*, 19.

58 Masheck, *Adolf Loos*, 169.

59 For a thorough examination of Loos's complex consideration of questions such as history and ornamentation, see Leatherbarrow, David, "Interpretation and Abstraction in the Architecture of Adolf Loos." *Journal of Architectural Education*, 1987, 2–9.

60 Loos, Adolf, "Ornament and Crime" (1908). Republished in Conrads, Ulrich, *Programs and Manifestoes on 20th-Century Architecture*. Cambridge, MA: MIT Press, 1970, 19–24.

61 The comments of Arnold Schoenberg about Loos were cited in Gravagnuolo, Benedetto, "Adolf Loos, Theory and Works." *Art Data*, 1995, 19.

62 Cited in Tomkins, *Duchamp: A Biography*, 83.

63 Tafuri commented about the relationship between Loos and various members of the Dada group, such as the poets Georges Besson and Paul Dermée, who translated some of the texts of the Viennese architect. See Tafuri, Manfredo, *Theories and History of Architecture*. Cambridge: Harper & Row, 1976, 35.

64 Cited in Taisto, "Modernity and the Historical Perspectivism," 141.

65 In the chapter "Everybody's Doric," Masheck discusses the difficult relationship between Loos and the modern movement. See Masheck, *Loos*, 147–171.

66 Cited in Rykwert, *The Dancing Column*, 24.

67 Quatremère, *The Historical Dictionary*, 254.

68 Cited in "Eleven Europeans in America," Sweeney, James Johnson (ed.), *The Museum of Modern Art Bulletin*, New York, vol. 13, no. 4/5, 1946, 20.

69 Rossi, Aldo, *The Architecture of the City*. Cambridge, MA: MIT Press, 1982.

70 Venturi, Robert, *Complexity and Contradiction in Architecture*. New York: Museum of Modern Art, 1998.

71 Arnell, P., and T. Bickford, *A View From the Campidoglio: Selected Essays 1953–1984; Robert Venturi and Denise Scott Brown*. Cambridge: Harper & Row, 1984.

72 Venturi, *Complexity and Contradiction*, 19.

73 About the house for his mother, Venturi commented that "maybe Mother's House should be known as Mannerist House." Venturi, Robert, and Denise Scott Brown, *Architecture as Signs and Systems: For a Mannerist Time*. Cambridge, MA: Belknap of Harvard University Press, 2004, 42.

74 From *Online Etymology Dictionary*. www.etymonline.com/index.php?term=ordinary. Accessed November 16, 2014.

**160** Type and Project—Alteration Tactics

75 Venturi, *Complexity and Contradiction*, 42.
76 The visual and conceptual relationship between Duchamp and the contemporary and pop artists is discussed in Kosinski, Dorothy, *Dialogues: Duchamp, Cornell, Johns, Rauschenberg*. New Haven: Yale University Press, 2005.
77 Venturi, Robert, and Denise Scott Brown, *Architecture as Signs and Systems: For a Mannerist Time*. Cambridge, MA: Belknap of Harvard University Press, 2004, 39.
78 Robert Venturi, Denise Scott Brown and Steven Izenour, *Learning From Las Vegas*. Cambridge, MA: MIT Press, 1972, 13.
79 Venturi, Scott Brown and Associates, Inc., "Times Square Plaza Design," description of preliminary design completed in 1984 as provided by VSBA.
80 Rossi, Aldo: "An Analogical Architecture." In Nesbitt, Kate (ed.), *Theorizing a New Agenda for Architecture: An Anthology of Architectural Theory, 1965–1995*. New York: Princeton Architectural, 1996, 348–352.
81 Rossi, "An Analogical Architecture," 348.
82 Rossi, "An Analogical Architecture," 349.
83 Rossi: "An Analogical Architecture," 349.
84 Rossi, Aldo, *A Scientific Autobiography*. Cambridge, MA: MIT Press, 1981, 2.
85 "Introduction" by Peter Eisenman in Rossi, *The Architecture of the City*, 8–9.
86 "Introduction" by Eisenman in Rossi, *The Architecture of the City*, 8–9.
87 Rossi, Aldo, *A Scientific Autobiography*. Cambridge, MA: MIT Press, 1981.
88 Rossi, *A Scientific Autobiography*, 5.
89 Rossi, *A Scientific Autobiography*, 7.
90 Moneo, Rafael, *Theoretical Anxiety and Design Strategies in the Work of Eight Contemporary Architects*. Cambridge, MA: The MIT Press, 2005, 362.
91 Kurt W. Forster, "Houses of the Engadine Valley." In Ursprung, Philip (ed.), *Herzog & de Meuron—Natural History*. Canadian Centre for Architecture & Lars Müller, 2002, 339.
92 From Herzog & de Meuron's website, accessed September 16, 2016, www.herzogdemeuron.com/index/projects/complete-works/326-350/327-porta-volta-fondazione-feltrinelli.html.
93 From Herzog & de Meuron's website, accessed September 16, 2016, www.herzogdemeuron.com/index/projects/complete-works/326-350/327-porta-volta-fondazione-feltrinelli.html.
94 Jacques Derrida describes the iconic silhouette of the "little house" as a collective construction, what turns it into a "metaphor of a metaphor: an expropriation, a being-outside-one's-own-residence, but still a dwelling, outside its own residence but still in a residence in which one comes back to oneself, recognizes oneself, reassembles oneself or resembles oneself, outside oneself in oneself." See Derrida, Jacques, *Margins of Philosophy*. Chapter "White Mythology: Metaphor in the Text of Philosophy." Chicago: University of Chicago Press, 1982, 253.
95 Forster, "Houses of the Engadine Valley," 346.
96 Forster, "Houses of the Engadine Valley," 346.
97 Comment by Jacques Herzog in *De Zeen* magazine, www.dezeen.com/2012/11/14/parrish-art-museum-by-herzog-de-meuron-2/. Accessed December 16, 2014.

# AFTERWORD

*It is self-evident that nothing concerning art is self-evident anymore, not its inner life, not its relation to the world, not even its right to exist.*

—Theodor Adorno[1]

Any discussion on the concept of type within the framework of architectural discourse should take into account the inaugural definitions by Quatremère de Quincy. There are two important issues that define the influence of Quatremère's conception of type on posterior generations. In the first place, it is remarkable that in just four pages[2] he managed to introduce a term of such complexity and sophistication, the narrative sliding from terminological definition to dialectical reasoning, from theoretical speculation to historical references. The other characteristic of Quatremère's definition of type is the utter *ambiguity* of many of his comments and thoughts. One might speculate that the continuous relevance of his theoretical corpus resides partly in the vagueness of his definitions, a prose that seems to invite—and demand—continual examinations and reinterpretations.

As discussed in Chapter 1, my primary understanding of the concept of type is based on readings of Quatremère de Quincy, who defined the term as: (1) the *origins* of architecture; (2) an instrument for *classification* of buildings; (3) related to the process of *imitation* or *mimesis*. Quatremère's definition of type as a *polysemic* term derives from three main sources: his 1785 (revised in 1803) essay on the origins of architecture, *De l'architecture Égyptienne*,[3] his 1823 essay, *De l'imitation*,[4] and his entry "Type" in the 1825 edition of the *Encyclopédie Méthodique*.[5] Quatremère's conception of type explains the complexity of any discussion of the subject, and the necessity of a continuous reevaluation.

Among the three meanings proposed by Quatremère, this study focused on the consideration of type as a process of *imitation*, which, in the Aristotelian sense,

**162** Afterword

implies the adoption and subsequent transformation of preexisting forms. The progression contemplates the passage between the knowledge and analysis of past forms, the selection of certain precedent, and the creation of new iterations derived from those preexisting forms. The history of art can therefore be interpreted as a continuous process of alteration of forms, where each generation adopts and transforms the typologies and iconographic vocabularies inherited from the previous generation: mannerism, for instance, adopts and transforms the Renaissance types; the Baroque undertakes a similar action with the mannerist forms, and so on.

The notion of developing the architectural project under the spectrum of type, which appears to be an almost universal condition, was intensively challenged by the rise of modern architecture. During the first decades of the twentieth century, avant-garde groups such as suprematism and de Stijl advocated a total rejection of all historical manifestations of art and architecture. The architectural project was approached as a *tabula rasa*, a blank and untainted sheet allowing for all kinds of formal and iconographic inventions. Rather than offering alternate design strategies, avant-garde groups proposed the cancelation of all artistic methodologies—a notion later consolidated as a modernist canon. As noted by Alan Colquhoun,[6] this position resulted in one of the major deficits of modern architecture: the lack of a methodological strategy for the realization of the architectural project. The question is particularly relevant if one considers the Bauhaus, a paradigmatic attempt to disseminate modernity through education by proposing a full integration of the arts and crafts. In spite of having a remarkable group of teachers—including some of the most celebrated modern artists, architects, and designers, of whom many had great interest in pedagogy—the Bauhaus was not able to advance a design strategy transmittable to the following generation of architects.[7]

Parallel to avant-garde and Bauhaus-related initiatives, an alternative path was explored by other early modern architects sharing a notable interest in utilitarian constructions, such as warehouses, factories, and grain elevators. With this initially casual, though later conscious gesture, this group of modern pioneers proposed dissolving the distinction between "high" and "low" architecture. The following step towards reassessing conventional architectural vocabulary was the consideration of typological and iconographic precedents derived from industrial machineries, such as automobiles, airplanes, and ocean liners—a question initially explored by the Italian futurists and later discussed and developed by Le Corbusier.

Beyond the question of selection of precedents, modern architecture's consideration of design methodology faced a more complex challenge. It soon became (tacitly) accepted that the "new" architecture should not continue appealing to traditional design strategies, such as the selection and formal alteration of types. Just like the pioneers of modernism managed to deploy a formal, spatial, and iconographic vocabulary with high doses of originality, why not expect that those same masters, or other innovators, would develop novel design strategies? Modernism's principal response was the development of the *prototype*, a method of standardization and integration of building units allowing limitless repetition. The prototype constitutes a paradoxical moment in modern architecture. On the one hand, it conveyed practical and ethical justifications: mass production appeared as the single option for developing efficient and economic collective housing. On the other hand, it was a reversal of one of the principal canons of modernity: the sheer originality of the artistic project.

To summarize, in the development of modern architecture, one can detect three design strategies. First, the search for formal invention, an approach that demands continuous generation of new and unprecedented solutions. While this position was initially advanced by early avant-garde groups, it was later validated by some of modernism's most paradigmatic projects, such as *Fallingwater*, by Frank Lloyd Wright, and the chapel of *Notre Dame du Haut*, by Le Corbusier. The second strategy was the prototype, initially used as a solution for developing collective housing, though soon adapted to other programs demanding standardized and normalized designs, such as office buildings and factories. And finally, the strategy that epitomizes modernism's ambivalent and contradictory position towards design methodology: the typological project.

Establishing a discussion on the typological project in modern architecture faces the difficulty that the overwhelming majority of modern critics and architects avoided any explicit mentioning of the term "type." As discussed in Chapter 3, a resultant incongruity was that many of the most emblematic projects by the principal pioneers of modern architecture[8] were developed appealing to typologically driven mechanisms, though simultaneously, the term "type" had been surreptitiously canceled from modern vocabulary.

Partially responding to modern architecture's methodological "vacuum," in the 1960s the concept of type was (re)introduced both as an instrument for considering the relationship between architecture and history and as the originator and propellant of the architectural project. Influenced by Quatremère's precisions, Giulio Carlo Argan argued that the architectural project could be developed through the process of selecting and altering typological antecedents. While the strategy advanced by Quatremère largely derives from the Aristotelian doctrine of mimesis, the range of precedents (i.e., the types to be selected) and the alteration mechanisms, argued Argan, are meant to be continuously reassessed. Seeking to clarify what he assumes may be modernism's main "prejudice" against type, Argan established a clear differentiation between the notions of type and style—that is, between form and ornamentation. The notion of type, he concludes, can become a determinant factor for the continual development of the modern movement.

Despite the "olive branch" offered by Argan, a camp of Italian historians and architects aligned with modernism, including Bruno Zevi, Leonardo Benevolo, and Giancarlo de Carlo, expressed an absolute rejection towards the presence of type in the architectural project. Historian Bruno Zevi launched the feud by harshly criticizing Argan's article, stating that "art is anti-typological, all architectural creation is inevitably the artist's individual interpretation, and it is style that defines type."[9] Soon after, this group of thinkers initiated a "counter-reaction" against the consideration of type in the design process, arguing its presence constitutes a deviation from modern architecture's fundamental principles.

**164** Afterword

Since the 1960s "Italian quarrel" and continuing to today, there are two opposed and irreconcilable positions on the concept of type. On the one hand, this study discussed critics and architects such as Aldo Rossi, Anthony Vidler, Alan Colquhoun, Rafael Moneo, Jean Castex, Álvaro Siza, and Herzog & de Meuron, as well as younger figures, such as Leandro Madrazo, Fernando Diez, Marina Lathouri,[10] Sam Jacoby,[11] and Hyungmin Pai,[12] who, while possessing different approaches, coincide by accepting the presence of type in the architectural project. On the other hand, contemporary architects and critics such as Tomas Maldonado,[13] Peter Eisenman,[14] Jeffrey Kipnis,[15] and Patrik Schumacher[16] have vehemently rejected any consideration of type as a design mechanism. As stated earlier, their positions are reminiscent of early twentieth-century avant-garde statements by Kazimir Malevich and Theo van Doesburg, who, for the first time in history, proposed a total rejection of any consideration of past forms and images.

★

This work discussed two interrelated questions. First, it argued in favor of an "expansive" understanding of the notion of typological precedent, not just a synthesis derived from a determined group of buildings, but also the possibility of considering as "types" all kinds of preexisting forms and elements sharing certain common features. In these terms, the fundamental condition of type lies in semblance and repeatability. Following the reevaluation of the notion of typological precedent, this study shifted towards the identification of the principal typological alteration mechanisms, such as *distortion*, *alteration of scale*, *juxtaposition*, *substitution*, *repetition*, and *displacement*. The typological project, therefore, operates as a procedure of selection and transformation, whereby the architect determines the point of departure and immerses into the process of creating new typological instances.

Among the listed tactics, typological repetition and displacement appear as the most enigmatic and perplexing. As noted by Gilles Deleuze, the notion of displacement implies the action of repetition, in itself an impossibility since two objects cannot occupy the same place and at the same time: "Does not the paradox of repetition lie in the fact that one can speak of repetition only by virtue of the change or difference that it introduces into the mind which contemplates it?"[17] The variation of meaning, therefore, is achieved through the repositioning of the object.

Procuring a better understanding of these questions, the last portion of this study discussed the affinities between typological displacement and the readymade as conceived by Marcel Duchamp—a correspondence settling the analogies between the notions of type and object. Revisiting Duchamp evokes the possibility of the *other* side of modernism, one that breaks away with formal and "optical" conceptions of art, instead reintroducing questions of language, meaning, voyeurism, humor, and erotism. It is within this context that one can observe how much of contemporary architecture appears fixated on the ambition of perpetually creating new and original forms, therefore proposing a marginalization of type in the architectural project. This position, which presumes building forms devoid of meaning, neglects the power of *desire*, *analogy*, *allegory*, *metonymy*, and *metaphor*. As posited by Alberto

Pérez-Gómez, "The poetic and critical dimension of architecture, like other relevant artistic products, addresses the questions that truly matter for our humanity in culturally specific terms, revealing an enigma behind everyday events and objects."[18]

The correspondences between typological displacement and readymade—and by extension, between Duchamp's works and ideas and the architectural project—introduce a final subject: the inevitable correlation between art and architecture. Passages of contemporary art, particularly those influenced by Duchamp's spell, reveal that the conception of an artwork is not necessarily—or exclusively—the gestation of new forms, but that it can also contemplate a range of mimetic tactics, such as *collage, assemblage, tableaux, combine*, and *readymade*. As demonstrated by the listed artistic tactics, the conception of the artwork doesn't necessarily depend on formalistic manipulations; the variations of meanings can be achieved through the selection, disposition, and displacement of conventional elements. Those artistic tactics suggest unexpected affinities with the notion of type, which like infinite echoes of Quatremère's originating statements, continues to be an elusive and evocative concept.

## Notes

1 Adorno, Theodor, *Aesthetic Theory*. London: A&C Black, 2013, 1.

2 Quatremère de Quincy and Samir Younés, *The Historical Dictionary of Architecture of Quatremère De Quincy*. London: Andreas Papadakis, 1999, 254–257.

3 Quatremère de Quincy and Antoine Chrysostôme, *De l'architecture égyptienne: considerée dans son origine, ses principes et son gout et comparée sous les mêmes rapports à l'architecture grecque*. Paris, 1803.

4 Quatremère de Quincy and Antoine Chrysostôme, *An Essay on the Nature, the End, and the Means of Imitation in the Fine Arts*. London: Smith, Elder, Cornhill, 1837.

5 Quatremère, *The Historical Dictionary of Architecture*, 254–257.

6 Colquhoun, Alan, "Typology and Design Method." In Nesbitt, Kate (ed.), *Theorizing a New Agenda for Architecture: An Anthology of Architectural Theory, 1965–1995*. New York: Princeton Architectural, 1996, 250–257.

7 As noted by Alan Colquhoun, the single modern architect who developed a set of "architectural rules for the new architecture" was Le Corbusier. Either through the "regulating lines," the "five points," or the implementation of the "Modulor," throughout his career Le Corbusier demonstrated a persistent interest in articulating a design methodology that could be transmitted to a next generation of architects. See Colquhoun, Alan, "Displacement of Concepts in Le Corbusier," in *Essays in Architectural Criticism: Modern Architecture and Historical Change*. Opposition Books. Cambridge, MA: MIT Press, 1981, 51.

8 In Chapter 3 I referred to some of the principal essays discussing how the most celebrated modern architects (e.g., Wright, Le Corbusier, Mies, and Aalto) appealed to typologically driven mechanisms.

9 Cited in Castex, Jean, "Saverio Muratori (1910–1973), The City as the Only Model: A Critical Study, a Century After Muratori's Birth." In Cavallo, Roberto and Susanne Komossa (eds.), *New Urban Configurations*. Amsterdam: IOS, under the imprint Delft University Press, 2014, 24.

10 Lathouri, Marina, "The City as Project." *Architectural Design*, Volume 81, Issue 1, 2011, 24–31. Special Issue: Typological Urbanism: Projective Cities.

11 Jacoby, Sam, "Typal and Typological Reasoning: A Diagrammatic Practice of Architecture," *The Journal of Architecture*, 2015, Vol. 20, No. 6, 938–961. DOI: 10.1080/13602365.2015.1116104.

**166** Afterword

12 Pai, Hyungmin, "The Diagrammatic Construction of Type," *The Journal of Architecture*, 2015, Vol. 20, No. 6, 1088–1104. DOI: 10.1080/13602365.2015.1117508.

13 Chapter 4 discusses Alan Colquhoun's essay, which quotes Tomas Maldonado defining type as "a cancer in the body of the solution." See Colquhoun, Alan, "Typology and Design Method." In Nesbitt, Kate (ed.), *Theorizing a New Agenda for Architecture: An Anthology of Architectural Theory, 1965–1995*. New York: Princeton Architectural, 1996, 254.

14 Peter Eisenman justifies his preference of the diagram over the type: "While type moves towards abstraction, it does so in a way that reduces the model, the copy, or the original. The diagram, on the other hand, contains more than the model. The type and the diagram are two different conditions of abstraction: type, the abstraction of a reduction to a normalization, and diagram, the abstraction that may generate into something more than the thing itself, and thus potentially overcome normalization." See "Diagrams of Anteriority." In Eisenman, Peter (ed.), *Diagram Diaries*, New York: Universe, 1999, 41.

15 Jeffrey Kipnis, a contemporary critic aligned with Peter Eisenman, challenged the relevance of type in the architectural project. He famously stated, "Diagrams underwrite all typological theories." See Kipnis, Jeffrey, "Re-originating Diagrams." In Eisenman, Peter, *Feints*. Silvio Cassarà (Ed.), Milan: Skira, 2006, 196.

16 In his "Parametricist Manifesto," Patrik Schumacher (principal of Zaha Hadid Architects) lists "familiar typologies" as a "condition" to be avoided: "Negative heuristics: avoid familiar typologies, avoid platonic/hermetic objects, avoid clear-cut zones/territories, avoid repetition, avoid straight lines, avoid right angles, avoid corners, . . . and most importantly: do not add or subtract without elaborate interarticulations." See "Parametricism as Style—Parametricist Manifesto," Presented and discussed at the Dark Side Club, 11th Architecture Biennale, Venice 2008, www.patrikschumacher.com/Texts/Parametricism%20as%20Style.htm. Accessed November 16, 2016.

17 Deleuze, Gilles, *Difference and Repetition*. Columbia University Press, 1994, 70.

18 Pérez-Gómez, Alberto, "The Relevance of Beauty in Architecture." In Emmons, Paul, John Hendrix and Jane Lomholt: *The Cultural Role of Architecture*. Oxon: Routledge, 2012, 165.

# BIBLIOGRAPHY

Ackerman, James S., *The Architecture of Michelangelo*. Chicago: University of Chicago Press, 1986.

Ackerman, James S., *Origins, Imitation, Conventions: Representation in the Visual Arts*. Cambridge, MA: MIT Press, 2002.

Adorno, Theodor W., *Aesthetic Theory*. London: Continuum, 2002.

Agrest, Diana & Mario Gandelsonas, *Agrest and Gandelsonas: Works*. Princeton: Princeton Architectural, 1995.

Alexander, Christopher, Sara Ishikawa, & Murray Silverstein, *A Pattern Language: Towns, Buildings, Construction*. New York: Oxford UP, 1977.

Argan, Giulio Carlo, *La arquitectura barroca en Italia*. Buenos Aires: Nueva Visión, 1984.

Argan, Giulio Carlo, "On the Typology of Architecture." In Nesbitt, Kate (ed.): *Theorizing a New Agenda for Architecture: An Anthology of Architectural Theory, 1965–1995*. New York: Princeton Architectural, 1996, 242–246.

Aristotle, *Rhetoric and Poetics*. New York: The Modern Library, 1954.

Arnell, Peter, Ted Bickford, Vincent Scully, & José Rafael Moneo, *Aldo Rossi, Buildings and Projects*. New York: Rizzoli, 1985.

Auerbach, Erich, *Mimesis: The Representation of Reality in Western Literature*. Princeton: Princeton University Press, 1953.

Aureli, Pier Vittorio, *The Project of Autonomy: Politics and Architecture Within and Against Capitalism*. New York: Princeton Architectural Press, 2008.

Banham, Reyner, *A Concrete Atlantis: U.S. Industrial Building and European Modern Architecture, 1900–1925*. Cambridge, MA: MIT Press, 1989.

Banham, Reyner, *Theory and Design in the First Machine Age*. Cambridge, MA: MIT Press, 1992.

Bandini, Micha, "Typology as a Form of Convention." *AA Files, No. 6* (May 1984), 73–82.

Barthes, Roland, *Elements of Semiology*. New York: Hill and Wang, 1968.

Baudrillard, Jean & Francesco Proto, *Mass, Identity, Architecture: Architectural Writings of Jean Baudrillard*. Chichester: Wiley Academy, 2003.

Benjamin, Andrew, *Art Mimesis and the Avant-Garde—Aspects of a Philosophy of Difference*, London: Routledge, 2005.

**168** Bibliography

Benjamin, Walter, "The Work of Art in the Age of Mechanical Reproduction." In Arendt, Hannah (ed.): *Illuminations*. New York: Schocken Books, 1969.

Benjamin, Walter & Rolf Tiedemann, *The Arcades Project*. Cambridge: Harvard University Press, 1999.

Bergdoll, Barry & Werner Oechslin (editors), *Fragments Architecture and the Unfinished*. London: Thames & Hudson, 2006.

Bonta, Juan Pablo, *Architecture and Its Interpretation: A Study of Expressive Systems in Architecture*. London: Lund Humphries, 1979.

Boullée, Etienne-Louis & J. M. Pérouse de Montclos (ed.), *Architecture: Essai sur l'art*. Paris: Hermann, 1968.

Braham, Allan, *The Architecture of the French Enlightenment*. Berkeley, CA: University of California Press, 1980. Brownlee, David H. & David Gilson De Long, *Louis I. Kahn: In the Realm of Architecture*. Los Angeles, CA: Universe, 1997.

Brownlee, David Bruce, Robert Venturi, & Denise Scott Brown, *Out of the Ordinary: Robert Venturi, Denise Scott Brown and Associates: Architecture, Urbanism, Design*. Philadelphia, PA: Philadelphia Museum of Art in Association with Yale University Press, 2001.

Bürger, Peter, *Theory of the Avant-garde*. Minneapolis: University of Minnesota, 1984.

Cabanne, Pierre & Marcel Duchamp, *Dialogues With Marcel Duchamp*. New York: Da Capo, 1987.

Castex, Jean, *Frank Lloyd Wright, Le Printemps de la Prairie House*. Liège: P. Mardaga, 1985.

Cavallo, Roberto, Susanne Komossa, Nicola Marzot, Meta Berghauser Pont, & Joran Kuijper, *New Urban Configurations*. Amsterdam: IOS, under the Imprint Delft UP, 2014.

Chareau, Pierre, Marc Vellay, & Kenneth Frampton, *Pierre Chareau: Architect and Craftsman*. London: Thames and Hudson, 1990.

Cohen, Jean-Louis, *The Future of Architecture, Since 1889*. London: Phaidon, 2012.

Cohen, Jean-Louis, *Scenes of the World to Come: European Architecture and the American Challenge, 1893–1960*. Paris: Flammarion and the Canadian Centre for Architecture, 1995.

Collins, Peter, *Changing Ideals in Modern Architecture, 1750–1950*. London: Faber and Faber, 1965.

Colomina, Beatriz, "Le Corbusier and Duchamp: The Uneasy Status of the Object." In Mäkelä, Taisto H. & Wallis Miller (ed.): *Wars of Classification: Architecture and Modernity*. New York: Princeton Architectural, 1991, 37–47.

Colquhoun, Alan, *Essays in Architectural Criticism: Modern Architecture and Historical Change*. Opposition Books. Cambridge, MA: MIT Press, 1981.

Colquhoun, Alan, *Modernity and the Classical Tradition: Architectural Essays, 1980–1987*. Cambridge, MA: MIT Press, 1989.

Colquhoun, Alan, "Typology and Design Method." In Nesbitt, Kate (ed.): *Theorizing a New Agenda for Architecture: An Anthology of Architectural Theory, 1965–1995*. New York: Princeton Architectural, 1996, 250–257.

Comas, Carlos Eduardo, *"Ideología Modernista y Enseñanza de Arquitectura."* Buenos Aires: Ideas en arte y Arquitectura, 1986.

Comas, Carlos Eduardo, *"Pampulla y la arquitectura moderna brasileña."* Buenos Aires: Summa +, 2006.

Comas, Carlos Eduardo, *"Precisões: Arquitetura Moderna Brasileira 1936–45."* Porto Alegre: PROPAR, 2002.

Comas, Carlos Eduardo, "Prototipo, monumento, *un* ministerio, el ministerio." Chapter of Perez Oyarzun, and Pedro Bannen Lanata, *Le Corbusier y Sudamérica: Viajes y Proyectos*. Santiago De Chile: Ediciones ARQ, 1991.

Conrads, Ulrich (ed.), *Programs and Manifestoes on 20th-Century Architecture*. Cambridge, MA: MIT Press, 1994.

Corona Martínez, Alfonso, *The Architectural Project*. Texas A & M University Press, 2003.

## Bibliography 169

Corona Martínez, Alfonso, *O Problema dos Elementos na Arquitetura do Século XX*. Unpublished Doctoral Thesis. Universidade Federal de Rio Grande do Sul, Facultade de Arquitetura, PROPAR, 2003.

D'Harnoncourt, Anne, *Marcel Duchamp*. Munich: Prestel, 1989.

Deleuze, Gilles, *Difference and Repetition*. New York: Columbia University Press, 1994.

Deleuze, Gilles, "Plato and the Simulacrum." *October, Vol. 27*. Cambridge, MA: MIT Press, 1983.

Derrida, Jacques: *Margins of Philosophy*. Chicago: University of Chicago Press, 1982.

Diez, Fernando, *Buenos Aires y algunas constantes en las transformaciones urbanas*. Buenos Aires: Editorial de Belgrano, 1996.

Diez, Fernando, *Crisis de Autenticidad: Cambios en los Modos de Producción de la Arquitectura Argentina*. Buenos Aires: Donn S.A., 2008.

Diller, Elizabeth & Ricardo Scofidio, *Flesh, Architectural Probes*. New York: Princeton Architectural Press, 2011.

Di Palma, Vittoria, "Architecture, Environment and Emotion: Quatremère de Quincy and the Concept of Character," *AA Files 47*, 2002.

Dos Santos, Jose Paulo & Wilfred Wang (editors), *Alvaro Siza Poetic Profession*. New York: Rizzoli, 1986.

Drexler, Arthur & Richard Chafee, *The Architecture of the École des Beaux-Arts*. New York: Museum of Modern Art, 1977.

Duany, Andres, Elizabeth Plater-Zyberk, & Robert Alminana, *The New Civic Art: Elements of Town Planning*. New York: Rizzoli, 2003.

Duany, Andres, Elizabeth Plater-Zyberk, & Jeff Speck, *Suburban Nation: The Rise of Sprawl and the Decline of the American Dream*. New York: North Point Press, 2001.

Duboy, Philippe, *Lequeu, An Architectural Enigma*. Cambridge, MA: MIT Press, 1987.

Duchamp, Marcel (Michel Sanouillet & Elmer Peterson eds.), *The Writings of Marcel Duchamp*. New York: Da Capo Press, 1973.

Duchamp, Marcel, Elena Filipovic, & Gonzalo Aguilar Moisés, *Marcel Duchamp: Una Obra Que No Es Una Obra "de Arte."* Buenos Aires: Fundación Proa, 2008.

Duchamp, Marcel, Richard Hamilton & Ece Bonk, *a l'infinitif (The White Box)*. New York: Cordier & Ekstrom, 1999. Durand, Jean-Nicolas-Louis, *Précis of the Lectures on Architecture; With, Graphic Portion of the Lectures on Architecture*. Los Angeles, CA: Getty Research Institute, 2000.

Eco, Umberto, "Function and Sign: The Semiotics of Architecture." In Leach, Neil (ed.): *Rethinking Architecture: A Reader in Cultural Theory*. London: Routledge, 1997.

Eco, Umberto, *La Estructura Ausente, Introducción a la Semiótica*. Buenos Aires: Editorial Lumen, 1968.

Egbert, Donald Drew, *The Beaux-Arts Tradition in French Architecture*. Princeton: Princeton University Press, 1980.

Eisenman, Peter, *Diagram Diaries*. New York: Universe, 1999.

Eisenman, Peter, "The End of the Beginning, the End of the End," *Perspecta, Vol. 21*, 1984.

Eisenman, Peter, *Written Into the Void: Selected Writings, 1990–2004*. New Haven, CT: Yale University Press, 2007.

Eisenman, Peter & Silvio Cassarà, *Peter Eisenman—Feints*. Milan: Skira, 2006.

Eisenman, Peter, Rosalind E. Krauss, & Manfredo Tafuri, *Houses of Cards*. New York: Oxford University Press, 1987.

Etlin, Richard A., *Frank Lloyd Wright and Le Corbusier: The Romantic Legacy*. Manchester: Manchester University Press, 1994.

Etlin, Richard A., *Symbolic Space: French Enlightenment Architecture and Its Legacy*. Chicago: The University of Chicago Press, 1996.

**170** Bibliography

Evers, Bernd & Christof Thoenes, *Architectural Theory: From the Renaissance to the Present: 89 Essays on 117 Treatises*. Köln: Taschen, 2003.

Fleming, Paul, *Exemplarity and Mediocrity: The Art of the Average From Bourgeois Tragedy to Realism*. Stanford, CA: Stanford UP, 2009.

Forty, Adrian, *Words and Buildings: A Vocabulary of Modern Architecture*. New York: Thames & Hudson, 2000.

Foster, Hal (ed.), *The Anti-Aesthetic. Essays on Postmodern Culture*. Port Townsend, WA: Bay Press, 1987.

Foster, Hal, *The Return of the Real: The Avant-garde at the End of the Century*. Cambridge, MA: MIT Press, 1996.

Frampton, Kenneth, *Alvaro Siza—Complete Works*. London: Phaidon Press, 2000.

Frampton, Kenneth, *Le Corbusier*. London: Thames & Hudson, 2001.

Frampton, Kenneth, *Modern Architecture: A Critical History*. London: Thames and Hudson, 1985.

Frampton, Kenneth & John Cava, *Studies in Tectonic Culture: The Poetics of Construction in Nineteenth and Twentieth Century Architecture*. Chicago, IL: Graham Foundation for Advanced Studies in the Fine Arts, 2001.

Frascari, Marco, *Monsters of Architecture: Anthropomorphism in Architectural Theory*, Savage, MD: Rowman & Littlefield, 1991.

Gehry, Frank O., Peter Arnell, Ted Bickford, Germano Celant, & Mason Andrews, *Frank Gehry, Buildings and Projects*. New York: Rizzoli, 1985.

Gombrich, E. H, *Art and Illusion: A Study in the Psychology of Pictorial Representation*. New York: Pantheon, 1960.

Gombrich, E. H., *New Light on Old Masters*. Chicago: University of Chicago Press, 1986.

Gombrich, E. H., *Symbolic Images: Studies in the Art of the Renaissance*. London: Phaidon, 1972.

Gorelik, Adrián, *La Grilla y El Parque: Espacio Público y Cultura Urbana en Buenos Aires, 1887–1936*. Buenos Aires: Universidad Nacional De Quilmes, 1998.

Gropius, Walter, *Scope of Total Architecture*. New York: Collier Books, 1962.

Haralambidou, Penelope, *Marcel Duchamp and the Architecture of Desire*. London: Ashgate, 2013.

Hays, K. Michael, *Architecture Theory Since 1968*. Cambridge, MA: MIT Press, 2015.

Hays, K. Michael, *Unprecedented Realism: The Architecture of Machado and Silvetti*. New York: Princeton Architectural, 1995.

Herrmann, Wolfgang, *Gottfried Semper: In Search of Architecture*. Cambridge, MA: MIT Press, 1984.

Herrmann, Wolfgang, *Laugier and Eighteenth Century French Theory*. London: A. Zwemmer, 1962.

Herrmann, Wolfgang, *The Theory of Claude Perrault*. London: A. Zwemmer, 1973.

Hitchcock, Henry-Russell, *Architecture: Nineteenth and Twentieth Centuries*. New York: Penguin Books, 1977.

Hitchcock, Henry-Russell, *Painting Toward Architecture*. New York: Duell, Sloan and Pearce, 1948.

Holl, Steve, "Rural and Urban House Types," (1983). *Pamphlet Architecture 1–10*. New York: Princeton Architectural Press, 1998.

Hubbard, Bill, *A Theory for Practice: Architecture in Three Discourses*. Cambridge, MA: MIT, 1995.

Hvattum, Mari, *Gottfried Semper and the Problem of Historicism*. Cambridge: Cambridge UP, 2004.

Ingraham, Catherine, *Architecture and the Burdens of Linearity*. New Haven, CT: Yale University Press, 1998.

Jacobs, Jane, *The Death and Life of Great American Cities*. New York: Vintage, 1992.

## Bibliography **171**

Jacoby, Sam, *The Reasoning of Architecture—Type and the Problem of Historicity*. Unpublished Doctoral Thesis, Technischen Universität Berlin, 2013.

Judovitz, Dalia, *Drawing on Art. Duchamp & Company*. Minneapolis: University of Minnesota Press, 2010.

Judovitz, Dalia, *Unpacking Duchamp: Art in Transit*. Berkeley: University of California Press, 1998.

Kahn, Andrea, "Is Like, Is Not: Towards a Non Oppressive Interpretation of the Concept of Type." In Rockcastle, Garth (ed.): *Type and the (Im) Possibilities of Convention*. Midgård Monographs, 1991.

Kaufmann, Emil, *Architecture in the Age of Reason; Baroque and Post-baroque in England, Italy, and France*. Hamden, CT: Archon, 1966.

Kaufmann, Emil, *Étienne-Louis Boullée*. New York: College Art Association of America, 1939.

Kaufmann, Emil, *Three Revolutionary Architects: Boullée, Ledoux, and Lequeu*. Philadelphia: American Philosophical Society, 1952.

Kipnis, Jeffrey, "The Cunning of Cosmetics." *Madrid: El Croquis 60*, 1996.

Kipnis, Jeffrey, "Twisting the Separatrix." *Assemblage, No. 14*, 1991.

Koolhaas, Rem, Bruce Mau, Jennifer Sigler, & Hans Werlemann, *Small, Medium, Large, Extralarge*. New York: Monacelli Press, 1998.

Kosinski, Doris, *Dialogues. Duchamp, Cornell, Johns, Rauchemberg*. New Haven, CT: Yale University Press, 2005.

Kosuth, Joseph, *Art After Philosophy and After: Collected Writings, 1966–1990*. Cambridge, MA: MIT Press, 1991.

Krauss, Rosalind, *The Originality of the Avant-Garde and Other Modernist Myths*. Cambridge, MA: MIT Press, 1985.

Krauss, Rosalind, *Passages in Modern Sculpture*. Cambridge, MA: MIT Press, 1989.

Krauss, Rosalind, *A Voyage on the North Sea: Art in the Age of the Post-Medium Condition*. London: Thames & Hudson, 2000.

Kubler, George, *The Shape of Time: Remarks on the History of Things*. New Haven, CT: Yale University Press, 1962.

Lathouri, Marina, "The City as Project." *Architectural Design*, Volume 81, Issue 1, 2011, 24–31.

Laugier, Marc-Antoine, *An Essay on Architecture*. Los Angeles: Hennessey & Ingalls, 1977.

Lavin, Silvia, *Quatremère de Quincy and the Invention of a Modern Language of Architecture*. Cambridge, MA: MIT Press, 1992.

Leach, Neil (ed.), *Rethinking Architecture: A Reader in Cultural Theory*. London: Psychology Press, 1997.

Leatherbarrow, David, *Architecture Oriented Otherwise*. New York: Princeton Architectural, 2009.

Leatherbarrow, David, "Interpretation and Abstraction in the Architecture of Adolf Loos." *Journal of Architectural Education*, Volume 40, Issue 4, 1987.

Leatherbarrow, David, *The Roots of Architectural Invention: Site, Enclosure, Materials*. Cambridge: Cambridge University Press, 1993.

Leatherbarrow, David, *Uncommon Ground: Architecture, Technology, and Topography*. Cambridge, MA: MIT Press, 2000.

Le Corbusier, *Towards a New Architecture*. New York: Dover, 1986.

Le Corbusier (& Ivan Žaknić, ed.), *Journey to the East*. Cambridge, MA: MIT Press, 1987.

Lee, Christopher C. M. & Sam Jacoby, *Typological Urbanism: Projective Cities*. Chichester: Wiley, 2011.

Lee, Pamela, *Object to Be Destroyed, The Work of Gordon Matta-Clark*. Cambridge, MA: MIT Press, 2000.

**172** Bibliography

Loos, Adolf, "Ornament and Crime" (1908). From Conrads, Ulrich: *Programs and Manifestoes on 20th-century Architecture*. Cambridge, MA: MIT Press, 1970.

Lyotard, Jean-François, *Duchamp's TRANS/formers*. Leuven, Belgium: Universitaire Pers Leuven, 2010.

Madrazo, Leandro, *The Concept of Type in Architecture: An Inquiry Into the Nature of Architectural Form*. Unpublished Doctoral Thesis. Swiss Federal Institute of Technology, 1995.

Madrazzo, Leandro, "Durand and the Science of Architecture." *Journal of Architectural Education*, Taylor & Francis, 1994. DOI: 10.2307/1425306.

Mahar-Keplinger, Lisa, *Grain Elevators*. New York: Princeton Architectural, 1993.

Mäkelä, Taisto H. & Wallis Miller, *Wars of Classification: Architecture and Modernity: Proceedings of the Colloquium "Reinterpreting Modernism" Held at the School of Architecture, Princeton University*. New York: Princeton Architectural, 1991.

Mallgrave, Harry Francis (ed.), *Architectural Theory: An Anthology From Vitruvius to 1870*. Malden, MA: Blackwell, 2006.

Mallgrave, Harry Francis, *Gottfried Semper: Architect of the Nineteenth Century*. New Haven, CT: Yale University Press, 1996.

Mallgrave, Harry Francis, *Modern Architectural Theory: A Historical Survey, 1673–1968*. Cambridge: Cambridge University Press, 2009.

Martí Arís, Carlos, *Las Variaciones de la identidad: ensayo sobre el tipo en arquitectura*. Barcelona: Fundación Arquia, D.L, 2014.

Masheck, Joseph, *Adolf Loos the Art of Architecture*. London: I.B. Tauris, 2013.

Masheck, Joseph (ed.): *Marcel Duchamp in Perspective*. New York: Da Capo Press, 2002.

McLeod, Mary, "Order in the Details, Tumult in the Whole?—Composition and Fragmentation in Le Corbusier's Architecture." In Bergdoll, Barry & Werner Oechslin (eds.): *Fragments Architecture and the Unfinished: Essays Presented to Robin Middleton*. London: Thames & Hudson, 2006.

Mendelsohn, Erich, *Amerika*. New York: Dover, 1993.

Meninato, Pablo, "(Dis) Assembling: Duchamp and Architecture." Marinic, Gregory & Mary-Jo Schlachter (eds.): *d3 dialog >assemble*. D3, 2012.

Meninato, Pablo, "Duchamp y la arquitectura." *Summa+ #104*, 2009.

Meninato, Pablo, "Tipología y proceso de diseño." *Summa+ #80*, 2006.

Middleton, Robin (ed.), *The Beaux-arts and Nineteenth-century French Architecture*. Cambridge, MA: MIT Press, 1982.

Moneo, Rafael, "Aldo Rossi: The Idea of Architecture and the Modena Cemetery." *Oppositions 5*, 1976, 107–125.

Moneo, José Rafael, "On Typology." *Oppositions 13*. Cambridge, MA: MIT Press, 1978.

Moneo, José Rafael, *Theoretical Anxiety and Design Strategies in the Work of Eight Contemporary Architects*. Cambridge, MA: MIT Press, 2004.

Moos, Stanislaus Von, *Le Corbusier, Elements of a Synthesis*. Cambridge, MA: MIT Press, 1979.

Muratori, Saverio, *Studi per una operante storia urbana di Venezia*. Rome: Instituto poligrafico dello Stato, Libreria dello Stato, 1959.

Nesbitt, Kate (ed.), *Theorizing a New Agenda for Architecture: An Anthology of Architectural Theory, 1965–1995*. New York: Princeton Architectural, 1996.

Nietzsche, Friedrich, *On the Genealogy of Morals*. New York: Knopf Doubleday, 2010.

Oechslin, Werner, "Premises for the Resumption of the Discussion of Typology." *Assemblage No. 1*. Cambridge: MIT Press, 1986.

Oppenheimer Dean, Andrea & Timothy Hursley, *Rural Studio: Samuel Mockbee and an Architecture of Decency*. New York: Princeton Architectural Press, 2002.

Pai, Hyungmin, *The Portfolio and the Diagram: Architecture, Discourse, and Modernity in America*. Cambridge, MA: MIT Press, 2002.

Panerai, Philippe, Jean Castex, Jean-Charles Depaule, & Ivor Samuels, *Urban Forms: Death and Life of the Urban Block*. Oxford: Architectural, 2004.

Panofsky, Erwin, *Idea: A Concept in Art History*. Columbia: University of South Carolina Press, 1968.

Panofsky, Erwin, *Studies in Iconology: Humanistic Themes in the Art of the Renaissance*. Boulder, CO: Westview, 1972.

Payne, Alina, *From Ornament to Object: Genealogies of Architectural Modernism*. New Haven: Yale University Press, 2012.

Paz, Octavio, *Marcel Duchamp, Appearance Stripped Bare*. New York: Arcade, 1990.

Pérez-Gómez, Alberto, *Architecture and the Crisis of Modern Science*. Cambridge, MA: MIT Press, 1983.

Pérez-Gómez, Alberto, "Architecture Is Not a Convention." In Rockcastle, Garth (ed.): *Type and the (Im)Possibilities of Convention*, Midgard Monograph, 1991.

Pevsner, Nicholas, *A History of Building Types*. Princeton: Princeton University Press, 1976.

Plato & Allan Bloom, trans., *The Republic*. New York: Basic Books, 1991.

Porphyrios, Demetri, "The Retrieval of Memory: Alvar Aalto's Typological Conception of Design." *Oppositions 22* (Fall, 1980), 55–73.

Quatremère De Quincy, *An Essay on the Nature, the End, and the Means of Imitation in the Fine Arts*. London: Smith, Elder and Co. Cornhill, 1837.

Quatremère De Quincy & Samir Younés, *The Historical Dictionary of Architecture of Quatremère De Quincy*. London: Andreas Papadakis, 1999.

Rabaté, Jean-Michel, *Crimes of the Future: Theory and Its Global Reproduction*. New York: Bloomsbury USA, 2014.

Rabaté, Jean-Michel, *Given: 1° Art, 2° Crime*. Brighton: Sussex Academic, 2006.

Rapoport, Amos, *House Form and Culture*. Englewood Cliffs, NJ: Prentice-Hall, 1969.

Rebella, Aníbal Parodi, *Escalas Alteradas, La manipulación de la escala como detonante del proceso de diseño*. Unpublished Doctoral Thesis, Universidad Politécnica de Madrid, 2010.

Ricoeur, Paul, "The Metaphorical Process as Cognition, Imagination, and Feeling." *Critical Inquiry 5*, Issue 1, 1978.

Ricoeur, Paul, *The Rule of Metaphor*. London: Routledge, 1977.

Riley, Terence (ed.), *Light Construction*. New York: Museum of Modern Art, 2004.

Rockcastle, Garth (ed.), *Type and the (Im)Possibilities of Convention*. Midgard Monograph, 1991.

Rossi, Aldo, "An Analogical Architecture." In Kate Nesbitt (ed.), *Theorizing a New Agenda for Architecture: An Anthology of Architectural Theory 1965–1995*. Princeton: Princeton Architectural Press, 1996, 345–352.

Rossi, Aldo, *The Architecture of the City*. Cambridge, MA: MIT Press, 1982.

Rossi, Aldo, *A Scientific Autobiography*. Cambridge, MA: MIT Press, 1981.

Rousseau, Jean-Jacques, *The Social Contract and Other Later Political Writings*. Cambridge University Press, 1997.

Rousseau, Jean-Jacques & Johann Gottfried Herder, *On the Origin of Language*. London: University of Chicago Press, 1986.

Rowe, Colin, *The Architecture of Good Intentions: Towards a Possible Retrospect*. London: Academy, 1994.

Rowe, Colin, *Collage City*. Cambridge, MA: MIT Press, 1984.

Rowe, Colin, *The Mathematics of the Ideal Villa and Other Essays*. Cambridge, MA: MIT Press, 1976.

Rykwert, Joseph, *The Dancing Column: on Order in Architecture*. Cambridge, MA: MIT Press, 1996.

Rykwert, Joseph, *The First Moderns: The Architects of the Eighteenth Century*. Cambridge, MA: MIT Press, 1980.

**174** Bibliography

Rykwert, Joseph, *On Adam's House in Paradise*. New York: Museum of Modern Art, 1972.

Saussure, Ferdinand de (Charles Bally & Albert Sechehaye, eds.), *Course in General Linguistics*. New York: Philosophical Library, 1959.

Semerani, Luciano (ed.), *The School of Venice*. London: Architectural Digest, 1985.

Semper, Gottfried, *The Four Elements of Architecture and Other Writings*. Cambridge: Cambridge University Press, 1989.

Semper, Gottfried, *Style in the Technical and Tectonic Arts, Or, Practical Aesthetics*. Trans. Harry Frances Mallgrave and Michael Robinson. Los Angeles, CA: Getty Research Institute, 2004.

Shearman, John, *Mannerism*. Harmondsworth: Penguin, 1967.

Silvetti, Jorge, "On Realism in Architecture." *The Harvard Architecture Review*. Cambridge, MA: MIT Press, 1980.

Siza, Alvaro & Antonio Angelillo (ed.), *Writings on Architecture*. Milan: Skira Editore, 1997.

Snodin, Michael, *Karl Friedrich Schinkel: A Universal Man*. London: Yale University Press & The Victoria and Albert Museum 1991.

Sola-Morales, Ignasi de, "The Origins of Modern Eclecticism: The Theories of Architecture in Early Nineteenth Century France." *Perspecta, Vol. 23*, MIT Press, 1987, 120–133.

Solà-Morales, Ignasi de, "Weak Architecture." In Hays, K. Michael (ed.): *Architecture Theory Since 1968*. Cambridge, MA: MIT Press, 2015, 616–623.

Summers, David, *Michelangelo and the Language of Art*. Princeton: Princeton University Press, 1981.

Summerson, John, *El Lenguaje Clásico de la Arquitectura—De L. B. Alberti a Le Corbusier*. Barcelona: Editorial Gustavo Gilli, 1979.

Summerson, John, *Heavenly Mansions*. New York: N.W. Norton, 1963.

Tafuri, Manfredo, *The Sphere and the Labyrinth: Avant-gardes and Architecture From Piranesi to the 1970s*. Cambridge, MA: MIT Press, 1987.

Tafuri, Manfredo, *Theories and History of Architecture*. New York: Harper & Row, 1976.

Tavernor, Robert, *On Alberti and the Art of Building*. New Haven: Yale University Press, 1998.

Taylor, Michael R. & P. Andrew Lins, *Marcel Duchamp, Étant Donnés*. Philadelphia Museum of Art, 2009.

Tomkins, Calvin, *Duchamp: A Biography*. New York: H. Holt, 1996.

Ursprung, Philip (ed.), *Herzog & de Meuron—Natural History*. Montreal: Canadian Centre for Architecture and Lars Müller Publishers, 2002.

Venturi, Robert, *Complexity and Contradiction in Architecture*. New York: Museum of Modern Art, 1977.

Venturi, Robert & Denise Scott Brown, *Architecture as Signs and Systems: For a Mannerist Time*. Cambridge, MA: Belknap of Harvard University Press, 2004.

Venturi, Robert, Denise Scott Brown, & Steven Izenour, *Learning From Las Vegas*. Cambridge, MA: MIT Press, 1972.

Vesely, Dalibor, *Architecture in the Age of Divided Representation: The Question of Creativity in the Shadow of Production*. Cambridge, MA: MIT Press, 2004.

Vidler, Anthony, "The Idea of Type: The Transformation of the Academic Ideal, 1750–1830." *Oppositions 8*. Cambridge, MA: MIT Press, 1977.

Vidler, Anthony, "The Third Typology." *Oppositions 7*. Cambridge, MA: MIT Press, 1977.

Vidler, Anthony, *Claude-Nicolas Ledoux: Architecture and Social Reform at the End of the Ancien Regime*. Cambridge, MA: MIT Press, 1990.

Vidler, Anthony, *Histories of the Immediate Present—Inventing Architectural Modernism*. Cambridge, MA: MIT Press, 2008.

Vidler, Anthony, *The Writing of the Walls—Architectural Theory in the Late Enlightenment*. Princeton: Princeton Architectural Press, 1987.

Vidler, Anthony & Annie Jacques, "*Chronology: The Ecole des Beaux-Arts, 1671–1900.*" *Oppositions* 7. Cambridge, MA: MIT Press, 1977.

Villari, Sergio, *J. N. L. Durand (1760–1834): Art and Science of Architecture*. New York: Rizzoli, 1990.

Vitruvius, *The Ten Books of Architecture*. Translated by M. H. Morgan. Cambridge, MA: Harvard University Press, 1914, The Project Gutenberg EBook no. 20239. www.gutenberg.org. Release date 31 December 2006.

Watkin, David & Tilman Mellinghoff, *German Architecture and the Classical Ideal*. Cambridge, MA: MIT Press, 1987.

Wittkower, Rudolph, *Architectural Principles in the Age of Humanism*. New York: Norton, 1971.

Wittkower, Rudolph, "Michelangelo's Biblioteca Laurenziana." *Idea and Image, Studies in Italian Renaissance*. London, 1978.

# INDEX

Page numbers in italics indicate figures on the corresponding pages.

Aalto, Alvar 66, 112, 146
abstraction 107–110, *109–110*
*Académie Royale d'Architecture* 14
Ackerman, James 97, 107
Adorno, Theodor 3, 161, 14n9
agro-industrial constructions 55–57, *56*
Aliamet, Jacques *18*
Allen Memorial Art Museum 146, *147*
alternative typological precedents 6–7
Althusser, Louis 72
"Alvar Aalto's Typological Conception of Design" 66
*American Academy of Rome* 80, 91n31, 146
*Amerika* 55–56
"Analogical Architecture, An" 79, 96, 149
*Après Le Cubisme* 64
architect-citizen 119
architect-poet 119
architecture: abstraction in 26, 29, 52, 79, 107–110, *109–110*, 114, 138; agro-industrial 55–57, *56*, 63, 74; conflicting interests in 1; element of 134–135, 158n36; four elements of 41–43; high *vs.* low 2, 72; juxtaposition in 110–111; origins of 14–15, 21, 39–40, *41*; prototypical modern 57–63, *58–61*, 162–163; real and relative scale in 102–105, *103–104*; science of 38–39; second typology 62; study of idea of type in 1–2; as taxonomy 24–26; three original types of 21; total 63–64; *see also* type

*Architecture of the City, The* 145, 150
Argan, Giulio Carlo 2, 4, 7, 87, 95, 163; on type in modern architecture 8n4, 73–75
Aristotle 23, 24, 33n52
*Arquitectura Popular em Portugal* 116
*Ars Poetica* 124–125
assemblage 138, 165
Aureli, Pier Vittorio 61, 66, 70n63
*Autobiografia Scientifica (A Scientific Autobiography)* 96, 150–152
avant-garde, the 3, 6, 8n12, 52, 53, 55, 57, 63, 72, 144, 162, 163, 164
Aymonino, Carlo 4, 7, 75–77, 85, 87, 88, 95

Banham, Reyner 51, 55, 85
*Barrières* 107–108, *109*, 122n40
Barthes, Roland 2, 72
Bauhaus 58, 63, 162
*Beires-Póvoa de Varzim* 116
Benevolo, Leonardo 163
Benjamin, Walter 52, 95
Benscheidt, Karl 55
Besson, Georges 144
Beuys, Joseph 4, 72
*Bibliothèque Nationale* 103, *103*
*Bicycle Wheel (Roue de bicyclette)* 128, *129*, 136
*Big Apple* 148, 148–149
biotechnical determinism 84
*Black Square* 53

Index **177**

Blatteau, John (and Paul Hirshhorn) 87, *87*, 89, 92n60
*Blind Man, The* 128
Blondel, Jacques-François 14, 22, 31n8
*Blue House* 154
Bohigas, Oriol 87, 89
Boon, Marcus 134
Boullée, Étienne-Louis 7, 25, 102, *103–104*, 103–105, 122n35, 138, 142
Bramante, Donato 59, 74, *75*
Brancusi 107, 128
Breton, André 132
Brownlee, David (and David De Long) 80
Brunelleschi, Filippo 2

Cabanne, Pierre 125
*Ca' del duca Palace 152*
"Caraib Hut, The" 40, *41*, 154
Carlos Siza house 116
*Casabella Continuità* 75–76
"casa chorizo" 89, *89–90*
*Casa Curutchet* 114, *115*
*Casa Malaparte* 110–111, *111*
Castex, Jean 66, 87, 89, 164
cave 6, 21, 22, 43
*Cénotaphe à Newton* 103–104, *104*
chains, typological 22
*Chaux* village 104, 108, *109*
*Chiat/Day* building 105, *105*
*CHICAGO. Grain Elevator 5* 55–56, *56*, 58
*Chicago Tribune* 7, 107, 142–144, *143*, 145, 152
*Church of Santa Maria* (Florence) 2
*Church of Santa Maria* (Marco de Canaveses) 118, *119*, 119–120
*Città Analoga (The Analogous City)* 79, *79*, 149
"classification" as one of the meanings of type 14, 22
*Clothespin 106*, 106–107
Cole, Henry 36
collage 79, 99, 138, 145, 165
*Collège de Louis-le-Grand* 19
Colquhoun, Alan 2, 6, 19, 66, 72, 87, 114, 162, 164; expansion of concept of type 8n3, 83–85; on Le Corbusier 60, 61, 68n30, 69n46, 112, 165n7; on Pevsner 65; on repetition 9n15; on structuralism 8nn8–9, 72
combine 165
*Commisaire des Salines* 108
*Comparative study of Philadelphia row houses 87*
*Complexity and Contradiction in Architecture* 145, 146

*Concrete Atlantis, A* 55
Consolascio, Eraldo 149
*Contra-Construction* 53–54, *54*
Costa, Lucio 66
*Cours d'Architecture* 14, 22
courtyards 4, 26, 116–118, *117*
Coustou, Guillaume 19
*Cow Byre faces south on the cool meadow, The* 138, *140*
Cret, Paul 80, 83
*Crystal Palace* 40, 52
cubism 53, 125–126, 127
Cuvier, Baron Georges 38–39, 43

Dadaism 144
Davanne, Maurice 127
de Carlo, Giancarlo 163
De Chirico, Giorgio 150
*De l'Architecture Égyptienne* 21, 161
Deleuze, Gilles 134, 164
*De l'imitation* 22, 132, 161
de Meuron, Pierre 5, 7, 136, 154–157, *155–156*, 163
Dermée, Paul 144
Derrida, Jacques 156, 160n94
*Der Stil in den technischen und tektonischen Künsten oder praktische Ästhetik (Style in the Technical and Tectonic Arts or Practical Aesthetics)* 37, 39, *41*
de Saussure, Ferdinand 2, 71
design process, type as 96–97
de Stijl group 6, 53, 54, 63, 162
*Deutsche Werkbund* 55, 58, 59, 63, 64
D'Harnoncourt, Anne 135
diagram, type as 28–31; 34n78; 48n37, 166n14
*Dictionnaire abrégé du Surréalisme* 132
*Dictionnaire d'architecture* 20, 22
Diez, Fernando 88–89, *89*, *89–90*, 164
*Difference and Repetition* 134
displacement, typological *see* typological displacement
distillation, typological 78
*Dom-ino* system 60, *60*, 61, 156; etymology of 69n37
doors and windows 134–136
Doric temple 22, 33n60
Duany, Andrés 88, 89, 92n62
Duboy, Philippe 136, 138
Duchamp, Marcel 4, 5, 7, 72, 125–128, *126–127*, 134, 138, 141, 164–165; attention toward architectural elements of doors and windows 135, 136; *Bicycle Wheel (Roue de bicyclette)* 128,

*129*; Dadaism and 144; *Fountain* 128, 131–132; influence in contemporary art 158n29, 90n5, 158n29; Loos and 144–145; pop art and 146; and ready-mades 157n15, 158n37; Richard Mutt and 128, 131–132
Durand, Jean-Nicholas-Louis 3, 6, 65; on architecture as taxonomy 24–26; compared to Quatremère 26–27, 33n65; development of science of architecture and 38; *Ensembles d'édifices résultants des divisions du quarré, du parallélogramme et de leurs combinaisons avec le cercle* 29–30, *30*; Gropius and 64–66; *Précis des leçons d'architecture données à l'École royale Polytechnique (Précis of the Lectures on Architecture at the École Royale Polytechnique)* 26–28; Semper and 36, 38–39; on type as diagram 28

*École des Beaux-Arts* 51, 57, 59, 65, 80
*École Gratuite de Dessin* 138
economy 58
*Eidgenössische Technische Hochschule* 36, 154
Eisen, Charles-Joseph-Dominique *18*
Eisenman, Peter 150, 164, 166n14
elasticity of type 97–99, *98*, *100–101*
element of architecture 134–135, 158n36
*Eléments et théorie de l'Architecture* 51–52
Éluard, Paul 132
*Encylopédie Méthodique* 3
Enlightenment period, the: antecedents of type in 13–16, *15*; Germany in 35; Laugier and 16–19; *see also* Quatremère de Quincy, Antoine-Chrysostome
*Ensembles d'édifices résultants des divisions du quarré, du parallélogramme et de leurs combinaisons avec le cercle* 29–30, *30*
*Escola Superior de Belas-Artes do Porto* 116
*Essai sur l'architecture* 5, 16–19, *18*, 104
*Et nous aussi serons mères 137*

*Faculdade de Arquitectura* 116
Fagus Factory 55
*Fallingwater* 163
*Feltrinelli Porta Volta* 154, *155*, 157
fire 40, 41
Foster, Kurt 154
Foucault, Michel 72
*Fountain* 128, *130*, 131–132
*Four Elements of Architecture, The* 6, 39–40, 47n18
Frampton, Kenneth 6, 39, 40, 64, 66, 85, 116
freedom 14

*Fresh Widow* 135
*Friedrichstasse* 152, *153*
futurists, Italian 58–59, 162

*Gallaratese* 78, *78*, 79, 149, 154
Gau, Franz Christian 36
Gaudí, Antoni 7; elasticity of type and *98*, 99, *100–101*
Gehry, Frank 105, *105*
*General Cultural History of Mankind* 40
Germany, Enlightenment period changes in 35–36
Giedion, Sigfried 3
Gleizes, Albert 125
Goethe, Johann Wolfgang von 35
*Goldman & Salatsch Store* 144
grain elevators 55–56, *56*, 57, *58*, 162
Grassi, Giorgio 75
Greenberg, Clement 3
Gregotti, Vittorio 75
Gropius, Walter 6, 52, 55, 57, 107; on type 63–66; on urban spaces 66
Guadet, Julien 51–52, 65, 70n59, 80)
*Guggenheim Museum* 66
*Guild House* 146

Hamilton, Richard 4, 72, 146
Hays, Michael 118
Hejduk, John 111
Herzog, Jacques 5, 7, 136, 154–157, *155–156*, 164
high *vs.* low architecture 2, 72
Hilberseimer, Ludwig 77
*History of Building Types, A* 65
*Hoftheater* 36
Holl, Steven 87–88, *88*, 89
Horace 124–125
*Hôtel Royal des Invalides* 25
*House and office of Inspector of Loue River 110*
Hübsch, Heinrich 36
Hunziker, Jakob 154
huts 2, 5, 6, 13, 16, 17, *18*, 19, 21, 22, 40, *41*, 60, 61,154
Hvattum, Mari 38–39, 43

*Idea* (Panofsky) 23
"Idea of Type: The Transformation of an Academic Ideal, 1750–1830, The" 85
imitation 22–23, 43, 132–133, 161–162
*Immeuble-Villa* 62–63
*inframince* 134
International Style 80
*In What Style Should We Build?* 36, 67n2
irony 141–145, *143*

*Istituto Universitario di Architettura di Venezia* (IUAV) 75, 76–77
Italian rediscovery of concept of type 73–75, *75*, 95

Jacoby, Sam 48n37,164)
Johns, Jasper 4, 72, 146
Judovitz, Dalia 124, 131, 132, 157n15
Julien, Pierre 19
juxtaposition 110–111

Kahn, Louis 7, 80–83, *81–82*, 91nn35–36, 112
Kant, Immanuel 13, 14, 20, 35
Kaufmann, Emil 138, 158n44
Kienholz, Edward 4, 72
Kimbell Art Museum *81*
Kipnis, Jeffrey 164, 166n15
*Kiss, The* 107
Klein, Yves 4, 72
Klemm, Gustav 40
knot as type 43–46, *44–46*
Kosuth, Joseph 132
Krauss, Rosalind 1, 5, 67n9
Kubler, George 5, 96, 104–105, 115, 133

*La Broyeuse de Chocolate Nr 1 (Chocolate Grinder)* 127, *127*
Lacan, Jacques 72
*La città territorio* (The urban territory) 77
*La formazione del concetto di tipologia edilizia* (The formation of concept of building typology) 77
*La Mariee mise a nu par ses celibataires, meme (The Bride Stripped Bare by Her Bachelors, Even)* 135
lantern type 2
*La porte de la chasse du Prince et l'étable* 138, *139*
*L'architettura della città (The Architecture of the City)* 76, 77, 96, 116, 149
*Large Glass, The* 135
*La Tendenza* 7, 77, 85
Lathouri, Marina 164
Laugier, Abbé Marc Antoine 5, 16–19, *18*, 31–32n16, 40, 60, 61
Laurentian Library, Florence 97–99, *98*, *100*, 102
Lavin, Sylvia 20, 24, 32n32
Leatherbarrow, David 99, 125
Le Corbusier 6–7, 52, 66, 68n23, 68n30, 80, 85, 105, 133, 146, 149, 162, 163; *Comparison between Greek temples and automobiles 59*; conceptions of "standard"

62; Gropius' influence on 57; *Immeuble-Villa* 62–63; *Maison Citrohan* 61–62, *62*, 63, 68n36; *Maison Dom-ino* 60, *60*; on objet-type 64; on ocean liners, automobiles, and airplanes as references in modern architecture 59–60; purism and 64–65; Rossi on 77–78; series of houses designed by 63; on silos 57; typological substitutions 112–114, *113–115* (
Ledoux, Claude-Nicholas 7, 104, 107–110, *109–110*, 122n35, 138)
Legrand, Jacques-Guillaume 26
Lequeu, Jean-Jacques 5, 7, 104, *139–141*, 149; on parallels between typological displacement and readymade 136–141
Le Roy, Julien-David 14, *15*; Durand and 26
*L'Esprit Nouveau* 57
*Les Ruines des plus beaux monuments de la Grèce* 14, *15*
Lessing, Gotthold 20, 35
Lévi-Strauss, Claude 2, 71–72
Libera, Adalberto 7, 110–111, *111*
Linnaeus, Carolus 14, 26
Loos, Adolf 5, 7, 77, 78, 105, 107, 136, 152; Duchamp and 144–145; presumed irony of 141–145, *143*

Madrazo, Leandro 29, 30, 164
magnification of types *102–106*, 102–107, 154
*Maison Citrohan* 61–62, *62*, 63
*Maison Cook* 63
Maldonado, Tomas 84, 164
Malevich, Kazimir 53, 112, 164
Mallgrave, Harry 37, 39
*Marche à suivre dans la composition d'un projet quelconque* 28–29, *29*
Marx, Burle 66
Masheck, Joseph 106, 144, 145
mass production 7, 52, 58, 61, 62, 63, 65, 85, 133, 163
*Mémoire sur l'architecture Égyptienne* 6
Mendelsohn, Erich 6, 55–56, 57, *58*; grain elevators and 55–56, *56*, *58*
metaphysical surrealism 150
*Métropole* 25
Metzinger, Jean 125
Michelangelo Buonarroti 7, 107, 116, 118, 146; elasticity of type and 97–99, *98*, *100–101*; magnification of type and 102–103; unexpected elements in work of 125

**180** Index

Milizia, Francesco 149
mimesis 4, 16, 22, 23, 95, 132, 161, 163
mimetic precedent 4, 46, 85, 137
misconstruction of urbanity 66–67
model *versus* type 24, 26, 27, 30, 80, 91n8, 132, 133
modernism 2, 3, 4, 5, 65, 72, 144; "apostles" of 9n14; beginnings of 52; classification of Loos and Duchamp in 145; Colquhoun and 83–85; Habermas on 8n12, 67n4; International Style in 80; Italian rediscovery of concept of type 73–75, *75*, 95; Kahn and 80–83, *81–82*; misconstruction of urbanity in 66–67; prejudice against type 163; prototypical architecture in 57–63, *58–61*, 162–163; redeemed relationship between type and city in 87–90, *87–90*; restarting history in 53–54; Rossi and 75–80, *78–79*; Schröder House 54, *54*; silos 55–57, *56*; and type, according to Gropius 63–66
Moneo, Rafael 2, 4, 7, 30, 164; on second typology 62; on Siza 117; on type and object 133; type as design process, according to 96–97; "On Typology" 4, 96
Monge, Gaspard 28
monumentality 118
*Mother's House* 146
*Moulin a cafe (Coffee Grinder)* 127
Mr. Richard Mutt (Duchamp) 128, 131–132
*Mura Spagnole* 154
Muratori, Saverio 7, 73, 75, 76, 77, 87, 95, 116
Muthesius, Hermann 64, 65

National Assembly Building of Bangladesh *82*
neo-rationalists 83, 86
Newton, Isaac 104
new urbanism 88
Niemeyer, Oscar 66
Nolli, Giambattista 27
*Notre Dame du Haut* 66, 163
*Nu Descendant un Escalier, no. 2 (Nude Descending a Staircase, No. 2)* 125, 126, *126*, 144

Obalk, Hector 132
objects: Duchamp and the secret life of 125–128, *126–127*; ordinary 145–152, *147–148*, *151–153*; prime 115; type and 133; used by Lequeu 136–141
Oldenburg, Claes 7, *105–106*, 105–107, 146, 148–149

*Opéra* 25
ordinary objects 4, 127, 132, 137, 145–152, *147–148*, *151–153*
"Originality of the Avant-Garde, The" 5
*Origini e sviluppo della città moderna* (Origin and development of the modern city) 77
origins of architecture 14–15, 21; Semper on 39–40, 42
*Ornament and Crime* 144
Ozenfant, Amédée 64

Pai, Hyungmin 164
*Palazzo dei Conservatori* 102
*Palazzo della Ragione* 77
*Palazzo Nuovo 102*
Panofsky, Erwin 23
Park Guëll, Barcelona 99, *101*
Parodi Rebella, Aníbal 105
*Parrish Art Museum* 154
Pascal, Jean-Luis 80
*Passages between row houses in Reading, PA 88*
Paxton, Joseph 40, 52
Payne, Alina 65, 69n54
Paz, Octavio 72
Pérez-Gómez, Alberto 3–4, 9n16; 164–165
Peterson, Steven 70n69
Pevsner, Nikolaus 64, 65
*Piazza del Campidoglio* 102, 117
*Piazza san Pietro* 117
*Pietà* 125
*Plan Voisin* 63
Plater-Zyberk, Elizabeth 88
Plato 23, 134
*Poetics* 23
Polesello, Giaungo 75, 95–96
*Politechnikum* 36
*Politecnico di Milano* 76
pop art 85, 146, 147, 149
Porphyrios, Demetri 66
*Porte, 11 rue Larrey* 135–136
*Prairie Houses* 66
*Précis des leçons d'architecture données à l'École royale Polytechnique (Précis of the Lectures on Architecture at the École Royale Polytechnique)* 26–28; on type as diagram 28–30
prime objects 115
*Proposal for a Colossal Structure in the Form of a Clothespin-Compared to Brancusi's KISS* 107
prototypical architecture 57–63, *58–61*, 162–163
purism 64–65

Quatremère de Quincy, Antoine-
Chrysostome 4, 6, 25, 62, 65, 73,
74, 77, 79, 85, 95, 96, 132–133, 145,
154; classical conception of art 25;
on classification 14, 22; compared to
Durand 26–27, 30–31, 38; definition
of type 3, 20–21, 161, 163, 165; on
imitation 22–23; influence on Semper
39–46; on origins 20–21; on type *versus*
model 24

"Rationalism" (Colquhoun) 60, 67–68n14
rationalization 58
Rauschenberg, Robert 4, 72, 146
readymade(s) 4, 5, 7, 130–132, 136, 145,
149, 157, 157n15, 164, 165; doors and
windows in 136; parallels between
typological displacement and 136–141
real scale 102
*Rectorado* for the *Universidad de Alicante* 116
*Recueil et parallèle des édifices de tout genre,
anciens et modernes (Collection and Parallel
of Buildings of Every Genre, Ancient and
Modern)* 6, 26
Reichlin, Bruno 149
*Reign of Terror* 20
Reinhart, Fabio 149
relative scale 102–105, *103–104*
resemblance 14, 22, 23, 24, 108, 131, 132
restarting history 53
*Restaurante e Sala de Chá* 116
riddles, typological 7–8, 154–157, *155–156*
Riegl, Alois 103
Rietveld, Gerrit 54, *54*
Rogers, Ernesto 76
Rossi, Aldo 2, 4, 5, 7, 65, 71, 87, 136, 164;
on fundamentals of the traditional
city 76–77; at *Istituto Universitario di
Architettura di Venezia* (IUAV) 75–76;
on Loos' irony 142; ordinary objects
and 149–152, *151–153*; parallels with
Venturi 145; rediscovery of concept of
type and 8n6, 75–77; Siza and 115–116;
type, according to 77–80, 96; Vidler and
85–86
Rousseau, Jean-Jacques 5, 15, 19
Rowe, Colin 63, 85
*Rudin house* 155–156, *156*
"rustic hut" 18–19
Rykwert, Joseph 144

*Saal da Bouça* 116
Saarinen, Eliel 107
*Sainte Geneviève Library* 126–127
*Salon des Indépendants* 125

Samonà, Giuseppe 75
Sant'Elia, Antonio 59
Sanzio, Rafael 103
*São Victor* 116
scale, real and relative 102–105, *103–104*
Scarpa, Carlo 105
Schiller, Friedrich 35
*School of Athens, The* 103
*School of Venice* 95
Schröder House 54, *54*
Schumacher, Patrik 164, 166n16
science of architecture 38–39
*Scope of Total Architecture* 63–64, 66
Scott Brown, Denise 146–149, *147*
Scully, Vincent 80, 82, 83
semantic operation 17
Semper, Gottfried 3, 6, 35, 36, 51, 52;
background and training of 36; "Caraib
Hut, The" 40, *41*, 154; context of
Enlightenment Germany and 35–36;
development of science of architecture
and 38–39; Durand and 38–39; on the
four elements of architecture 41–43,
47n18; on knot as type 43–46, *44–46*;
on origins of architecture 39–40, 42,
47n23; Quatremère's influence on 39, 43;
on the style paradox 36–38
*Shape of Time: Remarks on the History of
Things, The* 5
silos 6, 55–57, *56*
*simulacra* 134
Siza, Álvaro 7, 114–120, *115, 117,
119–120*, 164
Snake ornaments *44*
*Society of Independent Artists* 128
Solà-Morales, Ignasi de 87, 118
Sottsas, Ettore 105
Soufflot, Jacques-Germain 138
standardization 58
structuralism 71–72
*Studi per un'operante storia urbana di Venezia
(Study for an Operational Urban History of
Venice)* 73
style 3, 14, 19, 46, 51–52; Semper's paradox
of 36–38
substitution, typological 7, 52, 112–114,
*113–114*
subtle typological alterations 7, 118
suburban sprawl 88
Suhrawardy Hospital *81*
"Sul concetto di tipologia architettonica"
("On the Typology of Architecture") 73
Summers, John 97, 125
Sweeney, James Johnson 145
*Systema Naturae* 14

**182** Index

tableaux 133, 165
Tafuri, Manfredo 4, 75, 142, 144
Távora, Fernando 116
taxonomy, architecture as 24–26
*Teatro Faro, Toronto* 150, *151*
*Tempietto di San Pietro in Montorio* 74, *75*
*Temple à la divination* 138, *140*
"tent" as one of the original types
    (Quatremère) 6, 21, 22, 43
third typology 85–86
"Third Typology, The" (Vidler) 7
*Times Square* 148
Tinguely, Jean 4, 72
*Tombeau de Porsenna, roi d'Étrurie*
    138–139, *140*
Tomkins, Calvin 125, 132; on Duchamp
    158n29
total architecture, Gropius on 63–64
type: according to Aymonino and Rossi
    75–80; according to Gropius 63–66;
    according to Kahn 82–83; antimodern
    reaction and 4; behaving like language
    2; as classification tool 2–3, 14, 22;
    and the curtain wall 123n55; as design
    mechanism 3; as design process 96–97;
    as diagram 28–31, 34n78; disagreements
    over 163–164; early 20th-century art
    world and 3–4; elasticity of 97–99, *98*,
    *100–101*; as imitation 22–23; Italian
    rediscovery of concept of 73–75, *75*,
    95; knot as 43–46, *44–46*; lantern 2;
    magnification of *102–106*, 102–107,
    154; *versus* model 24; objet 65, 69n53;
    origins of 14–15, 21; other modernism
    of the 1960s and 4; Quatremère's
    definition of 3, 20–21, 161; readymade
    and 132–134; redeemed relationship
    between city and 87–90, *87–90*; study of
    1–2; subtle transformations in 114–120,
    *115*, *117*, *119–120*; as the very idea of
    architecture 2; *see also* architecture
"Type and Typology" 77
*Typisierung* 64, 65
typological chains 22
typological dislocation 154
typological displacement 5, 7, 152, 157,
    164, 165; Duchamp's readymade and
    132; parallels between readymade and
    136–141; secret life of objects and
    125–128, *126–127*

typological distillation 78
typological distortion 146–147
*Typological evolution-from the "Roman house"
    to the "casa chorizo"* 89
typological precedent 6, 52, 53, 74, 96, 133,
    141, 157, 164
"Typology and Design Method" 83
Tzara, Tristan 144

*Ueber Baustyle ("On Architectural Styles")* 37
urbanity, misconstruction of 66–67
U-shaped courtyards 116–118, *117*

van Bruggen, Coosje 105
van de Rohe, Mies 6, 65, 66, 112
van Doesburg, Theo 53–54, 164
*Variations "casa chorizo" according to the lot
    dimensions* 90
Vasari, Giorgio 125
Vattimo, Gianni 118
Venturi, Robert 5, 7, 136, 145–149, *147*,
    159n73
"Vernacular Classicism" 19
*Vers une Architecture* 57, 65, 69n56, 80
Vidler, Anthony 7, 14, 16, 28, 62, 87, 164;
    on Ledoux's design techniques 107–108;
    on Lequeu 138; second typology 62,
    85; third typology 85–86; on type and
    object 133
*Villa Karma* 144
*Villa Savoye* 63
*Villa Stein* 63
*Ville Contemporaine* 63
*Ville Radieuse* 63
*Ville Savoye* 63, 112–114, *113–114*
visionary architects 136, 138
*VitraHaus* 154
Vitruvius 16, 17, 44, 74, 82, 97, 121n17
von Moos, Stanislaus 66

Warhol, Andy 72, 146
weak architecture 118
weaving techniques 3, 6, 42, 43, *46*
Werkbund group 55, 58–59, 63, 64
*What Will Be Has Always Been* 83
*White on White* 53
Wright, Frank Lloyd 65, 66, 70n68, 112, 163

"zero hour" of history 53–54
Zevi, Bruno 163